RIVER
IN THE
HEART

INGRID WILTS

Contents

One Woman's Journey on a Road Leading to Love   5

Love is Stronger than Evil   6

Introduction   8

1. Back in Uganda   11

2. Opposition   25

3. Child Restoration Outreach   39

4. Johan   49

5. Suffering Street Children   58

6. Unexpected Provision   65

7. Insecurities   72

8. Church   77

9. Chased by Darkness   90

10. The Arrest   96

11. The Attack   103

12. Dealing with the Wound   115

13. Time Out   126

14. Jinja   133

15. Waiting   142

16. CRO Jinja   148

17. More Pain and Loss   164

18. Friends   170

19. The Beginning of the Inward Journey   181

20. Freeing Truth   191

21. Living out of Love   206

22. Winette   216

23. New Commissioning   220

24. The Process   225

25. New Beginnings   232

26. Sharing Father's love   241

27. Ministry Dogs   248

28. Orphans No More   254

29. His Thoughts are Higher   264

The Journey Continues...   277

Details of Ministries Mentioned in this Book   281

©2016

River in the Heart - by Ingrid Wilts
Published by Ingrid Wilts 2016

www.mto-moyoni.org

ISBN13: 978-15-34882-23-2

One Woman's Journey on a Road Leading to Love

From striving to patience,
From running to waiting,
From reasoning to listening,
From strength to vulnerability,
From fighting to surrender,
From bondage to freedom,
From loneliness to belonging,
From far off to close by,
From a Dutch culture to a Kingdom culture,
From pain to healing,
From fear to love,
From law to grace,
From visible to invisible,
From a heart of stone to a heart of flesh,
From a wink to an embrace,
With the Word and the Spirit,
From me to Him.
From my head to His heart.

Love is Stronger than Evil

It was early morning and I was still in bed when God asked me a question, "Ingrid, do you want to remove all the walls around your heart so that my love can brake forth out of you?" I panicked and said, "Oh no, don't You know what I have been through? Don't You know that I have been like a football that everybody has kicked around all the corners? I am sorry God, but I can't!" There was no response from God as I contemplated the question.

The following day when I woke up God asked the same question, "Ingrid, will you remove all the walls around your heart so that my love can brake forth out of you?" Again I said to God, "I am so sorry, but I cannot. I am too hurt; I cannot trust people anymore, I have no idea what will happen to me if I no longer protect my own heart."

God remained silent on the subject until the third morning when He asked the same question, "Ingrid, will you remove all the walls around your heart so that my love can brake forth out of you?" I became desperate; I so wanted to be obedient but I could not. The pain was too much. Finally I managed to answer Him: "God," I cried out, "I want to be obedient but I feel I cannot." As soon as I said the words, "I want to be obedient", God immediately spoke to my heart and said, "From now on Ingrid, will you believe that my love is stronger than all evil?" I strongly protested, "Lord, don't you see the wars in Africa, the AIDS and the hunger?" God simply replied, "My love is stronger than all evil."

Thoughts raced through my mind and the only response I could make was, "Please, make me a person that can receive as much of your love as my heart can contain so that I will always win."

Introduction

It was not my idea to write a book but somehow, here it is!

I wrote this not because I have a need to tell my story, but because I long for you to realise that God's love is stronger than any evil we pass through in life; that the Father's love is THE answer to all the 'why' questions we walk around with in our hearts, it's the missing piece in the puzzle of life.

I hope that you will see that we can't always understand Him but we can always trust Him. He has chosen to make His home in our hearts not in our heads. I hope that you will see that it is God's desire to be our perfect Father and for us simply to be children in His Kingdom. I hope that you will see that His love is always bigger and better than we think it is; His river of love in our hearts will never run dry! I hope that you will see that God is interested in every detail of our lives, not to condemn us but to love us back to life. I hope that you will see that it is not about how much we do for Him, but how much we dare to surrender to His love, that will lead us into our Divine destiny. I hope that you will see and experience the glorious freedom that children of God can walk in. A journey I am just beginning to discover.

I have used some fictitious names in this story, to protect people's privacy. For others I have not used their real names because I do not wish to hurt the people who hurt me. On the contrary, I am thankful now for these problems because they have driven me into the arms of my loving Father. Everything people meant for evil, Father is now turning around for good. He is just amazing!

I trust this book will help you to find that safe place in His heart for yourself.

I want to thank my parents, Martien and Dora Wilts for laying a strong foundation in my life and for their sacrifices in supporting my choice to live and work in Uganda. A huge thank-you to my siblings and their spouses: Marianne and Job, Harrie and Annemarieke and Carolien and Arie, for their continued help over the years; nothing was too much for you in responding to my needs, thank you for being such a faithful and caring 'support group'.

Winette, it has been a blessing to work with you for over ten years now. Thanks for being part of this story in reflecting the heart of the Father's to this wounded continent of Africa!

Thank you, to the team at Toronto Airport Christian Fellowship, I am challenged by your heart to share what the Father has entrusted to you with broken and wounded people like me. Your love and obedience to the Father has turned my life the right side up.

To the friends of Mto Moyoni, thank you for standing with us to see that the love of Father God spreads all over this continent of Africa and beyond.

Thank you Isla Brown, for the many hours you spent editing my Ugandan English. Thank you also for giving in to my wish to write satan with a small letter. The more I know Father God the more I see how satan has come to kill steal and destroy His plan in creation, so no capital letter for him in this book!

Gottfried Bernard, thank you for taking the risk of publishing a story of a person you do not know. I admire your step of faith in these times of economic crisis.

CHAPTER ONE

Back in Uganda

It was August 1989. As I woke up it was still early. It was not the first time I'd woken up that night. Somehow I kept on hearing unfamiliar things, making me feel tense. It sounded like shooting, but maybe I was mistaken and it was just insects. Every time I woke up it seemed as if somebody was walking around the house. It was dark. There was a power outage and I was all-alone. I consoled myself that I am *"the apple of His eye."*

The first sunbeam woke me up. I got up from the mattress on the floor and peeped through the window. It was a beautiful bright morning. The sun rose above the mountains and the birds sang their songs. Suddenly I realised that I was back in Uganda. Excitement took over as I realised that a desire of the last six years had been fulfilled.

I was in Uganda again; the place where I would live for the time being. I would be working for a local organisation, supporting development in Uganda and helping people in need. I would serve my God and His people in Uganda. I wanted to do useful things with my life and I was determined to make it work!

I looked around to see my few possessions; a mattress, a mosquito spray, four tins of detergent and my suitcase. I got up from my mattress on the floor. It was my first night in my new dilapidated house in Mbale, in the Eastern part of Uganda. Still sleepy, I walked to the kitchen, opened the door and I received a shock – the insecticide had done a great job – I counted more that 300 dead cockroaches. Never in my life had I seen so many cockroaches together. I felt nauseated. Would I have to share my house with them or would I have to kill them all?

I lit the paraffin stove. After more than half an hour the water finally boiled ready to make a strong cup of coffee! Once the coffee was in the cup and I had my first sip, reality dawned: I was back in Uganda, the place that never left my heart since I had first come here in 1981.

Looking around the house, I knew I would enjoy living here. It was in bad shape, run down, but with vim and disinfectant I could make it habitable. The former tenants had used charcoal to cook their meals and the walls, ceilings and windows were black with soot. The door frames were eaten by termites, the paint was fading and the floor cracked. In some places the roof leaked but the garden had a lot of potential and I enjoyed the huge, red flamboyant tree in the front yard. With a deep sense of thanksgiving, I enjoyed my first cup of coffee on a sunny veranda.

In preparation for going back to Uganda I had read a number of biographies of missionaries. One night I was reading Helen Rosevaere's book, *'Give me this mountain'*. She described how she was taken captive and raped by rebels. As I read, fear gripped me completely and with tears in my eyes I shouted out to God, "Unless you speak to me now, I will not go to Uganda."

I opened my Bible and my eye fell on the scripture in Zechariah 2:8. God spoke through His word and said, *"Whoever touches you touches the apple of my eye."* Tears of fear turned into tears of thanksgiving that night for God had spoken and I was ready to go.

Six months before I left for Uganda, the Director of a charity in The Netherlands, when he heard that I was going to Uganda, donated a container for my personal belongings and for other relief goods to be shipped to Uganda. I had packed my whole household, rented a van and drove the fully packed car to the container. I remember clearly talking to God in the car, "Lord, I am taking all my belongings to a country where people do not have anything. If I am taking too much, please let it not arrive in Uganda." I felt embarrassed taking so many personal things to a country where people were living in poverty.

Uganda was a country recovering from war. Banks, telephone, electricity and water were in need of lot of renovation. Occasionally they were working but more often than not they weren't functional.

I had arrived in a bus, from Nairobi, Kenya, and travelled with a huge amount of cash hidden in my shoes, shirt and underwear. I had received lots of warnings not to accept food or drink from anyone in the bus, because it is common practice that those 'gifts' are mixed with chloroform. Once you fall asleep, you lose your luggage. But I arrived safely and was met by Paulo who waited for me at the border between Kenya and Uganda. Paulo was the Director of the organisation I would be working for, a jolly man and a committed Christian brother. I looked forward working with him and his organisation. I had visited him earlier in the year to have a look at the work he was doing and to see if we would make a good team together. I had experienced a deep pain in a relationship with a Ugandan leader in 1981 and I wanted to avoid making another mistake like that.

I had a great time with Paulo during the month that I visited. We had fun, prayed and had fellowship together. Two things were made clear, however, in the time that I 'spied the land': I needed my own house and my own transport. I noticed that time had a different meaning in Uganda than I was used to and, at times I had been very frustrated having to wait for hours. Privacy was another concept that was interpreted very differently in the Ugandan culture. In all other things we could work together and make a difference in this broken nation.

The security situation in the country was still bad and almost every night gunshots were heard. Every house was riddled with bullet holes and almost every household had lost a relative because of war or AIDS. It was not difficult to see that the people were still suffering the aftermath of the war. It was seen in the roads full of potholes; it was seen in the houses pierced with bullet holes and neglected through lack of maintenance. And it was seen in the eyes of the people, which reflected their wounded hearts.

Uganda is a beautiful country in East Africa. The vegetation is green and lush, with a richness of flowers and trees. Churchill once called it the 'pearl of Africa.' It was clear that the pearl was no longer shining. The civil war had taken its toll. Almost everyone had lost a relative or friend. It was difficult to understand their smiles once you had heard their stories. *How is it possible for people to have such beautiful smiles while they have been through such intense suffering?'* I kept asking myself.

AIDS was the next threat. Many people were suffering from the disease and people lived with the idea that death could come any day so their attitude often was, 'why worry? Take what you can today because you cannot be sure if you will still be alive tomorrow.'

The country was destroyed and the economy had nearly died after Idi Amin (Uganda's President during the seventies) evicted all of the Asians, and because of its long history of civil war. The shops were empty; many people did not receive their salaries at the end of each month simply because there was no money. Banks were hardly functioning. Uganda was a hand-to-mouth economy. What was earned in a day was spent the same day on basics like food, soap, salt and sugar which were the only commodities found in the shops.

Hospitals had no doctors, no drugs and the beds were rusted.

Healthcare was barely available for the people. People died too young just because of the lack of medical facilities. I stored plasma in my fridge just in case I got involved in an accident and needed a blood transfusion.

The postal services were not functioning. At times the Post Office did not even have stamps. I had to go across the border into Kenya to collect my mail.

I would see children in school uniforms everywhere I went. It was clear that education was very important but it was sad to see that most schools did not have desks, textbooks or other educational materials.

Mbale is one of the bigger towns in Uganda, situated at the foot of the Mount Elgon mountain range. On the other side of the mountain is Kenya. Most of the people here made a living cultivating their own gardens to grow food. The slopes are very fertile and it's a beautiful sight to see the green banana trees all over the mountains. And, despite how the economy had been destroyed, the beauty of the lush nature still shone through.

Regardless of these circumstances, I was determined; I had come to make a difference in Uganda though it would not be easy.

After the second day of scrubbing and cleaning my house, I sat down with my cup of coffee, enjoying the big red-flowered tree in the garden. What a world of difference. Last week I was winding up my work as a TV producer with the Dutch Evangelical Broadcasting Company and now, here I sat, drinking coffee under an African sunset.

My thoughts went back to The Netherlands. I had enjoyed what I did. Along with my friend, Alma, I had travelled the world making television programmes about missionary kids. But I knew that it was time – God wanted me back in Uganda.

Uganda was not new to me. In 1981 I had worked in an orphanage in Jinja. After finishing school I had worked for five years as an Assistant Child Psychologist in an academic hospital and was ready for a new experience. I wanted to understand what it was like not to have the things many of us take for granted, so one of my criteria in selecting a country was that it needed to be a country where there was no Coca-Cola.

At that time Uganda had just come through a civil war and it was still unstable and dangerous. There were very few white people in the country. When you met another white person you would stop to ask what in the world they were doing in Uganda! And one could walk a whole day through the capital city and not find a single shop selling Coca-Cola.

I would hear shots being fired almost every night and it was almost common to see dead bodies lying in the streets in the morning. Twice I had guns pointed at my head.

My car was the only car for quite some distance. Back then children had been born in my car; children had died in my car. I had bonded with the pain and the suffering in the country. Now, after six years, I had come back to the country that had never left my heart.

Uganda was where I wanted to be, despite the fact that during a visit in 1986 I was robbed at gunpoint and held captive in a room with a number of other people. It was a scary experience but we all survived and we knew that this could happen in a country at war.

Now, after three days of intense scrubbing and cleaning I was ready to go to the office but I was in for a huge shock when I saw where I was going to be working over the coming years. The building that was going to be used for the school we planned to set up had no running water and there were no toilets. It was a 'go-down' partitioned by plywood. Everyone could listen in to every conversation; there was no privacy. The climate and the environment was completely different, to what I was used in The Netherlands.

I had to walk everywhere in Uganda, whilst in The Netherlands I'd had a car. There was hardly any food in the shops. My menu was maize and beans almost daily.

I remember the moment, after six months back in Uganda, when I was struggling with all the differences between cultures, I went to the butcher to buy a kilo of meat and the man cut a kilo of fat from the dead cow on the hook. I almost threw up; a kilo of fat! He wanted to give me the best, but that meant something very different to him. It was so frustrating to me that I was about to give up and go back to The Netherlands. I left the fat and continued home, meanwhile deciding that I would eat dry bread again that night.

While walking home I said to God, "Everything is different here, even the meat I buy. If I did not know that You are the same yesterday, today and tomorrow I would give up now and run home!"

Before I left The Netherlands I had bought a four-wheel drive car and packed it along with everything that I owned in the container. It was delayed on the way, taking seven months to reach Mbale! We were overjoyed when the container finally arrived. But that joy quickly turned to disappointment when I realised that half of the contents had been stolen. My TV, music system, washing machine and so many personal items were no longer there.

As we carried the empty boxes I realised with a shock that God had done what I had asked Him to do as I had packed everything up back in The Netherlands; He'd made sure I didn't have more than I needed here amongst people who had so little.

Though it was clear God had answered my prayers, I still felt the disappointment in my heart. I struggled with the fact that material things were still so important for me. I really wanted God to be number one in my life and not be disappointed with the loss of the things that were only meant to make life a bit more comfortable, in a country far away from home. I was so grateful when I saw the car at the back of the container.

At least, the car hadn't been stolen! When my Ugandan colleagues saw the car, they danced around it and shouted on top of their voices, "Our car! Our car!" I looked at them and thought to myself, '*"Our car?" No, this is MY car*'. Suddenly I realised how different our thinking patterns were and how much I wanted things for myself! Deep inside of me I hated my selfish attitude, but I did not want to pretend so I told them, "This is my car," and I hoped it would not bring any confusion in the future. 'Clear communication will avoid problems' was my motto, not realising that my clear, straightforward communication, was often interpreted as rude by the Ugandans.

The car was a small Toyota Landcruiser. I had bought it second hand in The Netherlands and was so happy with it. It had been a commercial vehicle so it only had two front seats. One day when I passed through a roadblock, the police looked at my car and when he saw only two seats, he commented, "Madam, you have a very selfish car." His comment took me off guard; I had never looked at it from that perspective, so I took the car to a garage and had two back seats fitted. I did not want a selfish car. I had come to serve the people of Uganda, even if it meant fitting nine people in a car that can officially carry only two.

The Ugandan and the Dutch cultures were miles apart. Almost everything was completely different. I lived in a house while others were living in mud huts; I had enough money to buy food while people around me went hungry; I had choices, they had no choice but to wait and see what the next day would bring. I remember thanking God almost daily that I was born in a country where it did not matter whether I was a girl or a boy. It hurt me to see how girls were getting fewer opportunities here and how women were exploited.

I didn't have a TV anymore so my only connection with the outside world was bad reception of a Dutch radio station when there was electricity. It was difficult to share my heart with people who knew nothing about my past and who were so used to the circumstances that were so new to me. Most Ugandans did not understand why I chose to live alone. People brought their daughters to stay with me but I decided that it was difficult enough to adjust to the culture outside my house, I wanted my own house to be a place where I could be myself; where I could wear trousers and shorts and play my kind of music.

It took me almost a week to make my house habitable after I arrived in Mbale. Then I started the work I had come to do. With typical Dutch zeal I worked hard, putting in long hours every day. It was my role to set up secretarial and tailoring courses for orphans, in what we called a Vocational Training School. With a lot of hours and a very good Ugandan counterpart, the Vocational Training School became a reality very fast. In the first months, we partitioned the 'go-down' to make classrooms. Teachers were appointed and advertisements made for this new school. Within the first six months we already had 30 students.

With my result-oriented work attitude I really made sure that there was progress. Little did I realise that in my striving, I bypassed my Ugandan colleagues. I knew how I wanted things done and did not take time to listen to the people I was working with. However, the school flourished. The children loved learning how to become tailors and secretaries. Our results were good and the school gained a name for itself within one year. The students liked to show off their European-designed uniforms. We were doing really well, or so I thought.

As much as the Vocational School was doing really well, I had no clue that the director was thinking differently. My workaholic attitude was difficult for him to handle and, unknowingly, my direct approach to things – both work and people – hurt him. I had already noticed that our relationship was not as open and free as it had been in the beginning. There were no jokes anymore, the atmosphere had become more serious, sometimes even tense but I didn't understand what had caused the change.

We had had some serious discussions about our developmental approach with one of the donors of the project and I had disagreed with him on a number of strategies he used to help the poor. What I didn't realise was that this man, who represented the donor organisation, took all our disagreements personally. He felt badly attacked by my ideas. In the evenings he held long meetings with the Director and, on one occasion when he was in Europe, he called my friends in The Netherlands and said that I was a danger for the development of the project.

Long phone calls were made to straighten out the disagreement. It resulted in a request from my friends in The Netherlands to apologise to him. Everything in me rose up and I felt it was terribly unfair for me to have to apologise. I believed in what I had said and felt that there was no reason to apologise for thinking differently.

"Ingrid, the lowest road is ultimately the highest," my Dutch friend said on the phone. That convinced me to write the donor a letter of apology. That apology was not fully accepted and this incident had negatively influenced my relationship with Paulo.

I felt lonely and misunderstood. I wanted to give up and leave but God encouraged me time and time again. I read somewhere, *"Success is nothing else than obedience and perseverance to God's calling for your life."* I persevered, not really aware of what was happening behind my back.

"Hey, Ingrid I am in Nairobi with a colleague, do you want to come for a weekend?" It was Alma; she had been making a TV programme in Zaire and was on her way back to The Netherlands. Alma was an old friend. We had first met in Africa and had travelled the world together. We were very good friends and her invitation came at just the right time. I needed someone to talk to; I was desperately lonely. I travelled the ten-hour journey just for the weekend in order to share my struggles with her. In the evening we decided to pray. Her colleague said that he wanted to baptise me in the Holy Spirit.

I was convinced that the Holy Spirit lived in me. I came from a spiritual background that had taught me when you accept Jesus you receive the Holy Spirit and He lives in you – end of story. Then, six years ago I had changed denominations because I had a deep longing to know more about Jesus.

I was taught as a child, that when Christians talk about satan, they give him honour. So therefore we never learned or talked about the enemy of God. I had committed my life to Christ when I was 14 years, but had never learned about the building work of the Holy Spirit and the destructive work of satan.

That weekend we had an intense time of prayer, in which many tears flowed. All those visible emotions made me sceptical; it was completely new to me. I did not understand it. That night's prayer meeting was very different than the prayer meetings I was used to. Alma's colleague insisted that it would be good for me to receive the Holy Spirit and without waiting for my acceptance he prayed for me. I felt forced to accept the baptism in the Holy Spirit, because it was done in such a pushy manner that it made me wonder if this really was of God. When I drove back from Nairobi airport, after saying goodbye to my friends, I asked God to forgive me if this was not His dealing with me. I knew that God was with me, but I felt very uncomfortable with what had happened that evening.

In that meeting God spoke about how He wanted to do a new

thing in me but I didn't have peace about it. I struggled with the whole experience. It was new to me and it had been forced on me. The man who had prayed with me told me that I would be dancing around my house and singing in tongues the whole day. But I did not feel like dancing and rejoicing at all. I was struggling and surviving and I felt that yet another burden had been added to my list. I now had to dance and speak in tongues when all I wanted was a shoulder to cry on. It made me feel unspiritual and instead of drawing closer to God, I withdrew from Him because my heart could not rejoice as He expected me to.

The word I'd been given about God doing a new thing was confirmed by one of my prayer partners on return to Uganda. I did not understand yet that, in order for God to do something new, the old had to be broken. That breaking process seemed never ending and was at times so painful that I felt I could not bear it any longer; I doubted the scripture that says that God does not give us more than we can bear.

Not long after this experience, the relationship with Paulo deteriorated and he sent a six-page fax to The Netherlands with all kinds of accusations.

"Ingrid, have you read the fax written about you?" the Chairman of the Board in The Netherlands asked when he rang me.

Telephone lines were often interrupted so I asked again, "A fax?"

"Yes, we received a six page fax about you and it is all bad stuff. Actually it is so bad that we have decided that you should come back to The Netherlands immediately."

"Who has written the fax and what does it say?" I asked, desperate.

The answer came, "It's better for you not to know at this stage. You will read it when you are in The Netherlands, just book your ticket."

I was devastated. In one day, two years of working 12 hours a day were taken away from me. I felt lonely, betrayed and deeply hurt. I doubted my experience in Nairobi. If I had committed myself again to God, was God not committed to me?

Many questions ran through my mind. I had given all that I had, done my best and had not held anything back. I knew my attitude was sincere and honest. How was it possible that my work was not appreciated? *'God where are you in all this?'*

I went back to The Netherlands, read the fax and cried. It was really bad. Many things were made up stories based on rumours. There were things I did not even know had happened or things that I knew about but I had no clue that Paulo was unhappy about them. The letter concluded that I was not capable to carry out the work required of me and that I needed to return to The Netherlands as soon as possible.

I wrote my defence but never had a chance to send it. I prayed and sought God; I was so disillusioned. After the initial shock was over and I felt able to open the Bible again, God encouraged me through Psalm 138:8, *"The Lord will fulfil His purpose for me; Your love, O Lord, endures forever – do not abandon the works of your hands."* That gave me the assurance that my work had not been in vain, that God would not abandon it, but that He would raise others to continue what I had started. This experience also marked the first time that God taught me an important spiritual truth: 'it is not what I do for Him but whom I am for Him that matters.

I had to learn that God's ultimate purpose for me was not the work I did for Him; it was for me to relate to Him and allow Him to be my closest friend. This was the first of many more very painful lessons to come.

I was thankful that my family and friends and the people in my church, continued to believe in me. In the two months that followed, we had many meetings in which we decided that I would go back to Uganda to discover what God had in store for me next. So I prepared to return to Uganda for the next chapter in my life.

CHAPTER TWO

Opposition

It felt so strange; what had happened to me in 1981 in Uganda had happened again. At that time I had worked in an orphanage in Jinja, the second biggest town in Uganda and I'd also lost that job. The lady who owned the orphanage made it suddenly very clear that she did not need me anymore. There was no other solution than to leave her place. Fortunately at that time I could help out in another place 15 kilometres outside Jinja.

I found it difficult to share my heart with people in The Netherlands. I felt that no one would really understand my situation. So I did a lot of thinking, *'God, why did you place me in a country where people communicate so differently, where they do not confront? Did you make a mistake sending me to a country where people don't disagree with one another openly?'*

As my mind was taken up with these kinds of thoughts I had to ask myself, *'Is Uganda really the right country for me to be in?'*

After many meetings with the mission committee from my home church, we had agreed that I would go back to Uganda for six months to see if God would open any doors. If no doors opened, I was to return to The Netherlands. I had received a great deal of love and support from family and friends during the time that I spent in The Netherlands but I was also excited to return to Uganda.

My ticket was bought and my suitcase packed, when a fax

arrived from Paulo saying that I was not welcome in the country anymore. All immigration offices were informed. It took me by surprise; what had I done to appear on the 'not wanted' list?

I prayed, discussed and decided with friends back home that I was going to go back to Uganda. Since none of the border posts were computerised at that time I knew it would be difficult for all immigration officers to be informed. In faith, I made the journey back to Uganda, all the time wondering how I would enter the country. There were no direct flights into Uganda, so I travelled through Kenya. It was an eight-hour flight arriving late at night. Early in the morning I took a bus to the Ugandan border. It was a journey of almost 24 hours from door to door. There was a level of uncertainty in my heart, but I was also looking forward getting back to my own place, after having shared houses with friends and relatives for two months.

I knew I had three different options to enter the country: if the Busia Border would not accept me, I would jump on a bus to the Malaba Border; if the immigration in Malaba would not allow me in the country that meant that I had to travel back to Nairobi and book a flight to Entebbe, the main airport in Uganda. I dreaded the thought that I may have to try all three of them but I also knew that if God wanted me back, He would make a way. My legs were shaking and I was nervous when I arrived at the Busia Border Post. There was a queue and I had to wait.

Suddenly, one of the immigration officers stood up from his desk, walked straight in my direction, looked at me and said, "Welcome back! Where have you been for so long? It's so good to have you back in Uganda."

Everything in me smiled and I said a silent '*thank you*' for the confirmation God gave me. I was in the right place at the right time. I continued my journey with a light heart, knowing God was on my side.

Isobel was waiting for me at the Ugandan side of the border. She also worked in Mbale. We were the only two white single ladies in the town. In the past two years Isobel and I had become friends and prayer partners. Although our personalities were totally different, we needed each other very much to deal with the big cultural issues. Isobel was a polite British lady, very relational, and she integrated very well in the culture, this in sharp contrast with me. I was much more result-oriented. In my difficult times with Paulo, Isobel always had a listening ear. We had become close friends.

It was so good to see her and it felt so good to be back in Uganda. As we entered Mbale, she looked at me and said, "Ingrid, the town is all yours. No-one can stop you from doing what God wants you to do!"

I knew it was true, but what did God want me to do? I had no idea, except that it was right for me to be back in Uganda. I prayed, *'God, You have six months to make it very clear to me what You want me to do.'*

I was confined to the house since the relationship with Paulo was very fragile. The rumours about me were so many and most of them were very negative. It was difficult to decide whom to listen to. Some people felt that they needed to share all the negative things they had heard about me and others came to tell me all kinds of bad things about Paulo. They came to my house with all manner of wild stories and dreams. I did not want to hear them. There was only one thing I could do to block my ears from allowing all the negative information to come in, I needed to know what God thought about me and what His promises were for my life.

I took my Bible and went through the New Testament marking all God's promises red and all that God wanted of me I marked in blue. I literally spent days in God's word, drinking in His truth.

At that time I was not aware that the red marked scriptures were going to be my lifeline in the future! I really had no clue that what I was doing was a prophetic act.

My self-esteem was dented and it was easy to begin believing the stories people told about me. It was a healing oil to realise that *'if God is for me no-one can be against me.'*[1] I read and re-read those scriptures, filling my mind with them. It was the only way to keep me from discouragement. God also warned me with the words, *"Do not be overcome by evil, but overcome evil with good."*[2] There and then I asked God to help me not to speak any evil about anybody. I learned to keep quiet and to cry out to God instead of confiding in people. It also marked the beginning of a silent and a very lonely road. I did not want to talk badly about anyone and be influenced by the negative, but at the same time, there were so little positive and good things around me. I was alone with my God and felt that no other person could reach my heart. I had lots of time to read and study, not knowing what each day and night would bring.

I heard a big bang. Frightened I looked up from the book I was reading to realise that bullets were flying through my compound. I hurried to get up as soon as I could and dive in the corridor, the only place in my house without windows. I lay with my face flat to the ground. The shooting went on for what seemed like ages. All I could do was pray that the gunman would not enter my house. I felt vulnerable as a lady, alone in the house and all I could do was call on heaven to protect me. I knew I could do nothing if they entered my house. After what felt like an eternity, it fell silent again. When I enquired the next day about the shooting the people just laughed. Bullets were part of life; it didn't seem to worry the Ugandans too much.

I had already made contact with a few street children when I

---

1   *Romans 8:31 and Hebrews 13:6*

2   *Romans 12:21*

was still working with the Vocational School. One afternoon a week I would walk to the market, buy bananas and we would eat together, sitting on the pavement. Language was a problem but that was soon overcome if there was food on offer! There was no building, no structures but there was a relationship with the kids and the relationship grew. Since I had a lot of time, and was not sure what the next step was that God had for me, I decided to spend more time with the children on the streets.

They got to know me by name and we had fun times together. There were a large number of street children in the town and no project addressing their needs. I knew that spending time on the streets with them wouldn't be enough to really meet their needs. Was it perhaps the time to formalise things? I prayed about it and was aware of the great responsibility to begin a new organisation. *'Who would help me; how would it be funded; how could we be sure that it wouldn't die after a few years?'* Many uncertainties and questions went through my mind. My faith however took over when God led me to a scripture in Samuel, during one of my times with Him. It came to life as I read, *"Whatever you have in mind, go ahead and do it, for the Lord is with you."*[3]

Once the project proposal was ready, I gave it to a few pastors in the town to comment on it. One of them came back with the words, "When are we starting?" Simon Peter Emiau became not only the Chairman of the Board of Directors but also a very dear personal friend. He invited two other people to become board members before we started implementing the project proposal.

One day someone gave me a scripture from Isaiah 58, *"You will be called Repairer of Broken Walls, Restorer of Streets with Dwellings."*[4] I took this as another confirmation so we began to lay the foundation of Child Restoration Outreach (CRO). In faith we

---

3   *2 Samuel 7:3*
4   *Isaiah 58:12b*

rented a small house and in December 1991 we had our first board meeting on a mat in an empty house but with a vision from God.

Three people were appointed to work together with me in setting up the organisation: a Cook, a Social Worker and the Manager, Christine Kamiti. She turned out to be a woman of calibre. Just before she was appointed, God gave her a dream that she would work with children. The moment she told us, we knew that she was the right person for the job. As we began working together I soon realised that one of her many strengths was her ability to bridge the gaps that I created with my direct Dutch approach to communication.

One of the decisions the board made was to inform Paulo about our plans to start a new organisation in Mbale. A proposal was sent to him and he reacted in his own way...

"Ingrid, the town clerk of Mbale wants to see you." The secretary to the Town clerk had sent me a little note.

'Why does the town clerk want to see me?' I wondered.

When I arrived at the Town Clerk's Office I asked the secretary what the reason for the meeting was.

"He received a letter about you and wants to find out more about it".

Curious, I asked her, "A letter from whom?"

She did not answer the question; instead she opened the door to the Town Clerk's office and said, "You can now see him."

Nervously, I entered the big office where the Town Clerk sat behind a huge desk; he was busy writing. I greeted him and he kindly offered me a seat.

"Sir, I understand that you want to see me?" I asked as politely as I could, by now fully aware that politeness is not one of the strengths of the Dutch.

"Yes, I see you around town and I am wondering what you are doing?"

As quickly as I could I replied, "I can imagine that you want to see me, because I understand that you received a letter about me. What does the letter say?"

He looked puzzled and said, "But you received a copy of the letter."

I said that I did not know that the letter existed and that I had not received my copy. He opened his file, took the letter out and gave it to me to read. The letter indicated that I had received my personal copy but it had never arrived.

Paulo had written three pages of lies and accusations. My mind went into overdrive when I read all the lies. I knew that there was no way I could defend myself against these accusations. Some of them had a political undertone, which could be dangerous. I did not like what I was reading but I also did not know how to respond. My heart cried out to God to help me.

I read the letter and said to the Muslim Town Clerk, "Sir, there is no way I can defend myself against these accusations. It will be his word against mine. When I was reading this letter, I had to think about Jesus, who was falsely accused and crucified but He choose to keep quiet. I would like to keep quiet too and ask you to observe me for three months and make your own judgement. I am not going to defend myself against these accusations."

The moment I spoke these words, the door to the office opened. The Medical Officer of Health entered the office with the words, "Let me just greet my Town Clerk."

When he saw me sitting in the chair at the desk he walked straight to me, shook my hand firmly and said, "Ingrid, thank you so much for what you are doing for this town, we need more white people like you in Mbale."

I smiled from deep within. The Town Clerk asked, "What *are* you doing?"

I explained that we had just started a project with the street children. I had not finished my explanation when he said, "I want to see it. Can I come and visit?"

That same afternoon the Town Clerk drank tea with the street children of Mbale, seated on a mat on the floor. And my name was vindicated, or so I thought.

The same letter had been copied to many other Government Officials in the town, and copies were also sent to the Immigration Office and the Registry Board of Non-Governmental Organisations (NGOs) in Kampala. I decided to look up all these people and to introduce myself. All I could do was to show them that I had nothing to hide.

Everybody was very helpful; they promised support if I needed it. I was encouraged. One of the government leaders, when he found out that I had not received my copy of the letter, even promised me his letter so that I could make a photocopy. He told me he would let me know when I could get it. I was thankful for the positive responses I received. Little did I know that there were some strings attached.

It was dark and quiet when my phone rang unexpectedly at 9.30pm. A week had passed and I was still wondering what the consequences of the letter would be for the future. It was the Government leader calling to tell me that I could come over to his house to get a copy of the letter. Since he lived nearby, I decided to walk over. I moved fast; night time was not a very safe time to be out walking; gunshots were often heard, mostly far away but sometimes very near.

He opened the door and I noticed that he was not very stable on his legs. He looked tipsy. He invited me in and I took a seat on the couch. I saw the letter on the table. The man moved to the couch, sitting too close to me. He put his hand on my leg and confided in me that he had just been transferred to Mbale and that he was in need of a girlfriend. His preference was for a white lady this time.

I didn't know how to get out of this situation quickly. I told him briefly but very clearly that I was not available. I grabbed the letter from the table, thanked him for it and made my way out of the house as fast as possible.

On my way home, I smiled to myself, *'God, for sure, You use strange situations to help me out!'*

Three weeks after this incident I received an invitation to this man's wedding. I just couldn't get it into my head. How can you ask someone to be your girlfriend while you know your wedding is in three weeks? I was too annoyed and refused to attend. How could he have the guts to invite me to his wedding? I wouldn't appreciate just how deeply this man's ego was grieved until four years later...

We needed to streamline the operations of our NGO in Uganda and that meant travelling to Kampala again to meet with Government officials. It was a four-hour journey. As usual, I travelled to Jinja the day before and stayed the night with friends. This made it easier to be in Kampala early in the morning. Telephones usually didn't work so it was difficult to make appointments.

The Ministry was located on the 14th floor in one of the tallest buildings in Kampala. Unfortunately the lifts were out of order; it was a good morning exercise to walk the stairs to the 14th floor. After every three floors I needed to rest. I looked through the broken windowpanes at all the buildings in the capital, full of bullet holes. I was tempted to ask anybody coming down if the Official I needed to see was in the office. Once I reached the 14th floor, I needed a few minutes to get my breath back. I stood in the corner panting until I could talk again. The secretary invited me in. When I asked if the Official was in his office she said, "Sorry, come back this afternoon."

In those days many people had more than one job. They would leave their jacket hanging on the chair pretending they were in the building, while they had already moved on to their second job. I knew waiting was useless; I would just have to come back in the afternoon. *'At least walking back down the steps was simpler,'* I thought to myself on the way to the next government office. When I returned again in the afternoon, I silently prayed with each step that I climbed, that the right people were going to be in their offices.

The Immigration Office in the capital city had also received a copy of the letter. I knew I needed to change my work permit but I could not do that unless CRO was officially registered. My previous experiences with the Immigration Office had not been very positive. When I had first arrived in Mbale, the Immigration Officer said he originated from Mbale and if I wanted a work permit, I needed to meet him on a particular day at 8 o'clock in the evening in a hotel in Mbale. I'd been in Uganda long enough by then to understand that this was an appointment with physical strings attached and had got upset.

I stood up and said, "Sir, I am not the kind of lady that calls on men in hotels at night," and walked out. I closed the door to his office a bit too loud, but that was my only regret. However, it had upset the Immigration Officer and he lodged a complaint with Paulo. Now, once again, I had to go to the Immigration Office and I dreaded it.

Though it shouldn't have surprised me, it did: my file was lost. Usually this meant that some money needed to be given to find the file, but I was not willing to sustain a corrupt system. I knew exactly what they wanted but I was not ready to give it to them so I told them that I would come back in two weeks to give them time to find the file, otherwise I would go to a higher authority.

After two weeks, the file was found but there was a letter in it with bad news. The letter stated that I was expelled from the country. I had two weeks to pack my bags and leave. I could not believe my ears and argued with the Immigration Officer. I was upset and annoyed and felt the deep injustice of the situation. Expressing my feelings did not help either, so I decided to go to the Inspector General of Government, a body that checks corruption in the Government. I was seen by a staff member in the IGG's office and he told me to write a letter of appeal and copy it to seven other people in this country or alternatively he suggested that I bribe the Immigration Officer with two million shillings. The Government would give me this money so that they could lay a trap for this officer. I could not believe my ears, *'Had an officer fighting corruption in this nation just asked me to bribe an Immigration Officer with Government money?'*

I felt very uncomfortable; all the years I had lived in Uganda I had never bribed anybody. How could I do it? Was it right to do it? I talked to my Ugandan friends who were not at all in favour and discouraged me from following this route. "Unless the Inspector General puts in writing that you are doing it on his behalf using Government money, stay clear of it," they advised.

I decided against it; if I was to be in Uganda, God again had to make a way so I moved into a higher gear of faith. That same afternoon, upset, tired and angry I went back to the Immigration Office and asked to see the highest authority. The Office of the Commissioner of Immigration was busy and I had to wait for my turn to be seen by the top man. Armed policemen and staff walked in and out of his office while I was waiting to see him.

After half an hour he invited me into his office. The man looked very impressive and important. He wore big golden chains around his neck and golden bracelets on his wrists. It was clear that he was the man who held the power in this building. Two of his staff members were sitting at his desk and I was offered a seat on the couch. Despite my presence he continued disciplining his staff and informing them that they were being punished for forging immigration files. Now and then he glanced at me to see if I understood how powerful he was. He made his staff write a confession and after that, they were handcuffed and led to prison.

Then he graciously bowed to me and said, "What is your problem?"

"Sir," I said, "I found a letter in my file that I am expelled from this country and I would like to know why I have to leave Uganda."

"If the file says you leave, you leave, simple as that."

I don't know where I got the courage from but I told the man, "Sir, the letter says that I have two weeks to leave this country but I am not going."

He laughed sarcastically and said, "If the letter says you go, you have no choice but to go." His voice became stronger, "Pack your things. You do not need two weeks; I am reducing the time to one week for you to leave this country."

I persisted and told him as politely as I could but with a hint of anger, "Sir, I am not going! I cannot understand why you want me out of this country unless you are interested in my possessions but otherwise I have not done anything that deserves expulsion. I am not going!"

"Why are you refusing to go?"

"Sir," I told him "I know you are a powerful man but I know that God has called me to this country and that He is more powerful than you are."

He laughed, "You mean to say that your God is going to tell me to keep you in this country?"

"I am not saying He is going to do it, I am saying that He is able" I replied firmly.

His laughter became more sarcastic as he said, "Did you see the police officers handcuff those people? I can call the same policemen to handcuff you and take you to the police so that you sleep in the cells tonight!"

By that time I lost my cool. I stood up and said, "Come, let's go to the police now and we will see who sleeps in the cell tonight. I have done everything your office told me to do and I have not broken any law in this country. Let's go to the police now and we see who'll be sleeping there, you or me!"

He smiled when he saw my outburst and cooled down. I was invited to take the chair opposite his. He enjoyed my vigour and I knew I had to take advantage of it. With a very soft tone he almost whispered, "I know why you want to be in this country you must have a boyfriend in Mbale."

I looked him straight in the eye and said, "Sir, I am a too difficult a woman for any Mugisu man."[5]

He laughed and said, "Okay, okay. I will give you a Mugika[6], they are stubborn too, and I will also give you one year to finish your project."

I took his hand, told him I did not need his Mugika man but I thanked him for the one year he gave me.

Then I continued with a polite voice, "Sir, if you are so powerful that you can give me one year, you can also give me two years."

"My sister", he answered, "you should be happy with one year."

"My brother," I answered again, "I will be much happier with two years."

At that moment the door to his office opened and his secretary walked in. I smiled at her and said, "Madam, you have a great boss, he wanted to send me out of the country but now he gives me a two year work permit!

This did the trick, and I got my two-year permit. I walked out of the office feeling a mixture of victory and anger. I had used all the strength and the tricks I could think of, but deep inside I

---

5   *A Mugisu is a man born in Mbale*
6   *A man born in western Uganda*

ultimately knew that this was God showing up again and telling me that my time in Uganda was not yet over.

CHAPTER THREE

Child Restoration Outreach

CRO was doing really well; we were getting an average of 40 street children coming to the centre on a daily basis and the number grew steadily. Trust developed between the children and the staff.

The first thing CRO received, as a donation was a small picture from one of my prayer partners it said, "Before the cloth began, God gave the thread."

We used some of my savings for the initial costs, until a friend in Kampala donated US$3,000 for the operational costs. That was the beginning of amazing things happening.

I had quickly forgotten that God loves me for who I am and not for what I do. I loved what I was doing and soon I was back to my 14-hour-long working days. I wrote proposals, raised funds, made sure CRO was known to authorities and enjoyed every opportunity for networking. I loved planning and most of the time I was living my life in tomorrow and forgetting to live today.

My days were busy and I tried to encourage our Ugandan staff with my Dutch zeal. I did not realise that sometimes this fervour was a threat to them, especially when I expected them to work as I did. I had a 'gift' to push people to do things they normally would not do. If things went differently than I expected, I became easily upset and made judgements in my heart that I would never speak out.

Luru was one of the faithful children. He loved coming to school, loved all the attention he got during the counselling sessions and he was grateful for a healthy cooked meal every day. He had been on the streets for many years but was very happy that now he had a chance to go to school. I felt so bad when one day he appeared with a terribly swollen head which made it difficult to recognise him and so I asked him what happened.

"My mother beat me because I came to CRO and did not bring money home!"

I was so shocked. CRO was created to assist the children and not for them to be beaten up when they came home!

This revealed one hidden truth about the street children: Luru did not spend time on the streets out of his own will. His mother sent him and Luru sustained her alcoholism with the money he received begging.

This incident led us to the slums of Mbale, an area of mud huts closely built together. The smell of alcohol almost made me feel drunk as we passed people gathered around a pot of local brew. Long straws were sticking out of the pot where men and women sat in a circle sipping the whole day. We discovered that most of the children had mothers. Fathers were absent or weren't involved with their families because of polygamy. Suddenly we realised that we were fighting a symptom but that we were not addressing a major cause that led to so many children being on the streets: the mothers. It was very difficult to find a sober woman. The women were either drinking or brewing. Luru's story and what we saw, heard and smelled that day, were the catalysts for a project we developed for women in the slum area.

After our first assessment of the slum area, we quickly decided that the mothers needed as much attention and teaching as the children needed and so we planned to spend two afternoons a week in the slum area. We became regular visitors in order to build relationships with the mothers of the children. On one occasion it had rained and we were wading through the mud in the slums. We jumped over rivers filled with garbage and human waste.

"Mama, come and see." We were called into a small grass-thatched hut. Around it many women were sitting in the mud, crying very loudly. It was the first time I entered a hut in the slum area and was overtaken by the smell of alcohol.

"A baby has just died," our Social Worker said, "come and see the body."

My eyes needed to adjust to the darkness. On the mat in the middle of the hut sat a mother waling with grief. Next to her laid the body of a nine-month-old baby. The child had died because of diarrhoea. I looked more carefully, overcoming my reluctance to pry into other people's pain and privacy. I saw the body of the child and everything in me wanted to cry out, '*This child should not have died. This death could have been prevented.*'

I moved closer and, once my eyes were fully adjusted to the dark, I could see that there was no life left in this small, beautiful body. But when I looked again, I saw something move near the nose. As I focussed I felt nauseated, seeing worms coming out of the child's nose. That's when I knew that we had to start with health and hygiene lessons.

It took a long time to win the women's trust. After about four months the biggest step forward was that they no longer hid the alcohol when we came to visit the slums. But through persever-ance the women's club started influencing the environment and a number of women accepted Jesus as their Saviour. Over time their homes improved and these women became examples in their communities.

In the first months when we came to the slum we usually told Bible stories, sang and prayed with the people. During one of our first visits we found a good place under a tree. It was centrally located which gave people the possibility to stop and listen in to what we were teaching.

The following week as we gathered in the same place, an old man from a nearby house came charging at us with a big stick. He was beating everybody who came within his reach. I ran with the others. When I asked our Social Worker what the problem was she translated, "The man says that we made his gods angry last week and he does not want us in the area".

We found another place to meet and as soon as we had settled, a woman with one leg came walking on crutches, straight towards me, half drunk. She looked at me and said, "Pray for me; I want two legs." I did not have that faith to pray for a new leg but I prayed blessing over her life.

After five months we had a regular group of about 30 women who met twice a week. One lady offered for us to use her compound for the meetings, but soon the women decided that they needed a clubhouse. In a joint effort they built their own clubhouse.

The problems in the slum area were so many and so serious. One of the mothers ended up in prison after killing her own child. She had been drunk and was fighting with a man. Instead of beating the man, she killed her own child. Because of her experience we gained access to the prisons and were able to visit her regularly and to share the Gospel with her and with the other prisoners. Steadily CRO grew and expanded its activities into the community.

Paulo was very unhappy about the existence of CRO in Mbale and tried to undermine everything we were doing.

"Aunty, tomorrow we are not coming to CRO because we are invited by Uncle Paulo for sweets."

I was worried; why would Paulo want the CRO children to come to the Vocational School?

The following day, no children appeared at the project. They had all moved to my former work place. We learned that Paulo was hosting people from the National Council for Children and the Registry Board of NGOs.

We were still not officially registered so when I learned of their visit, I looked for them in the town, to invite them to our project, in the hope that their visit would alleviate any remaining concerns about the letter they had received about me. We had problems getting CRO officially registered as an NGO because of the letter that was circulating about me. If the officials from Kampala were in Mbale, I wanted them to see what we were doing so that we could have our official paper work done. When I saw the group from the capital city, I was so happy to recognise a good friend of mine among them.

I greeted her and said that I came to invite them to see what we were doing in the town with street children. She could not make a promise since Paulo was in charge of their programme, but said they will try to pay us a visit the next day.

Early in the morning, the following day, a car parked outside the project house and out came the officials from Kampala. I was pleasantly surprised; this visit could be vital for CRO's future as a legally registered organisation since the damaging letter about me was still in the Registry Office in Kampala.

The Chairman of the party was a Catholic priest; he listened to our vision and spent time with the children. Paulo, who was his host, stayed in the car, not ready to see what CRO was doing. The priest, however, called him out of the car and said, "You need to see this project and, not only that, I also want you to pray a blessing over this project!"

Paulo got out of the car reluctantly. He stayed in the doorway, not willing to enter and prayed a quick prayer for CRO. He did not look at me, but as quickly as he could he went back to the car and waited for the rest of the party to join him.

We were indeed blessed, not only with growth but also with our official NGO certificate! We were now legally operating in the country!

I looked for different training opportunities and found a very good cross-cultural course in Nairobi, which I thought would be good for Christine and me to follow. We came from such different backgrounds and we really had the desire to work together as a team, understanding each other's strengths and weaknesses.

We had just returned from the 10-hour journey from Nairobi when the phone rang. It had been a tiring bus journey and I was already in bed.

"Hi Ingrid, I am in Nairobi and would like to see you." It was the director of a charity from The Netherlands.

"I am so sorry I have just returned from Nairobi, there is no way I can go there again tomorrow, I wish you had informed me earlier, I would have stayed a day longer," it was too much to do the 10-hour journey again the following day. "But our Chairman is travelling to Nairobi tomorrow, can you meet with him?" I asked.

We agreed that Simon Peter would meet the Director in a Nairobi hotel. He returned from Nairobi with a big smile on his face. He explained that the Director was sick and could not see him. He was asked if he could wait in the lobby and, soon after, an envelope was brought to him. He opened it and could not believe his eyes; it contained a cheque for US$10,000! This again was a sign that God was committed to supplying all our needs. Soon after this we received a message from Internationaal Christelijk Steunfonds, a charity in The Netherlands, with a positive reply to our project proposal. They were willing to support our whole annual budget!

Banks were not very efficient those days and so the money was deposited in an account in a foreign exchange bureau. The bureau belonged to a Muslim friend of mine. I had known him since 1981 when I worked in Jinja. He operated a petrol station and we used to have long and deep discussions about God. He was looking for more in his faith and I just knew that Christ was the 'more' he was looking for. There was a deep desire in me to introduce the Way, the Truth and the Life to him and his family.

I wanted to give him the business, because I knew that he would give us honest service. I had been banking with him for all these years because he gave us favourable exchange rates and our banking with him was always straightforward, a rare thing in Uganda. We had become personal friends and often I visited his home or stayed with his family when I was in need of accommodation in Jinja.

Their commitment to Islam challenged me; they were living out their faith in a way I had not seen many Christians do. They were so hospitable to me, a Christian woman. They gave me space to thank my God for the food in their home. They were very accommodating to me. At the same time there was a pain in my heart when I heard them share that they needed to earn everything by doing good. We would talk together but the 'Way, the Truth and the Life' could not penetrate their hearts and minds. There was this big stumbling block for them; Jesus, the Son of God. I so wanted these committed Muslims to get to know the Christ that I believed in. I prayed and fasted for them.

I had just concluded three days of prayer and fasting when God gave me the confirmation that He was concerned with this family. He made it clear that He was going to reveal His true identity to them but that I had taken their salvation to heart. God challenged me when I read Isaiah 45:11, *"Do you question me about my children, or give me orders about the work of my hands?"*

That's when I realised that I had made their salvation a personal effort. I laid aside my Bible and repented of my strife and acknowledged that conversion is the work of the Holy Spirit and not me. I continued to read and a few verses later God gave me the answer to my request.

"The products of Egypt and the merchandise of Cush, and those tall Sabeans – they will come over to you and will be yours; they will trudge behind you, coming over to you in chains. They will bow down before you and plead with you, saying, 'Surely God is with you, and there is no other; there is no other god.'"[7]

In faith I accepted this as God's word for my friends, but I did not realise how severe the spiritual warfare was going to be. I knew God was at work with these people, when out of the blue, my friend told me that he had been cheated and lost all the money. This meant that a huge amount of CRO project funds were lost! Without doubt, this was part of the spiritual warfare I was engaged in.

"Lord!" I cried out, "Here I am praying and fasting for my friends and as a reward all our project funds are lost!"

I panicked. This was surely not what God meant after my days of prayer and fasting? *'God where are you in this?'* I wondered. All I could do was go back to my Bible and read the scriptures marked in red.

I did not want to tell anybody about the problem, because he was my friend and I did not want him imprisoned. I felt responsible because I had made the decision to bank with his foreign exchange bureau alone. I also did not want to tell the donors, because we would lose credibility as an organisation. It was the end of the year and our books were going to be audited at the beginning of the New Year. How was I going to explain the loss of these funds? I confided in Simon Peter and told him of the only

---

7 *Isaiah 45:14*

solution I could think of.

I made an emergency call to The Netherlands and asked how much money I had in my savings account. I was so surprised to hear that the amount in my savings account was exactly the amount that was lost. This was a sign to me that God was right in the midst of this problem and that He allowed it to happen for a purpose. I learned once again that He wanted me to be fully dependent on Him and I knew He was testing me on how firmly I wanted to hold on to my own money.

My savings arrived in the country two days before the financial year closed and the auditors never knew what had happened. God took care of all our needs. I felt so thankful that we were able to carry out all the planned activities in the CRO centre without any financial constraints and that our reputation was not damaged. I also learned that, from that day on, God would take care of me with or without my savings account.

God did even more in the relationship with my Muslim friends. One night I was praying and I heard a voice saying, "Your friend is dying." I was not familiar with hearing voices and wondered, *'Is this satan wanting to make me fear or is this God wanting to get me to pray?'* I decided to do the latter. I prayed until three in the morning. The phones were not working so there was no way to get in contact with them.

The following morning, the telephones had started to work again. I called his office early; he had not yet arrived. He was late that morning, but the secretary did not say anything to suggest he had passed away. I told her that I was passing though Jinja that day and wanted to see him.

When we met, he looked tired. I asked, "What happened yesterday?"

"Why are you asking?" he said. I told him to tell me first what happened, after which I would tell him the reason behind my question.

"Yesterday," he said, "my best friend died. When I was washing the body, the spirit of my friend visited me and told me to come where he was. Yesterday I faced death and I feared it so much. It was at three in the morning that I was able to sleep." My eyes filled with tears, because I had learned a new lesson in my relationship with the Lord. He had used me to prevent my friend's death through prayer!

I decided to share with him what I'd experienced with God the night before; I told him that God had literally told me, with an audible voice, to pray for him and that I was only released to go back to sleep at three in the morning. At that moment his eyes became wet and I knew that his heart was touched. I left Jinja thinking, '*Surely God, You must have great plans with this family!*'

However, my friend could not handle the fact that he had disappointed us and he left to find answers in Pakistan. He was out of the country for many months. But God encouraged me with the scripture, *"'For my thoughts are not your thoughts, neither are your ways my ways,' declares the Lord. 'As the heavens are higher than the earth, so are my ways higher than your ways and my thoughts than your thoughts.'"*[8]

A few days later He showed me another Scripture: *"Forget the former things; do not dwell on the past. See, I am doing a new thing! Now it springs up; do you not perceive it?"*[9]

I accepted God's word in my mind, because it was His truth, but somehow it did not minister to the pain in my heart; I missed my friend and had to make a deliberate choice that this family's salvation was now no longer my responsibility.

---

8   *Isaiah 55:8-9*
9   *Isaiah 43:18-19*

CHAPTER FOUR

Johan

Another of my friends, Johan, I knew from my earlier years in Uganda. He was an adventurous man who had driven from The Netherlands all the way through Africa in his Land Rover. He loved the beauty of Uganda from the moment he arrived in the country and had fallen in love with the River Nile, so he decided to stay in Uganda. In the early eighties I had helped him to find work and a place to live. A Ugandan lady from the same village was asked to do house work for him. Not long after that, they fell in love and married. Now they had three beautiful children.

He loved his children and spent time with them, teaching them various survival skills. Johan was a Dutchman who had adjusted well to a simple African lifestyle. He knew a lot about the stars and it was always a joy to sit out with him at night and learn about the universe. On a number of occasions we went out on a safari to the game parks. He would bring his telescope and teach us about the universe.

There were times that he did not have work so money was very scarce. I usually stopped to greet him on my way to Kampala, have a cold drink and catch up on new developments. We were good friends.

One day I showed him a piece of land that I had been able to buy very cheaply. It was a beautiful plot on the shores of the River Nile. Although the land was very bushy and many people laughed at the piece of 'bush' I had bought, he loved the place and decided to buy a piece of land next to mine, with money that I lent him. We both saw the potential the land had.

Since he did not have a job, he offered to develop the land into a campsite. I had no plans for the land yet so I agreed to the plan. With a lot of enthusiasm, Johan began developing the campsite. The bushes were replaced by grass, the ground was levelled to be able to put up tents and he built latrines. But tourism was not a booming business, too many people were still associating Uganda with Idi Amin and with AIDS, it was not a holiday destination at all at that time. This meant, unfortunately, that the campsite did not bring any income for him and his family. Since he was a builder, he suggested that he build a house for me, so that he had an income and I had a house. It was an offer I could not refuse!

In my spare time and at weekends, we planned the design of the house. He had a book with all kinds of different designs and I choose one and adjusted it to my liking. I left money for the work with Johan and he enthusiastically started with the foundation of the house. I was amazed that after six months the foundations and the walls were already up to ring beam level.

One Saturday afternoon we had a long talk. We were sitting down by the river and he was telling me of his passion for the River Nile. He shared his deep dream with me of wanting to be the first man who ever rafted this stretch of the river. He wanted to make the headlines in the newspaper that he conquered the Great River Nile. I was worried when he told me that he used a small toy boat to go down the river. Although he was wearing a life jacket, he did not have a helmet.

He would put four jerry cans filled with water, representing his weight, in this toy boat to test if he could pass a particular rapid. If the jerry cans did not fall out of the boat in the rapids, he would go in the boat himself.

The Nile is a mighty river. I was not very happy with his story and told him that he was a father of three children and that it sounded to me an unsafe and dangerous venture. I told him, reinforcing my point as I repeated it twice, "Johan, you can win against the river many times, but you can lose only once!" Three days later he lost.

I was filling up with diesel at a petrol station in Jinja when someone ran to the car and shouted, "Ingrid, do you know Johan is lost?"

"Lost? What do you mean, lost?"

"Yesterday he went rafting and he never returned, they found the boat, and the life jacket but they did not find him. His wife is in the hospital with a bad infection in her leg, she cannot walk and is worried because he did not come to see her yesterday night."

My breathing stopped, *'Was this not what we talked about just last Saturday?'*

'No Ingrid,' I told myself, *'No time to reflect, you need to act now.'*

As fast as I could I drove to the hospital. His wife was in pain, both physical and mental. She asked me to go to the house and lock all the doors. In the meantime she would prepare herself to go home and wait for Johan there.

I rushed to her home and found the villagers already with radios and cameras in their hands. I lost my cool and like a mad woman I told all the villagers to keep their hands off this property. I brought all the valuables to the first floor in the house and changed the locks on the doors. I had no experience with this aspect of the Ugandan culture but was shocked to see how quickly people came to help themselves to stuff of people who had died.

As soon as I had brought all their property in safety, I drove back to the hospital, and brought Johan's wife home. In the meantime a search party was organised to look for the body. He had gone on the river with two Ugandan fishermen. The police had arrested them and locked them in the cell. I rushed to the police and pleaded with them to allow the fishermen to join the search party. They walked the shores of the river and asked the villagers around to alert them when they found Johan's body.

It had been three days and Johan's body had not been found yet. I decided to stay as much as possible with Merida, his wife, and slept in the same room with her and the children. The house and compound were full of mourners. A fire was lit in the middle of the compound and the whole night people were crying. It was like I was living in a dream. This could not be real – I had landed in a movie.

People were lying everywhere – on the floor and around the fire – to wait for the news that Johan's body had been found. In the middle of the night Merida would have nightmares, beat me and say, "Yes, I hear him, Johan has come!"

It broke my heart and I cried, knowing that we would never see him alive again. Once more it was a time where I cried out to God, *'God, where are you in all this? Is this Your will? Are you truly Love as You say you are?'* I had too many questions and no answers.

The nights were long and many spirits attacked Merida. I prayed and called on the Name of Jesus. When I did so, she would sleep; when I fell asleep, she woke up shouting, with strong panic attacks. I had never seen the reality of demons so clearly before.

After four days I was completely worn out. No sleep, hundreds of people walking in and out of the house. I needed to rest, myself, so I drove to a friend's place. On my way the police, who had been using Johan's car to search for the body, waved me down. Four men jumped out of the car and told me that they had found the body, but they were not ready to release it until we paid them a large amount of money. I felt like running mad; with a loud voice I asked them to repeat their request just to make sure that I was not going to beat them for the wrong reason.

The men were lucky that, at that moment, a Dutch priest stopped and asked me what was going on.

"They have found Johan's body but are not willing to bring it unless I give them money."

Full of emotion, I told the priest the amount they wanted for the dead body of my friend. The priest told me to go and rest. He would handle the matter further. I went to rest, but could not. After a few hours, I went back to the house. The body had not yet arrived.

As it approached midnight we heard the sound of a car. I overheard people say, "Johan has come." Before I realised it, Johan's eldest son, seven years of age at that time, jumped up to see his father. Michel was a great friend with his father. He had a beautiful twinkle in his eye every time he saw his father. I was too late to stop him; he ran to the casket and saw his father's lifeless, disfigured body. After he had glanced in the casket, he ran outside as pale as a ghost and sat in an old car tyre, completely in shock.

I walked up to him and asked, "Michel, what are you thinking?"

"I am thinking about Jesus," he replied

"What are you thinking about Jesus?"

"That Jesus will now take care of us," he told me, simply.

Tears rolled down my cheeks and I broke down and wept for the first time that week. I knew it was the truth, but I could not understand it. Along with Johan, the twinkle in Michel's eyes had also died.

Johan's body could not stay in the house. The mortuary had just been renovated so we took the body there until his family could come from The Netherlands for the burial. I met the priest at the mortuary and he told me the horrible story that the fisherman had hidden Johan's body in order to get money from us. Since he was white, they wanted to cash in on him. They had kept his body in the water to catch more fish. I was nauseated and wanted to vomit, '*Where is their humanity? Has hell come to earth that things like this can happen? God where are You? Is this still Your world?*'

I could not recognise Johan anymore, except for his swimming trunks and his wedding ring.

My heart broke, the following day, when I bought a newspaper. There he was, with a big headline on the front page, "*Dutch drowns in River Nile.*" He had made the headlines, but in a much different way than he would ever have anticipated or hoped for.

All flights to Uganda were fully booked, as it was approaching Christmas. It took three days before Johan's family could come to Uganda for the funeral. I went to the airport to collect them. We cried and consoled each other. We drove straight to the home. Merida was able to walk with a stick, her leg was slowly healing.

It was one of the most painful funerals I had ever attended. Looking at Merida and the children, questions kept on coming and there were no answers. I felt lonely and abandoned with no one to talk to.

After the funeral I went with Johan's family to the place of the accident. As we parked the car, a man walked up to us. He showed us a fresh wound on his face. It was clear that he had been fighting and most probably he had been drinking too, the smell of alcohol was all over him. In broken English he told me how he had struggled to get Johan's body out of the water.

"Can you see the wound on my face it's because I got the body out of the water, I risked my life and I need money."

It was purely God's grace that I did not give the man a kick where it would hurt him most. I managed to control myself for the sake of Johan's parents, who fortunately, did not understand what the man had said.

Exactly one week after the accident, I was back in my own home in Mbale. However, it took much longer to recover from this black week in my life. Not only had I lost my Muslim friend, now I had also lost my dear friend, Johan; two of my closest friends gone in three weeks. As if that was not enough I also received a letter from another friend who wrote that our friendship could not be sustained and that this would be the last letter.

I was an emotional wreck; it was almost too much to handle – three friends gone in four weeks. *Lord, this is too much! Am I supposed to go through life alone? Don't You know I need people to support me and to share with? Are You truly love? Do You really exist?'*

I lost my faith, *'If God really is who He says He is in His word, how can things like this happen?'* For two whole days I battled with the question of God's existence. These days felt like years. Everything felt black – I was too fearful to get out of bed. I felt as if God had deserted me completely, but I was too scared to ask Him if He had.

After two days I got up, but was not able to pray and I had stopped reading my Bible. I was angry with God; I just could not handle His so-called 'love'. I continued going to our prayer breakfasts with Isobel and two other missionaries but told my prayer partners that I was unable to pray. They faithfully prayed for me.

The longer it took, the more I became aware that God was watching over me with a little smile on His face, knowing that His rebel child would come back to Him. And I did, I could not go on without Him. After three long months in a spiritual desert, I opened my Bible and was deeply touched when God showed me a scripture from the book of Isaiah. It just lit up from the page when I read, *"As a bridegroom rejoices over his bride, so will your God rejoice over you."*[10]

How was it possible that God would rejoice over me when I stopped reading the Bible and praying to Him for more than three months? I continued reading and another scripture sank deep in my spirit, *"And you will be called Sought After, the City No*

---

10 *Isaiah 62:5*

Longer Deserted."[11]

I wondered to myself, *'God, seeking after me? I, who only had questions for Him; who did not understand Him and in my heart did not want to be close to a God who could cause so much pain and suffering?'*

My heart filled with peace as I finally realised how much God loved me despite my angry attitude. His love is truly unconditional. I repented of my attitude and picked up my journey with God again. I knew with my head that I was no longer deserted but, at the same time, struggled to truly accept it in my heart.

A month later I no longer felt the heavy burden of pain in my heart. It was a quiet Saturday afternoon, and I was enjoying the beautiful view over the mountains. I wanted to experience more of who God is in my life. I knew now that He was seeking after me but how could I experience more of that?

"God I need more of you," I said while relaxing in my chair. I sensed something but did not know what it was. It was a holiness that surrounded the veranda where I sat. I just knew that I had to kneel down in reverence.

As I was facedown on my knees, a thought passed quickly through my mind, *'I hope no-one sees me lying here on the ground for no reason.'*

Just then a small voice whispered to my heart, "Stop smoking and pay your telephone bill."

I had been a regular smoker in Holland but when I came to Africa where smoking is not tolerated as a Christian, I had drastically reduced to just one or two cigarettes each evening. I only smoked when I was alone in the home because I did not want to upset anyone. Since there were no cookies or sweets available in the shops I reckoned it was okay to smoke a few cigarettes just for my enjoyment, until this moment. It became very clear that my

---

11 Isaiah 62:12

time smoking was over!

I stood up, took my packet of Marlboro's and flushed them down the toilet. A strange feeling of relief came over me as I watched the little white sticks turning brown in the water and disappearing. I then realised that all along I had felt like a little school kid trying to hide my bad habit.

The telephone bill was another story. I had lived in my house for four years, and had never received a telephone bill. I had reminded the Post Office on several occasions, but they had not given me a bill for all those years. I had resolved that it was their problem and that I wouldn't pursue a solution any longer.

I made some quick calculations and was shocked when I realised that I had a backlog of charges amounting to at least US$3,000. I had made many calls to The Netherlands in times of crisis. I remember making one phone call that lasted at least three hours. I so desperately needed to talk to someone, that I had not worried about the costs involved, or perhaps, in my heart, I knew I wouldn't get a bill, so it did not matter to me how long my phone calls were.

Early on Monday morning, I went to the Post Office and requested my bill. I waited for almost two hours as they went through all the files to look for my bill. I was determined to be obedient to God. In my heart, though, I struggled, *'This is a lot of money, do I really have to pay everything - isn't it their fault? Why should I have to push them to give me a bill?'* When they could not find it, I told them that I would come back later to pick it up. Three days later, I went back and there was still no bill.

The third time, I went into the Post Office with a true desire to settle the money matters. The manager told me, "Just pay for a new connection and from now on, we will send you a bill." I gladly parted with US$40 and paid my bills regularly ever after. I smiled as I realised that God had once again wanted to test my obedience.

CHAPTER FIVE

Suffering Street Children

CRO had acquired more assets and more staff. We had worked on the job descriptions and begun to structure the first initiatives. A lady called Beatrice was appointed as one of the Social Workers. She lived at the project house. One night there was a lot of noise and she realised that thieves had come to break into the office. She did the only wise thing she could do and hid quietly in the corner of her room. Most thieves in Uganda are armed. They don't fear killing people, if you raise the alarm. The following morning we found out that the thieves had taken all our kitchen utensils. Fortunately we did not have very expensive equipment, but in a country like Uganda everything is precious.

We went to the police to make a statement. The police told us that Beatrice had to come back in the afternoon to make another statement. At 4 o'clock in the afternoon she had not yet returned to the project so Christine and I decided to check on her. We were so shocked to find her locked in the cell. *'Beatrice behind bars? She who loves and cares for the street children so much!'*

When we talked to the police officers they told us that Beatrice was the first suspect and that they would work on her case on Monday. Everything in me protested; we couldn't leave her, innocent as she was, in a cell for the whole weekend! We argued with the police and felt strongly that they had done this because they were looking for some extra money to spend at the weekend. We knew that if we bribed the policeman Beatrice would be out in five minutes. But we just would not give in to a corrupt system. We told the police, "If you do not release her, we will also stay here over the weekend!"

Christine and I sat down on a bench on one side of the bars while Beatrice with ten other people sat locked up on the other side of the bars. We were encouraging ourselves when the story of Paul and Silas came to my mind. "Why don't we sing and praise our God?" I asked. We decided to follow their example and started singing praises to God, believing that the walls of the prison would fall. After half an hour, the policemen were so fed up with us. They came with the key, opened the cell and released Beatrice from prison.

Honesty requires me to admit that our singing was not the nicest and the motive of our song was not only to praise our God but also to draw attention to our cause. However, the doors opened and God performed the same miracle as He had in the book of Acts!

After working with the children for a few months, we realised that they were having problems with the police on a regular basis so we decided to make pictures of all the CRO children in order to give them identity cards. In case they landed in trouble with the police they could identify themselves as being part of CRO and we could then go to the police and speak on their behalf. Street children do cause problems but they are also an easy scapegoat for all the problems in the town. The identity cards would help the children to show the rest of the community that they were associated with an organisation that was working with them towards their rehabilitation and resettlement to their homes.

We had printed two pictures of each child, one for their identity cards and one picture for our notice board. We wanted to keep track of all the children CRO worked with. The children were so excited, they had never had their pictures taken and it made them feel valued and important. We called the children in one by one and said, simply, "Find your own picture and we will glue it on your identity card." The first child entered, he was excited and saw all his friend's pictures. He started naming all the children, but when he reached his own picture, he skipped it to name the next picture. I did not think anything of it but when the second and the third child did the same thing, I suddenly realised that the children had no clue how they looked, themselves. They did not recognise their own faces.

That's when it dawned on me that the children had never seen a mirror, or a window; they had never looked at their own face in still water; they had never seen their own reflection. Now I also understood why, often, when I parked my car anywhere in the town, the car mirrors were turned downwards – in order for children to see what they looked like.

The first thing we did after we discovered this was to buy a huge mirror and put it on the wall. The mirror was constantly in use!

One of the biggest problems we were confronted with was that most of the children were addicted to glue or petrol. I visited all the petrol stations in the town and requested that the owners stop selling petrol to the children. For 5-dollar cents the children had enough fuel to be high for the whole day. Most owners admitted selling fuel to the children and it shocked me that they did not see anything wrong with it.

The children knew that we were in disagreement with them over their use of addictive substances and therefore they had to make a daily choice: "Am I going to use petrol today or am I going to school". If they decided to come to CRO they had to part with their little bottles filled with addictive. When they would see us in the town they would hide from us when they were drunk or they pretended not to see us. The fuel made the children aggressive, drunk and wild.

Paul was one boy who reacted strongly to petrol. On one occasion, as I walked down to the market I heard Paul's voice behind me shouting, "This is the mzungu who beats children; this is the mzungu who beats children." Mzungu is the Swahili word for 'white person' so there was no doubt that he meant me.

Some of the other street children saw me coming and ran away from me meanwhile hiding their petrol. People stopped their activities to see who this white person was that beats children. I laughed it off, straightened my back and walked as if nothing had happened.

Emeremere was the most 'famous' beggar in Mbale town. He was a young boy; we guessed that he was about five years of age. Everybody knew him because he had a distinctive mark on his body. When he was a baby, his parents who were drunk, fought over some meat that was on the fire. Unfortunately when the father beat his mother, the mother dropped the baby in the fire. He was terribly burned but he did not die. He'd been laid on his side. The wound was open and it took many months for it to heal. Once it had healed, his shoulder was joined to his chin. He did not have a neck so it was difficult for him to see beside and behind him. He was severely disabled.

A team of Dutch surgeons were coming to a nearby town to carry out free plastic surgeries. We wanted to register Emeremere for an operation, but were confused when his mother refused. She told us that the boy was bringing in a lot of money and that she could not do without her source of income. I was so upset – this had never occurred to me; refusing a free operation that could bring freedom for your child, because he is your source of income! I pondered about it the whole day and decided not to give up on her. Fortunately we had a few weeks before the operation, and we counselled her every day.

Another big problem was that she was not allowed to drink in the hospital, so she could not go and stay with the boy. In the hospitals in Uganda it is common practice to bring a relative or a friend to care for you and to cook the food. Mama Emeremere finally agreed for her son to be operated on the condition that somebody else would stay with the boy in the hospital; she was not willing to give up her drinking. Another mother from the slum area was willing to care for the boy in the hospital and, when the day of the operation came, we drove to the next town.

Emeremere was sitting on the back seat in the car. Suddenly I heard a very excited voice shouting in a language I did not understand. When I asked for a translation the social worker laughed and said, "Emeremere has never seen houses running so fast!" I realised that the boy had never sat in a car before. I surely took a lot of things for granted!

The community attitude towards street children was very negative. Some people found it difficult to understand why we worked with thieves and pickpockets. Street children were blamed for most of the crime committed in the town. Many children were involved in petty theft, not necessarily because they wanted it but because circumstances forced them too.

There were sudden round-ups in the towns where the police arrested all street children. CRO's social workers spent whole days in the police station, pleading on behalf of the children. Often the police released the children who were connected to CRO after the children made a commitment to attend our centre on a daily basis. We developed a good working relationship with the police in Mbale.

Magombe was one of the bigger street boys in the town. He must have been 14 years old. For as long as I'd known him, he had lived on the streets of Mbale. The streets were his home. He never told us where his relatives were and he had no desire to reveal his past to us. Almost every day he passed by my office window to greet me. His whole life he had been stealing and it was difficult to stop the habit. Every one called him a thief.

He refused to go to school. Over time I realised that his greetings through the window changed; he started to look at me seductively, giving me very dirty looks. I decided not to tolerate this kind of behaviour and asked him to come in the office. Christine and I asked him what was happening with him and why his behaviour towards us had changed.

He opened up and admitted that he started flirting with me because he now knew what sex was and how you could convince women to give in. He then told us that he had a partner, a primary school child, who slept with him every night for only 30 cents. He was not using condoms; they were too expensive. Magombe was knowingly exposing himself to the deadly disease, AIDS. As we probed further, we reached his heart. He admitted that his life was rotten but he didn't have the inner strength to change it. He did not believe that God could do it for him. My heart cried out for him. Here we were, willing to help him reach his potential but he closed the door to our help right in our faces. '*Why would someone refuse help?*' I asked, silently.

Early one morning, we found him at the entrance of CRO all covered in blood. He had a deep cut on his head. His brains were almost visible. As fast as we could, we rushed him to the hospital for treatment. When we arrived at the hospital the doctors said, "This is an assault case, we are not allowed to treat this boy without a police report." I felt like shouting, '*This boy is dying and needs treatment now!*' But I knew that shouting would have the opposite effect, so I kept quiet and rushed the boy to a private clinic where they worked to close his wound. He needed three weeks of rest in the CRO medical room, but after one week he escaped back to the street. He would wave at me in the town but had no desire to leave his lifestyle on the streets.

I felt like Habakkuk, and cried out to God, *"How long, O Lord, must I call for help, but you do not listen? Or cry out to you, 'Violence!' but you do not save? Why do you make me look at injustice? Why do you tolerate wrong? Destruction and violence are before me; there is strife, and conflict abounds. Therefore the law is paralysed, and justice never prevails. The wicked hem in the righteous, so that justice is perverted."*[12]

Everything seemed to be a struggle and breakthroughs in the behaviour of the children were taking so long. How I longed to see 'greater things than Jesus did' that the Bible promised!

---

12 *Habakkuk 1:2-4*

CHAPTER SIX

Unexpected Provision

Many more children became part of CRO and after one year the house we had rented had became too small. A house with eleven rooms in the town was available for rent. As the number of children increased so did our activities. There was growth and God blessed the work of our hands despite the setbacks with some of the children.

Soon after we had moved into this big house the board decided that it would be good to purchase our own premises. The rent increased often; rental contracts were not so respected in Uganda, so there was a chance that we could be evicted without notice. Landlords were not happy when they found out that their premises were used to assist 'criminals', as the street children were often labelled. The number of children kept increasing and soon our rented house became too small for all the activities that were going on in CRO.

We identified a huge building, right in the centre of town as the ideal place for our own drop-in centre. It was near the bus park, the place where most of the street children were hanging out. Collectively, we began trusting God for this building. We walked around the building praying and fasting for it, claiming the property for God's work. The owners wanted US$90,000, which was a lot of money for a building that needed to be completely rebuilt. But the space was great, the location even better. All the board members, staff and children felt this was the ideal place for our own premises. The building also had an option to rent out shops, which would help raise an income for the project.

A representative of a Dutch donor agency was passing through Mbale on his way to a project that they sponsored in the next town. I sent him a message and asked if he could stop by so that we could talk to him. One Saturday evening he came by. Simon Peter and I met with him to discuss our need for our own premises. His organisation was not focusing on social issues so he wondered how he could be of help. We explained that we needed a one-off grant because our on-going support was already secured. However much he wanted to help, he was bound by the regulations of his agency. Suddenly he said, "I may know an option but the money is not meant for a church building, and you are not allowed to use it for evangelism."

I wanted to be honest and told him, "But we are praying with the people." He answered, "But which African is not praying?"

'That's true,' I thought, *'Africa is a spiritual continent.'*

When he confirmed that he saw an option to help us, I offered to take him to the slum area so that he could see the community component of our work. The following morning we picked up Beatrice and went into the slums together. She knew the women better and could help us to translate. We walked the slum area and entered the hut of a very sick lady. She was terminally ill with AIDS. When we entered the hut, the smell of death had almost taken over the place. She was lying on a mattress made out of rags. Beatrice took her hand and spoke encouraging words to the dying lady. Then she turned to us and said with joy in her voice, "She gave her life to Christ last week!" Instead of rejoicing over a lost soul, I panicked because the donor had said we were not supposed to do evangelism and I feared our money would disappear. I felt so bad that this was my first thought and repented of that later. We prayed for the lady before we left. I suggested to the donor that I show him the building we would like to buy. He agreed but also said, "I do not need any more convincing, I have seen that you need it." God had either closed his ears to the evangelism, or he saw the need for evangelism. Whichever it was he gave us US$100,000 to purchase the building!

My heart overflowed with thanksgiving. This was wonderful, US$100,000 in less than two hours! That had never happened to me before; it could only be God. I was so encouraged that God had shown me again that He is the ultimate provider.

Once the paperwork was done, and we were the true owners of the building, we needed more funds to renovate the building. My former employer, the Evangelical Broadcasting Company, agreed to make a documentary on our project for fund-raising purposes. This programme, together with donations of three other donors raised the US$250,000 we needed for the renovation works.

We were the happy owners of a dilapidated building in one of the main streets in the town. We had fenced the building with iron sheets, until we had the funds to renovate the place. Thieves had used the building as a hiding place, but now that we were the owners, we did not want to have any illegal actions taking place in it.

"There is a lot of blood coming from our new building," one of our children shouted, running into our office. I feared going there; I had seen enough blood and death over the last years. Christine, courageous as she is, went to check out what had happened. Someone had been knifed and killed inside the building. The police searched the body for any clues. They found an identity card in the pocket of the murdered man and it had my address on it! I was scared. *'Who is playing games with me?'* I wondered.

Once again I felt very vulnerable and under attack. *'Who is using my address, why was this man murdered and how am I associated with it?'* Many questions filled my mind, but again there were no answers.

The police ordered some prisoners to take the body out and to clean the building. The identity card issue had no further consequences apart from the fact that I knew satan was not happy and was using all means to steal away my peace.

In Uganda it is common to sacrifice an animal or sometimes even a person while building a new building, to invoke the spirits to bless it. When we started the renovation works, the community said that we did not need to offer a sacrifice anymore, since someone had already been killed in our building. This statement hurt me so much. This building was going to be used for God's Kingdom and satan had to take his hands off. All the staff, board members and children walked through the building to dedicate it to God. While walking through the ruins I knew deep in my heart that this building was going to be a blessing to many children.

After four years in operation CRO had become known as a 'women's venture'. All people in leadership positions were women, except for some of the board members. Sometimes being females helped, sometimes we were a threat to the dominant male society. This became clear when we started the renovation works. The work was tendered and we found a local construction firm to do the rebuilding and adjustments. I was to supervise it but did not have any building experience, I only knew what I liked or didn't like and I knew how to pretend as well!

Every day I would check on the work. One morning, when the renovations had been underway for five months and the new interior walls were going up, I entered the building site. One of the workers greeted me, "Good morning, Ssebo", which means 'Sir'. Sometimes they call women Ssebo as a sign of honour but I did not think that this worker wanted to honour me. The workmen on the site really struggled with the fact that a woman was in charge of the decisions made on a construction site. So I asked, "Truly, am I a Sir?" He looked at me and smiled saying, "No, no, you are in the middle!" Soon it was rumoured that my nickname had become, 'The iron lady of Mbale'.

It was a time in which I questioned God why He had chosen a woman to do this kind of work. The construction work did not appeal much to my femininity and I did not like it at all.

After eight months of renovation, it was time to celebrate the opening of our own premises. Dignitaries and other officials, as well as pastors and donor agencies were invited for the opening ceremony. It was a great occasion where we celebrated God's goodness and provision. However, the only 'compliment' we ever received about CRO that day, was in a speech given by a man from the local authorities. He commented, "We waited for you women to fail."

Another typical man's job that I had to do was clearing my new vehicle with Customs in Mombasa, Kenya. God had blessed me with a new car but it needed to be cleared and brought into the country. There were clearing agents who were able to do that work but they would charge huge sums of money, so I calculated that it would be cheaper if I did it myself.

The new car was a real miracle. My good friends Hans and Christine were visiting me a few months before. On our way to one of the game parks, my car broke down in a remote area, which was not very safe. We managed to get the car to a police station where it could stay for the night while we took a bus to Jinja. They saw my struggles with the car and on their return to The Netherlands they initiated a fund-raising drive for a new car. Now that it had arrived I was excited; no more struggles, no more fear of a breakdown. It was brand new – I had never owned a brand new car before!

Memories about my old car came back to me on the 1000km bus journey to Mombasa. I remembered the time that it broke down in the middle of nowhere, in an area where there were lots of robberies and it was getting dark. Frantically I tried to stop the few cars that were passing. No one stopped; I felt so unsafe and vulnerable.

It was almost dark when a taxi passed me at high speed. I tried to stop him but the car was driving too fast. I sighed with relief when I saw two break lights in the dark. Then the reverse lights came on and the taxi came all the way up to me and asked what the problem was. We towed my car to the next town and parked it at the police station for the night. I jumped in the taxi to find a place to sleep in the next town. That's when I heard the conversation that had taken place in the taxi when they saw me waving down the car, "This is a lady from Mbale, you need to stop and help her," a passenger had said. The taxi driver had replied, "I have also stopped her once and she did not stop for me." The passengers knowing that this was a dangerous spot convinced the driver to stop and assist me.

On the dock in Mombasa, I was the only woman amongst hundreds of men. I needed to find a listening ear as I tried to locate my car. What on earth was I doing with these masses of men who were trying to clear their goods? People couldn't even see me; they didn't even expect women in this area. Finally I found one man who wanted to help me, no strings attached, and in three days I was on my way to Uganda happy with the new car but frustrated with the way I had been treated as a woman.

Ever since I'd returned to Uganda it had been a long, lonely struggle and I wondered once again why I seem to have to do all these things alone. I even wondered if God had not made a mistake in creating me as a woman. I knew it was a funny question, but

I was so fed up having spent three days amidst hundreds of men without even a single toilet for women anywhere in sight! It was a difficult trip back from Mombasa to Uganda despite the fact that I was very happy with my new car.

While driving back to Uganda, I remembered another journey to Mombasa in 1982. I was with my friend Alma and we had to clear an 8-tonne truck with relief goods. There was no one I knew who could drive it so I volunteered to do it. She joined me in Nairobi. We had so much fun! Here we were, two ladies in their mid twenties, driving a big truck through Africa. People laughed at us and so did we of ourselves. Truck drivers stared and made their jokes about us but we did not care. We had fun! The truck went slow and we had to stay overnight on our way to Uganda.

The road we were on was muddy and very slippery. Before we realised what happened the truck slid off the road into a ditch. It was almost dark. We were on our way to the hotel in a remote village. Within a few minutes many people had surrounded us and were giving us advice on what to do. Some people suggested that we emptied the truck, but it had a customs seal on it and we would be in big trouble if we opened it. We were literally stuck! Fortunately there was an army barracks nearby and they had a tractor. We managed to hire the tractor but it did not have the strength to pull the car out.

At 10 o'clock at night we managed to get another tractor from the Mayor of the nearby town and by midnight the truck was pulled out of the ditch. So many people assisted us. We invited them to the hotel for a drink, in order to say 'thank you' to them. Little did we know that a drink would inevitably go together with food! The following day we continued our journey completely broke after paying the huge restaurant bills. We still had fun but we were not as naïve anymore as the day before!

CHAPTER SEVEN

Insecurities

In the meantime, the foundations of my house in Jinja were rotting away. I did not have the time, or energy to continue to build the house after Johan's death and I didn't have the money to hire a construction firm. I also knew that my priority was with CRO and I could not split myself into two. I was tired of renovation and building.

Whenever I travelled to Kampala I would usually stopover in Jinja and check on the compound; every time something went wrong. As soon as I entered the dirt road leading to my house, my imagination would go wild. *What would be stolen this time? What might have gone wrong?* I could do nothing besides expect the negative.

The watchman told me, one day that he'd seen a big black Mercedes entering the compound, followed by another car. An important looking man got out of the car and started giving him instructions to pay more attention to his work. This man pretended to be the owner of the land and wanted to sell it behind my back. I just knew I could not continue to struggle this way. The only option was to ask God to really help me. If I was His child, I should not suffer so much! I felt lonely, abandoned and stressed.

I went with some friends from The Netherlands to Jinja to pray specifically for the house and the compound. I had fallen in love with the environment so quickly that I had not even asked God

His opinion when I bought the land. Perhaps I had run ahead of Him once again. We prayed and I gave the whole place back to God. If it meant giving it away, I was ready; if it meant selling, I was ready; if it meant developing it further I was ready, but I was not willing to continue struggling with it the way I did. At the end of the weekend God gave me a scripture and I knew it was meant for this situation: *"Do I bring to the moment of birth and not give delivery?"*[13] I knew that God was going to help me out! It was also the first time that I got a strong sense that God had given me this property for a purpose.

That same week I got in contact with a very reliable plumber and he offered to continue to supervise the building work. I could trust him with a little money every time I passed through Jinja and within a period of four years the house was built. The struggle was not completely over and the process was slow. There were still times that I wanted to give up; it was sheer perseverance and nothing else that made me to continue.

An engineer friend came to see the house. He looked at it, admired it but then said, "Ingrid, you have a very big problem; your roof is sagging and very soon it will collapse." The house was designed for nice thin black slate roof, available in the USA but not in Uganda. I had searched for tiles resembling the dark slate and I found them. The only difference was that each tile was five kilograms and I never thought about the consequences of the increased weight on the roof. The foundations for the pillars had to be rebuilt and, with five car jacks and ten strong men, the whole roof was lifted and a heavy metal beam was put underneath the roofing tiles.

I wanted a good view of the river and, at the same time, strong security bars so the plans for the house included long windows with small windowpanes. The best way to achieve this was to make

---

13 Isaiah 66:9

strong steel windows frames with small glass panes. These were ordered but unless one sat next to the welder, nothing happened! I did not have the time to sit next to the welder so I waited for about three months before the windows were ready.

When they were finally fitted in the house I realised that something was wrong. On one side of the house the windows were nine inches and on the other side the windows were eleven inches. I lost my cool and called the welder; he was a small man. I asked him if he saw what was wrong. He did not see it. So I told him, "Try to climb through this window," pointing at the nine-inch window, he tried and failed.

"Try to climb through this one," I said, pointing to the eleven inch window. He climbed through easily.

"You are making my windows burglar proof with heavy steel, but so big that any thief can climb through." I was upset but the man looked at me and had no idea why I lost my cool! All the windows had to be re-done and it took another two months for it to be completed.

I was desperate to see the house finished but almost everything had to be done twice. I do not remember how much blood, sweat and tears were shed over this house! But it was also amazing to see how the right people came at the right time to give me help, suggestions and ideas on how to improve on the design. It was a tiresome process and nothing was straightforward but it became a real homemade house. Somehow I knew that one day God would make it clear what He wanted me to do with it, but for now my place was in Mbale.

Although the security in the country was so much better, there were still incidents taking place. On a number of occasions I had hid in my corridor because the shooting was so near the house that I felt the bullets could come through the window anytime.

It was approaching Christmas, 1994. My good old friend Hans

came to visit. I had known him for the past 15 years and we had always stayed in touch. He would usually come once a year with a pile of books to make use of my hammock for two weeks. We were on our way to the airport and passed through the capital city, Kampala. In Uganda, Christmas is the most important feast of the year and everyone prepares for it in his or her own way. The town was busy, it was drizzling and there was a huge traffic jam. Suddenly we heard a lot of shooting nearby. The car in front of my car was an open pick-up full with people. Suddenly all the people jumped out of the car and they laid flat on their stomachs on the wet and muddy road. That is when I realised how serious the situation was. I saw policemen running with their guns. To my amazement they were running away from the fight instead of helping to solve it.

"Get down!" I shouted at Hans as I dived underneath the dashboard. A thought passed my mind to get out of the car, but I realised that someone else could take advantage of that and steal my bag! I had just been to the bank to prepare for my own Christmas!

As fast as we could we got down and squeezed ourselves under the dashboard. I remember thinking, "I must turn my buttocks to the door, it is easier to remove a bullet from my buttocks than from my head!"

When I looked at us squeezed under the dashboard it was so ludicrous that I could only laugh. Hans wondered if I always laughed when faced with death.

Ambushes on the road still happened, though not as much as many years back, but it was still a force to reckon with, especially approaching Christmas time or on certain routes to the North. My house in Mbale was a stopover place for either a drink or a place to sleep for a number of people who worked in the North, before continuing their journey.

Early in 1995, on one of their stopovers, I shared the Kampala experience with some of my missionary friends who were on their way to Karamoja in Northern Uganda, where they were working. We had a drink and a laugh together, celebrating that we were all still alive and sharing stories about our experience dodging bullets. It was just a brief stop because they wanted to get home. They had a seven-hour journey ahead of them. I waved them goodbye and wished them a safe journey.

The following morning early, a hooting car waked me. The driver jumped out and told me that my friends were ambushed and that their Ugandan colleague, who was with them in the car, had died. I was broken and shocked, *'I am so tired of death. Lord, where are You? Are You aware that these things happen to Your children?'* My head knew the truth of His word, *"God is good,"* but my heart could not grasp it.

I sat outside and consoled myself by looking at the beautiful sunrise above the mountains of Mbale and tried to understand God.

CHAPTER EIGHT

Church

The 'born again' churches in Africa are often loud churches. People sing, dance and shout. Being a born again Christian in Uganda somehow meant that you belong to a selected group of people. When born again Christians meet in Uganda the first greeting is "Praise God". As soon as you say, "Praise God," you are considered part of this select group. There used to be this unwritten rule that you needed to behave in a certain way too; there was a dress code, a clear rule about what you were allowed to eat and drink and sometimes even where you bought things. If you didn't stick to the rules there was judgement. In my struggle with God, I wanted to be honest with myself and also with Him. I did not feel like pretending. There were times when it was too difficult for me to say "Praise God".

From the moment I started living in Mbale, I knew it was important to be a member of a local church. Not only because it is written in the Bible, but also to get to know my Ugandan brothers and sisters and to share our lives together. The church services were very different than what I was used to. Church in Uganda is also a social happening and it is not strange for announcements to take half an hour. On most occasions the service would also be used to distribute mail to church members. Fundraising activities often took place after the service.

Other missionaries who worshipped there introduced me to the church that I attended. They told me that this was one of the most accommodating churches for foreigners in Mbale. I had taken their word and decided to make it my church for as long as I was in Mbale. Each Sunday morning began with Sunday School at 9.00am, with the main service starting at 10.00am. Most times it was 2.30pm before we would leave church and often I skipped the fundraising that was done after the service. Every evening of the week there was an activity; Bible study, prayer meeting, cell group, worship and, once a month, overnight prayer.

I just knew I would not be able to attend all the church meetings. It was too difficult to keep up with all the programmes in the church at the same time as having a full-time job and also staying in touch with family and friends at home. Letters were all hand-written and there was no quick e-mail communication yet. I had made a decision that CRO was the reason I had come to Mbale and therefore that was my first priority.

Sunday was my only day of rest and soon I decided that as much as I knew I needed to be part of a church I could not sit for five hours in a Sunday service so I gave myself permission to leave after three hours. Often the sound was so loud, that I found it difficult to concentrate and find God in the church service. I struggled to go to church and often left feeling guiltier than before. I felt that people were watching me, that I was not giving enough, not involved enough, not attending the extra activities, not praying enough, not singing loud enough and not fasting long enough. I did not go to overnight events and I did not dance and shout.

I stood and watched all the people dancing and I felt distant from God. I had so many questions for Him. I wanted my answers so I really tried staying in the church service longer, fasting longer and reading more of my Bible, but it did not help my wounded heart.

One of the Elders of the church stopped me in the middle of the road one day and told me, "Ingrid, we are really praying for you so that you will stay longer in the church."

This upset me; God was not giving me answers and the church had not helped me either, it had only made me feel guiltier. With my blunt Dutch communication style I answered, "I am really praying for you that you become good stewards of time."

It was reported back to me that I had been disrespectful to the Elder of the church. Somehow I felt, whatever I do for or in the church I would never do it well enough. I continued going to church out of sheer obedience to God's word.

Another Christmas was approaching. One day, in October 1995, the Pastor asked me if I wanted to host his visitors. Without asking any questions I answered, "Sure, they are welcome." I was shocked when I found out that they were a family with two children and that they were coming for two weeks during Christmas and the New Year! I felt cheated and panicked as well, *'How could I handle four extra people, care for them, work full time, organise Christmas parties for the children and for the staff of CRO, maintain my relationships in Holland by writing almost 100 Christmas cards and share the Christmas season with people I did not even know?'*

I was already tired and was looking forward to some quiet time on my own. But I had said yes and had to keep my word; *"Let your 'Yes' be 'Yes', and your 'No', 'no',"*[14] it was underlined blue in my Bible.

The visitors came; it was their first time in Africa and they experienced a complete culture shock. Early in the morning when I woke up the children were drinking Coca Cola and eating chocolate biscuits from the UK because they did not like the Ugandan food. They feared anything new so they spent most of their days indoors. I did not have the energy to make it a wonderful Christmas for them; I had nothing left to give. They felt so out

---

14 *Matthew 5: 37*

of place in Uganda that they tried, for the whole of Boxing Day, to call the airline to change their ticket and return to the UK sooner than planned. Again I felt a failure; I had not been able to encourage them, to give love to them and I had failed miserably to make their Ugandan Christmas a great experience. Just before the New Year they left; in my heart I hoped that the New Year would bring them more fun that this last Christmas had done.

In the next six months after Christmas I was without visitors for just three weeks. I was looking forward to some time on my own. I needed it. I loved visitors but it was also a lot of work on top of a full-time job. As I returned from the airport where I had just said good-bye to some of my friends, the thought of going back to an empty house really appealed to me! I decided to stop in Jinja to check on the progress of my house. Strangely, there was a tent on the campsite.

When I came closer I recognised a Dutch lady called Irene. I had seen her once before. She was a friend of the late Johan and had come to visit his wife and the children. I walked over to greet her and when I asked how she was doing, she said she felt sick and wondered if she could come with me to Mbale. I struggled; I so longed for time on my own and decided to tell her, that actually I really needed time alone. For the first time I dared to protect my own needs.

"Usually I am hospitable," I said "but I have had so many visitors of late that I am really looking forward to some time on my own."

"I am really not feeling well can I please come with you?" she asked.

That's when the little voice in me said, *"Surely you can make one exception; you can't let her be here on her own when she is not feeling well."*

It was Friday. I had a free weekend ahead of me and really looked forward to it. Was I going to make that sacrifice to take somebody

I don't know with me to Mbale? I relented out of obedience to the little voice, but deep in my heart I did not agree with the things I heard my mouth say.

During the trip to Mbale there was deathly silence in the car. I was having a strong discussion with heaven, *'Lord, why do I always have to be there for others? Don't You see that I am tired?'*

When we were approaching Mbale, I knew I had to repent of my complaining attitude and after repentance my conversation with the Lord changed. In my heart I prayed, *'Lord, now that Irene is here, will You make Yourself known to her? Will You use this time to reveal Your salvation to her?'*

Just before dark we reached home. After we unloaded our bags from the car we poured ourselves a cold drink and relaxed from the long journey on the veranda.

We had just settled when I heard a knock on the gate. It was dark and I could not see who was at the gate, but the night watchman opened it and I recognised the voice of the pastor of my church.

I wondered to myself, *'What has he come for at night?'* He was not alone; the assistant pastor was with him. In a country where security is not good it is rare to receive visitors at night, unless there is an emergency. I was concerned, thinking, *'There must be a purpose for their visit and it must be urgent otherwise they would not come at this time.'*

I rushed to the fridge to put my cold drink back. I did not want to offend the pastor – alcohol and being born again were incompatible in the Ugandan Church. I welcomed them, introduced Irene to them and invited them to come into the house. Irene remained on the veranda, enjoying the cool of the night. After the traditional greetings, I prepared some tea for them since it was the first visit of the assistant pastor to my house. Ugandan culture had taught me that you need to give a first-time visitor at least some refreshment, if you are not able to give them a meal.

After I had served the tea, and we had exchanged small talk, they revealed the reason for their visit. They said there was a lot of sin in the church and they had visited a number of church members who were living in sin and, this coming Sunday, their names would be read as members who were going to be expelled from the church. I felt I wanted to disagree with this doctrine, but decided to listen and not to speak.

"We have come," the pastor said, "because there is a lot of sin in your life."

I was shocked, *'Yes I know I am a sinner; I also know that I am saved by grace and that it takes a lifetime to become the person God wants me to be, but speak up I am ready for change,'* I thought to myself.

He opened his briefcase and got a piece of paper out, which spelled out at least six serious sins. I listened and got very concerned about Irene, who was sitting on the veranda listening to the conversation through the open window. Just two hours ago I had prayed that God would reveal Himself to her. She had already confided in me that she found it hard to become a Christian because of the behaviour of so many Christians. I was fully aware that what was happening in this room was one of the reasons why she had not embraced Christianity.

I was dumbfounded; I had nothing to say, so I listened. After each sin was discussed in detail, the pastor ticked it with a pencil and the following sin was analysed. It was approaching midnight when the pastor looked me in the eye and said, "And, you are also deeply involved in witchcraft."

'Me, witchcraft?' I had been long enough in Uganda to know that witchcraft is an almost unforgivable sin so I asked the pastors why they felt I was involved in witchcraft. I once had heard a sermon that rebellion is the same as witchcraft, and I knew my fighting spirit, in the Ugandan culture, could easily be interpreted

as rebellion. Was that the reason why they said I was involved in witchcraft?

Many thoughts ran through my mind and I could not think of any incident that could be the source of this rumour, I only remembered that the pastor had preached against witchcraft in the church and that he knew there were people in his own church that were involved in witchcraft. Never, ever had it occurred to me that he was actually speaking about me!

The pastor continued, "We heard that you were planning to take a child to The Netherlands to sacrifice it and when you took the street children for a camping trip you met with a red snake and you told the children to worship that snake. Since that time you have put a red roof rack on your car and you are often wearing red clothes. You also bought land near the river and that is where the demons live. In addition to that, you have Muslim friends and Muslims are deeply involved in witchcraft."

The assistant pastor continued and said, "Ingrid, I had to pray for two weeks before I dared entering your house for I thought you would have red lights and red tables everywhere."

I laughed in disbelief and told the pastors, "Look, I have red toe nails and the red roses you see there are from my sister because she loves me."

All the while Irene listened through the open window...

Witchcraft was the last item on the long lists of sins I allegedly had been involved with. It was approaching half past midnight when I decided to speak.

"Did you hear anything positive about me?" I asked.

"That is not the reason why we are here," was the pastor's answer.

"Pastors, I want to pray with you because you have a big problem in your church with gossip and jealousy. I do not recognise myself in any of the things you discussed with me. The last four hours I felt you were talking about another person and not me."

I prayed with them, then we loaded their bicycles in my car and I took them home. When I came back it was well after 1.00 am and Irene was still sitting on the veranda. We got our cold drinks out of the fridge and talked until we heard the Mosque calling the Muslims for prayer and saw the sun rise above the mountains. She was shocked about the whole conversation and wondered why I had not asked these people to leave my house. I did not want to defend the attitude of the Christians but at the same time I also did not want this incident to be a hindrance for her to meet Christ. That night I pushed my hurt aside, hardened my heart against all the allegations and was 'strong in the Lord' because I did not want to be another stumbling block for Irene. But it surely was a painful experience.

Before I entered my bedroom I concluded our conversation, saying that we were all sinners and in need of a Saviour.

We slept in. I woke up with a funny feeling trying to recall what happened the previous night and I knew it was the conversation with the pastors. The following day was a Sunday and I was supposed to go to church. *'Should I go? What if my name was going to be read as a sinner needed to be expelled from the church?'* I decided to be courageous and go to church. Personally I knew that there was no known hindrance in my relationship with the Lord and that I had repented of all the known sins I had committed in my life.

At the end of the service names were being read. It was so painful to hear how good friends of mine were called forward to be publicly disciplined. I felt tense, was my name also going to be read out?

I was not on the list. I wondered why, but dared not ask and no one dared tell me. My leave was approaching and this issue was hanging like the Sword of Damocles above my head. I needed to know if I was going to be expelled from the church and would I be welcome again after I came back from The Netherlands?

Two days before I went on leave I ran into the assistant pastor of the church in town and with all the courage I had in me I asked, "Pastor, I am going on leave, I just want to know if everything is fine between the church and me. Since your visit to my house I have not heard from you anymore."

"Oh yes," the assistant pastor said, "The morning after our visit to your house we had a meeting in which we praised God for your spiritual attitude. Everything is fine!"

I had no reason to doubt their judgement. With a relieved heart I went to The Netherlands, knowing that I hadn't left an unresolved issue behind me. I enjoyed the company of family and friends and realised once again how much energy living in another culture takes. I enjoyed a time of good company, fun, nice food.

During my leave I met with different people who loved to come to Uganda and visit the children. Some of them came a few months later, after I had returned to Uganda. They were travelling missionaries who wanted to share the gospel with our street children. It was a wonderful time. The children were singing, dancing, praying and enjoying the preaching. God was moving among the children and my heart filled with thanksgiving. This is what I wanted; to see God at work, changing the lives of street children towards Him.

Halfway through the celebration I was handed a letter. The envelope was sealed. I was curious and opened the envelope wondering who would hand deliver a letter to me. I saw a familiar letter headed paper and realised that it was a letter from the church. I read the short letter and tears appeared in my eyes. The letter read that, *'due to my dubious testimony I was no longer considered a member of the church.'* The letter was copied to the Pastor's Fellowship in the town and to the CRO Chairman.

I walked out of the room. Some staff members were following me; they noticed that something was wrong. I went to my office and cried. The staff read the letter and understood my tears. One of them took the letter raised it up to heaven and prayed over it, just like Hezekiah when he received a letter with bad news. They encouraged me and told me it was the work of the enemy.

All I knew to do was to run to my friend and CRO Chairman Simon Peter. Over the years he had become a very good friend and counsellor. As one of the leading pastors in Mbale he was aware of most of the things that were going on in the churches in Mbale. I knocked on the door of his office and entered with teary eyes. He looked up from the letter he was reading. I recognised the letterhead on the paper he had in his hand. He had just received his copy of the same letter. The moment he saw me, a big smile appeared on his face and he spoke words that I will never forget, "Ingrid, you are going to be a strong Christian."

"But I don't like it," I said half laughing, half crying.

"Jesus, did not like to die for us," was his simple answer.

I swallowed my tears, smiled and strengthened myself, remembering how Joshua needed to be strong and courageous. I would be strong and courageous too and made an inner decision that no one would see me hurt. This was part of the price I had to pay to become like Jesus, a prayer I had so often prayed. Had I not told my Lord to do what He needed to do to make me more like Christ? Yes, I had prayed it, but surely this is not what I meant!

Sometimes I even wondered if God had made a mistake in sending me to Uganda. I tried to adjust to the Ugandan culture but even my trying was not good enough. It was so difficult for my Dutch approach and my direct character to blend in with the polite, never confronting Ugandans.

'Lord, will I ever change?'

"Yes, you will," was His answer, *"But not your way, My way."*

'My conscience is clear, my conscience is clear,' I had re-read the letter and the thought came again, *'My conscience is clear.'*

It occurred to me that this was a scripture somewhere in the Bible. I looked it up and realised that it was actually part of what the apostle Paul wrote to the Corinthians and I knew that this scripture was my reply to the letter I had just received.

I wrote to the pastor, *'God has given me the grace to accept your decision but I would like to say with Paul that "My conscience is clear, but that does not make me innocent. It is the Lord who judges me. Therefore judge nothing before the appointed time; wait till the Lord comes. He will bring to light what is hidden in darkness and will expose the motives of men's hearts. At that time each will receive praise from God."'*[15]

A missionary pastor from Tonga offered me a place and time of healing in his church. He had been involved with CRO and knew what we were doing. He was shocked when he had read the letter and came to my house to invite me to become a member of his church. I was grateful that I was not completely isolated from the body of Christ in Mbale.

One sermon he preached really touched me, *"If your enemy is hungry feed him."*

I bought a bunch of green bananas, the staple food of that part of Uganda, and a kilo of fresh meat and had it delivered to my former pastor's house. I knew we were not really enemies but I also knew we were not friends. I wanted the relationship to be restored but really did not know how to do it. His reaction, so I heard was, "I will accept this food only because it is not cooked but otherwise this woman could poison me."

It hit me; I had not seen that the problem was so deeply rooted. I really wanted reconciliation but stopped initiating it. I had tried my best but for reconciliation to take place, two parties are needed.

---

15 *1 Corinthians 4:4-5*

The time came when this pastor was to transfer to Kampala and a new pastor filled his place. He invited me back to the church. I kindly requested him to put it in writing since one of the accusations towards me was insubordination to the church leadership.

Many months later, Christine, Simon Peter and I were in a meeting in Kampala and we visited the pastor. We had a good time of fellowship together and I got the impression that everything was forgiven and that our relationship was healed.

But the stories did not stop. My Ugandan friends would come and tell me that they heard that I was hiding a human skull in my bedroom and that I had a fridge full of human blood.

Where people could not encourage me, God did. I received a letter from my youth leader of many years ago in The Netherlands. A month previously he and his wife had visited their children in Northern Uganda and stayed a day with me to break the long journey. We had spent a whole night talking and sharing. It was so good to have a listening ear.

The letter said, *'When we spent time with you, I noticed that you have changed. I asked myself, "How or what has changed Ingrid. Has she become older? Wiser? I came to the following conclusion, using grammatical terms: In years past, Ingrid was the 'first person' for Ingrid and the Lord was the 'third person', now the Lord is the 'first person' and Ingrid 'third'." Congratulations. Continue on this road!'*

It encouraged me but it was also a bit hard to swallow, because I never realised that apparently I found myself very important in the past. Yes, I was outgoing, and I knew I could dominate others, but I thought I was also a social person, ready to listen to others too.

In my heart, I was happy that it was becoming visible to others that God was changing me and, more importantly, that both He and I were committed to the process of making me more like Jesus.

Two years later, three weeks before I left Mbale, I finally received the letter from the new pastor welcoming me back and

I visited the church once more. The congregation welcomed me with applause, but I felt awkward and thankful at the same time; thankful that this painful chapter of my life was closed.

CHAPTER NINE

Chased by Darkness

Irene had enjoyed Uganda so much that after her one-month visit it remained in her heart. Once she was back in The Netherlands she decided to apply for a full time job in Uganda. She found a job in Northern Uganda, a war torn area; a difficult place to be. We remained in contact after our nightlong spiritual conversation but she had not made a commitment to Christ. So now and then she would come to Mbale and we would spend weekends together; times in which we would catch up on the good and the bad in our lives.

Usually she travelled back to Kampala early in the morning with the first taxi but this time I was planning to go with my own car in the afternoon. Travelling with a personal car is much safer so I asked her to join me in the afternoon but she insisted she wanted to go in the morning.

I repeated my offer, and finally she accepted it. She was going to join me in the afternoon. When we travelled on the smooth new road we came across a burned-out car wreck. It was clear that the accident had happened not long before. Many people were gathered around the taxi. We stopped to find out what had happened. The people told us that this was the first taxi that had travelled from Mbale to Kampala that morning. Eleven out of 14 people died instantly. It was clear to both of us that Irene had escaped death that morning. Dumbfounded we continued our journey.

The second time she escaped death was at my house in Jinja. We were spending a relaxing weekend with a group of people in the half-finished house. The hot afternoon was great for swimming down in the river. Irene had already jumped in the river when suddenly a huge two-metre-long black cobra appeared in the water. The three of us who were still standing on the shore saw this big snake swimming in Irene's direction. We shouted on the top of our voices telling Irene to come out as soon as possible. She heard us shout but did not know why we were panicking. The shouting made the snake change his direction and we sighed with relief. She could now safely reach the shore.

With a quick breast crawl she swam to the shore. But, all of a sudden the snake changed direction again and began swimming in Irene's direction. I was trembling on my legs and my voice failed; I was holding my breath just waiting for the confrontation to happen.

She lifted her head above the water and that's when she saw the huge snake passing by her at a distance of only 50 centimetres. As if someone told her, she held back her hand otherwise she would grab the snake by his head. God again protected her and she began seeing His hand on her life. It would take a third confrontation with death for her to commit her life to Christ.

Although the overall security in the country improved steadily, the security situation around my house in Mbale deteriorated. I had been on a business trip to Kampala and when I returned to Mbale I found my night watchman in shock. Three thugs with sticks and knives had attacked him the night before and they had locked him in the garage. When he realised that they had no guns, he made a lot of noise, scaring off the thugs. Thankfully they hadn't entered the house. He reported the matter to the police, but the police did not act.

Right after this incident my friends from the UK came to visit me. I felt very unhappy that this had happened just before they came because I wanted it to be a nice relaxing holiday for them. They had saved a long time to be able to make the journey and I did not want to disappoint them. We had a great time together and I managed to keep quiet about the incident so as not to scare them.

I heard a strange sound in the middle of the night, the sound of metal touching metal. It woke me up. My heart was beating wildly and I could not breathe. What was going on? Who was making this noise?

I opened the curtains and saw two men working on my car. Quietly I pushed the curtains aside so that I could see better; they had already cut out the rear window, climbed in the car and opened the bonnet. They were busy removing all the good parts from the engine.

I stiffened, *'What do I do?'* They had not seen me; they had no idea that I was watching them. My breath stopped. What was the wise thing to do? I contemplated and carefully checked if they had a gun.

My watchman had the night off, so I knew there was no one in the compound. I looked carefully but I did not see a gun. At least that was positive sign. *'Should I go out and invite them in for coffee?'* I had heard a story of a missionary who had the courage to do that and the thieves came to faith that same evening.

I decided, being a woman living alone in the house that, the best thing to do was to keep them as far away from me as possible. Like a mad woman I shouted on the top of my voice through the open window, "Thieves, thieves! Toka, toka," which is Swahili for 'get off'! One of the very few useful words I knew in Swahili.

The men heard my voice, jumped out of the car and disappeared in the dark. I quickly dressed and ran to the door to assess the damage that was done to my car. I had completely forgotten about my friends who were staying with me in the house. As I ran through the sitting room, I found them there, white as snow and shaking on their legs. They had just said to one another, "Do you think she is still alive?" before I stormed into the sitting room. My voice had sounded so terrible that they thought I had been killed. We went outside to check the damage. The rear window had been taken out and the battery was on the ground. In their haste the thieves had left all the valuable parts from the car behind. This was the second attack in less than a month. It was strange and I did not like it at all. We went to the police and reported the case, but the police did not act.

I came back from church one Sunday, about a month later and noticed that the glass in one of my sitting room windows was broken. The burglar-proof was left untouched. *'Had someone tried to enter the house or were they just intimidating me? And how did the glass break, had someone thrown a stone?'* Many questions, but I didn't have the answers. Again, I reported it to the police, but they did not act.

The next Sunday when I came from church, three windows were smashed. I reported to the police, yet again, but they did not act.

It made me nervous, it was clear that somebody was watching me. They knew when I was out and when I came in. I inspected the fence behind the house and discovered some holes. That same Sunday afternoon, I changed the fence, and had the windows repaired, but I still felt very vulnerable.

I was under attack and it did not feel right. I knew I was a conqueror in Christ and that satan could not get me to stop what God wanted me to do, but at the same time he once again managed to steal my peace-of-mind.

There were four other attempts to brake in, in the space of two months but I did not report them to the police anymore because they never acted.

I learned some of the enemy's tactics. It was true that I was in the front line of a spiritual battle. Bringing street children from darkness into the light does not make satan happy. I didn't know much about satan's tactics before I came to Uganda and most of what I had learned came through personal experience or through teachings in the local church. Although I did not fully agree with all of the teaching, I could no longer deny that satan was active and it was clear that he was going to give me some 'real-life' lessons.

One of those lessons came during a strange night. I just could not sleep, because of a heavy thunderstorm and lightening. On-going lightning lighted up the mountains of Mbale and it was as if the thunder was stuck behind them. It was a long and very heavy thunderstorm. Finally, long after midnight, I fell asleep, my fingers still in my ears to shut the terrible thunder out. At three in the morning I felt something funny moving on my shoulder. The storm had cut the electricity so it was pitch dark as I looked for my torch. When I switched on the light I saw a huge cockroach, about 5 centimetres long, enjoying his peace on my shoulder! I felt horrified.

My room usually is very clean and I had not seen a single cockroach in my bedroom in the past four years. I had managed to keep my house almost cockroach free since the first week I moved into the house. I brushed the insect off and killed it. Before I went back to sleep, I inspected the room and saw another big one climbing towards my feet in the bed. *'Surely, this is not normal,'* I thought to myself, *'Two big cockroaches in my bed?'* It had never happened before. It was strange. I killed the second one and went back to sleep.

After another hour I woke up again and felt something in my hair. I got the torch again and reached with my hand to where I had felt it. At that moment a huge cockroach flew from my head to the floor. My peace was completely gone, as I killed the third cockroach that night. What on earth was happening? I decide to leave the torch on and instead of sleeping I decided to pray. Something from within prompted me to resist the devil. I had never done that before and it sounded a bit funny to me. These are cockroaches and not devils, but I obeyed the prompting and said, "In the name of Jesus, satan, go!" My peace returned and the rest of the night I slept without being disturbed by cockroaches.

I began to see that satan was using seemingly 'normal' things to unsettle me. One morning I woke up from a terrible dream; one of my loved ones in The Netherlands had drowned. It has always been difficult for me to remember my dreams but this one was so vivid. My heart was heavy, knowing that any time the phone could ring and give me the devastating news. I walked to my phone, but as so often happened, there was no dialling tone; there was no way I could get in contact with The Netherlands.

I dressed, drank my coffee and went to work. But I could not concentrate; for all I knew I might have lost a loved one in The Netherlands and no one could get in contact with me. I decided to go home and pray. I had never experienced such a heavy feeling in my heart before so I prayed, "God if it is You who is speaking to me, perform a miracle and let the phone work, but satan if this is you who is giving me this heaviness, in the Name of Jesus go!"

My skull began to tingle and this feeling moved down over my whole body and it left through my toes. The heaviness was gone; all fear had disappeared. In that instant I knew that nothing had happened in The Netherlands and that everyone was okay, which was confirmed the next time I had contact with the people in The Netherlands. Satan obeyed the name of Jesus and I had learned a new spiritual lesson! Jesus had given me the power! I was deeply amazed. It was a lesson that I had to practice many times in the years to come. It actually saved my life a year later.

CHAPTER TEN

The Arrest

It was 1996, election time, and the whole country were full of political fever. Politics was the talk of the day. Security was tight and everybody was eagerly waiting for the day that they could elect their new president. Campaigns were in full swing and campaign posters were everywhere. When I came to work one morning I saw our CRO building covered with presidential campaign posters. I was very upset, we had just spent millions of shillings painting this property and now the posters spoilt it. On top of that, we were not a political project but a Christian project. Soon it showed that this was my typical Dutch reasoning. I did not know that during election times in Uganda, everything is labelled political.

I instructed a few of the CRO children to remove the posters from the walls, but I was not aware that this was a grave mistake. Within half an hour a police Landrover stopped in front of the building. Three armed policeman and three plain-clothes policemen entered the office and asked for the 'mzungu'. Christine asked them if she could be of help, but they ignored her, passed by her and stormed my office with their guns aimed at me. I had no clue what the problem was until they told me that I had instructed people to remove the campaign posters from the building. They asked me if I had a car so that I could follow them to the police station. I had come on my bicycle to the office, that day so I told the police that I would ride my bicycle and they could meet me at the police station. I was not allowed to go on my own and in full view of the whole street I was ordered into the police Landrover. Dozens of people had already assembled to see what the police invasion was about. People whispered their comments in a language that I did not understand but it was clear that I was the highlight of the day for many people in the street.

They took me to an office and I was interrogated.

"What were my hidden motives?"

"Why did I remove the posters?"

"Was I against the government?" Questions were fired at me all day.

I repeated the same thing all over. I was sorry; no I never meant to upset anybody. No, I was not against the government. On the contrary, we were very happy that the government were supporting our initiatives for street children. We had no political affiliation; we were a Christian organisation, fully aware that it is God who has instated leadership, so we need to obey the government. The man wrote my statement and then told me to bring the children who removed the poster. Everything in me protested and I informed the police officer that I was not able to do that. I could not handle the thought that children, who were already mistreated so much in life, were to be subjected to fierce questioning. The children had acted on my instructions and I was fully responsible for what had happened.

In the meantime the project premises were searched for political materials, but there was none. Police invaded the building, interviewed the children and searched for any incriminating materials.

Christine and all the staff had panicked; this was the way former regimes had worked in the past; back then when people were abducted they would never return. She ran to the Mayor as fast as she could and told him that the police had taken me to an unknown place. In the panic of that moment no one realised that the country had changed for the better. Although the questioning was very stressful, I was treated well by the police. When I returned to the office late in the afternoon, the people in the street clapped their hands and welcomed me back from the police station. The arrest of a mzungu had been the public entertainment for the day.

Although the police had cleared me, I noticed that some things had definitely changed. Every time I picked up the receiver to make a phone call, or when I received a call there was a funny click on my phone line. Could it really be possible that they were tapping my phone? I could not believe my ears. *'Who would want to tap my phone? I have nothing to hide.'* The people at the post office were my friends so I reported it to them. They laughed a little, did not look me in the eye but said, diplomatically, "We are able to tap anybody's phone."

All the letters in my mailbox were opened and taped up again. I showed these to the postmaster and asked him what the problem was. He denied any knowledge of tampering with my mail.

Wherever I went the intelligence services were there; I was shadowed everywhere I walked. It was scary and I almost became paranoid. At each corner of the road intelligence people were posted to observe what was going on in our project. We had nothing to hide and continued our work as transparently as possible. All of us tried hard to ignore what was going on. But without me knowing it, without me wanting it, without my participation it looked like I had become an enemy of the state.

The only thing we did more than ever was to pray. But in my heart I had this deep question, *'God where are You in all of this?'* I felt vulnerable and very alone. *'God, the only reason why I am in Uganda is to serve You! What have I done to deserve a treatment like this?'* My heart complained bitterly to God and I could not believe that this was my reward for working so hard in His Kingdom.

One Sunday, two weeks after the arrest the resident State Attorney, who was a member of the church I attended, came to me after the service.

"Ingrid, your file is on my desk and it really looks bad. It says that you are moving with some policemen who are rebels. A Government official has been to my office three times already and asked me why I have not yet arrested you and put you in prison. You need to do something, they want you behind bars. Please do not come to my office because people may think that you are bribing me. If you need information, contact my wife."

I quickly asked him the name of the Government Official. A piece of the puzzle fell into place when he mentioned the man's name; it was the same man who wanted me to be his girlfriend! It seemed like his time for revenge had come!

Immediately I wrote a fax to the Dutch embassy and told them of what had happened; that a file had been opened against me. In the evening I went out for a meal in the Mbale Hotel with my friend Isobel. I needed a change of environment and to relax a bit after the stressful week and I also wanted to share with her what had been happening.

I entered the hotel, and the first man I met was the Government Official. He greeted me warmly. With my heart beating in my throat I returned his greeting. Then he took my hand and pulled me over to a corner. He said, "Ingrid, I need your help, I have a sister and she is somehow saved like you, so I thought you can give her a job." Here I was eye to eye with the man who wanted me behind bars and he is posing as my friend? I wondered if I could ever trust people again. I lost my sense of reality; all of a sudden I felt like a lead character in a book of which I didn't know the author. It was a weird and confusing feeling.

At 8.30 the following morning my phone rang, it was the Dutch

Embassy. They had read my fax and were very concerned, asking if I could come to Kampala immediately. I packed my bag and went off to Kampala.

I told my story at the Embassy and they listened. It was a so good to be with people who believed me and who were in a position to act on my behalf. It was such a relief that I could share my story with people from the same cultural background; people who understood what this kind of stress did to my heart and who would stand up for me. The Ambassador acted fast and called the Minister of Internal Affairs.

After she finished speaking to the Minister she wrote a letter to him, asking for his help. I was grateful that she acted so fast, and I was happy that she took the case so seriously. With the letter in my hand I jumped in the car and drove straight to the Ministry of Internal affairs. As I waited to be allowed into the minister's office I prayed and really asked God to make a way for me. I felt trapped in a story that was not mine. The minister himself was not in the office so I was shown in to see the second in command at the Ministry. The man greeted me and that's when I realised that I knew him.

His first question was, "Are you the one accused of being a rebel?" There was a surprised tone in his voice. It was clear that he also recognised me.

"Yes sir," I replied, relieved that he recognised me. We had served on a board for an Umbrella organisation together. *'Thank God that You haven't deserted me, after all'* I thought.

"Who is accusing you?" I gave him the name of the person and he said, "What dealings have you had with this man?"

"I met him once, when he helped me to solve a problem and then….."

"…And then he wanted to go to bed with you," the Minister finished my sentence. I nodded my head but did not have to speak because immediately he continued.

"Those people and their sex," he commented. Without asking any more questions, he walked to his desk and wrote a note.

"Give this to the Inspector General of Police."

I thanked him and left the ministry building, in my heart thanking God that He had come through again at the last minute.

The Inspector General of Police was already aware of the interrogations that had taken place in Mbale. Looking at his face I could see that he had no idea what to do with a mzungu woman rebel leader. I gave him the note from the Minister. After he had read it, he was visibly relieved that the Minister had cleared me. He asked me what I wanted him to do. I told him that I needed some protection, I felt very vulnerable.

He wrote a short note to the Regional Police Commander saying: *"Assure this lady that nothing will happen to her during her stay in the district."*

"Please give this to the Regional Police Commander in Mbale and you will be fine," he instructed me. I left his office happy that something had been done and that my name was cleared.

I returned to Mbale and gave the note to the Regional Police Commander.

"Who is the man accusing you?" the police officer asked. I mentioned his name and he asked, "Do you want to see him?" I agreed and we went to his office.

The police commander knocked at the door and when I entered the office behind him the government official looked surprised, "Ah, Ingrid," he said, "Long time no see! What brings you to my office, is it the poster issue?"

"No sir, the poster issue is already solved but I am now being accused of moving with rebels."

"Accused of moving with rebels? Who is accusing you?" He sounded surprised.

Very briefly and clearly I said, "It is you, sir!"

He started turning on his chair very uncomfortably and said to the Police Commander, "It can't be me; Ingrid and I have been long time friends. She is visiting me in my house and I am visiting her in her house, it is not me."

I interrupted and told him, "Sir, I have been in your house only once and you have never been to my house. That is not what I understand by friendship." He changed the statement and began revealing all the stories the people had told him about me. I had worked for somebody in the opposition in the early eighties; Paulo had told him that I had come to Uganda with a hidden agenda. Suddenly everybody was blamed for the situation. He had heard so many stories about me and since he had the power, he needed to act and arrest me.

As he was talking, I stood up, I had heard enough. As I walked out of his office I said, "Sir, this is a high office in the district, it should not be an office of abuse. Good afternoon." It was perhaps not the wisest reaction but it came truly out of my heart.

I sent a message to the wife of the State Attorney and we made an appointment to meet somewhere far away in a village church. No one could be allowed to see me discuss the developments with her. We needed to avoid any possibility of someone accusing me of bribing the State Attorney.

I needed to know if there were more activities taking place behind my back. I was desperate to know what the Government had decided about my case. I was relieved when I heard that the Director for Public Persecutions in Kampala had cleared my file.

My phones weren't tapped anymore and no mail was opened. Things went back to normal. I was so thankful to God that this chapter in my life was closed, after three stressful months.

CHAPTER ELEVEN

The Attack

In June 1996, Hans and Christine were coming to visit. I looked forward to their second visit. It was so good to be able to share my heart with good friends, who'd known me for so long, and who did not doubt my integrity. This time they came on a mission to 'spy the land'. They were thinking of moving to Uganda and were checking out different opportunities. It was great to have old friends around and I was happy that they were thinking about moving to Uganda. They planned to live in Kampala, only a few hours away from me. I had missed friends from my past and at times felt very lonely.

Yes, I had good friends among the Ugandans and I had my prayer partners, but none of these people knew anything about my past, they did not know how I had changed and what I had gone through in life. It was as if we were all people without a history, and that made the relationship different. All of us represented our different cultures and together we were looking for a Christ-like culture. But to have a friend who knows with one word what you want to say, that I had missed for many years.

The three of us had many deep heart-to-heart talks and one evening I confided in Christine; "I am going to tell you something that you need to keep to yourself until the time it is right to speak. Every time when I pray I feel like I am going to die a violent death in Uganda. I don't understand it but in case that happens please say this to my family..." I gave her my last words for my parents and I also gave her the words for my funeral.

"At the same time," I told her, "I have been telling God that I am still too young to die; I am not ready to die. I want to believe that God's power is stronger than a gun." Christine looked at me without saying a word. I am not sure what she thought at that moment but I know that she pondered those words in her heart.

Three months later Irene and I travelled together from Kampala to Mbale. I had spent a few days with Hans and Christine to help them settle in. They had moved from The Netherlands to start working in Kampala. Irene was in need of some rest after many months of hard work in the war zone so we decided to travel together to Mbale. Once settled on the veranda with the beautiful view of the mountains, we started catching up with each other's stories; we both had a lot to share. In the middle of our conversation a man came to the gate. He was selling all kinds of locally made crafts and he was wondering if we wanted to buy some.

I was not impressed by the things he was selling, except for one wooden sculpture that I quite liked. It had a nice face but only one arm.

I asked, "Why does this sculpture only have one arm?"

The man laughed and said, "In the village people believe that when you have pain in your arm, it will heal your arm when you rub it."

I also laughed and said, "This does not have any influence on me since I am a born again Christian." I offered him some money for it and I said, "This is what I'll give you for it; take it or leave it, I am not going to bargain for it." The man took my money and I put the sculpture on a shelf in my sitting room.

My night watchman had his day off and after we had cooked some food, Irene and I were preparing ourselves for a good evening of catching up on each other's lives. With a little candle giving us the light we needed and with the plates of food on our lap; we enjoyed a cool evening on the veranda.

Suddenly I heard footsteps. I stood up to say "Karibu" which means welcome in Swahili. Since the gate was locked I was sure this must be my colleague who lived with his family in the boys' quarters on the compound.

I stretched my hand out in greeting, when I heard a big bang and a voice shouting, "Kaa chini!," 'Sit down!'

I sat down and looked at my arm. I had never seen a hole in somebody's body as big as the hole in my arm. I had never seen such big drops of blood in my life. We sat down as quick as we could. Then reality hit me; I'd been shot!

I looked and there were four thugs, one with a gun and two armed with big knives. "Give us money," they demanded. Quickly I stood up to get money and immediately they aimed the gun ready to shoot me again.

As loud as I could and on the top of my voice I shouted, "In the Name of Jesus, you people, go, go, go!"

Four pairs of arms were thrown into the air and the men moved backward. As if an invisible force pushed them away. I took advantage of the confusion and ran inside the house, to get my money. But the thugs were already on their way out. One of them grabbed my purse and ran with it. I had little money in my house but fortunately it was in small denominations, so it looked like a big amount. Since it was dark, it was difficult for the thugs to check the bank notes and they did not want to take the time. Someone unseen was chasing them.

We locked the door as fast as we could and looked at the damage done to my arm. The whole house had a trail of big drops of blood. The hole in my arm was more than five centimetres wide and I began to panic. I would die because of loss of blood if we didn't do something soon.

Down on the floor, staying low just in case the thugs were still around, we crawled to the kitchen to get a towel and tied it around my arm. We continued to crawl to the telephone and dialled the number of the police, "Please, come we have been shot we need help," I shouted in the receiver.

A sleepy voice answered, "You have dialled the wrong number try this number." I tried the other number, and got the same message again. "You have the wrong number."

I shouted in the phone, "I am shot, you need to come I am bleeding to death!" All the response I got was, "You have the wrong number."

Looking at how much blood I was losing, my panic grew. Here I was, trying to ring the police for assistance and in the meantime I imagined dying with the phone still in my hands. All kinds of scenarios rushed through my mind. I tried three times to call the police before we realised our help needed to come from a different source.

We rang some of my friends. None of them was at home. What more could we do? Irene and I looked at each other not knowing what to do anymore when the phone rang. It was my South African neighbour, a man who had a real interest in guns and anything to do with shooting. How did he know?

"Our house girl just rang and told us that you called us and your voice sounded strange. Is there something wrong?"

"Yes, I am shot and I am losing too much blood. We need help!" Within five minutes three cars arrived at the house. All I could do before I left the house was to shout through the window to my colleagues in the boys' quarters, "I am shot and I am going to the hospital!"

They had heard the commotion, the footsteps of the thugs and they heard the shot that was fired. All they could do was hide, fearing for their lives. The three cars had parked in front of the gate with their headlights on. When I saw one of our friends jump the gate, we took courage and opened the door of the house. Another man was keeping watch on top of the gate. It was such a funny sight that we joked to one another, "The A-team has come to rescue us!" The situation resembled this hilarious TV programme so much. Everybody felt the sense of humour and there was a moment of relieved laughter.

Irene and I were taken to the hospital, while other people watched over the house. I looked at my arm and held it carefully. The hole was so big that it felt as if my arm could fall off at any time. In the car we learned that some of the expatriate community were together for a meal when the message of the attack came. It was a miracle in itself to have so much help so fast. A fourth car had gone to the police to collect the Police Officers.

On the way to the hospital I prayed a deep, sincere prayer, *'Lord, erase this experience from my memory, I refuse to live the rest of my life in fear.'* In the hospital, strangely, we had so much fun together even though it took about half an hour before we found a doctor. It was approaching 9.30pm. The first thing the doctor prescribed was blood transfusion. I refused the doctor's advice and told myself to trust God for enough blood. I feared accepting blood transfusion in a country with a high HIV infection rate. The doctor was upset that I protested against his decision but I did not change my mind.

I asked my friends to look for the doctor whom I used to play tennis with. They went to the sports club and within 20 minutes he arrived in the room. "At least you cannot beat me on the tennis court anymore," he joked as soon as he saw the damage done to my arm. He knew I had never beaten him, he was one of the best players in the town, but he wanted to make sure I was at ease. I needed a surgeon so he advised us to look for another doctor.

At midnight the surgeon came. It was four hours after the

attack. He cleaned out the wound. I had not felt pain at all and was amazed at how the body reacts to such a shock but when he began cleaning the wound, it was very painful. I lay on the bed moaning and groaning, when I heard one friend say to the other, "She resembles my wife, when she was in labour." We all laughed, humour was such a healing medicine!

The doctor said that I needed to wait until the morning for an X-ray to show what damage the bullet had done. No artery was hit he stated so there was no need to fear that I was bleeding to death. The private wing in the hospital had just been renovated and we were thankful for our own room. In the general wards more than 30 patients share a room and there is no privacy at all. Despite the privacy of our room, we did not sleep at all that night.

At 6.00am Christine entered our room; she had tears in her eyes as we told her our story. From that moment on people started flocking the room. From the highest person in the district to the dirtiest child in the street, all came to see me. In three days over 200 people visited me in the hospital. It deeply touched my heart.

My house girl came to the hospital later that first day. She had arrived at the house and when she saw the blood, she ran out of the house, shouting that I had died. She feared going to the hospital because she knew I could not have survived this kind of blood loss. She sent a message to the night watchman and the two of them finally got the courage to find out what actually happened.

I was taken to the X-ray room. The equipment looked old, but I was thankful that there were X-ray films available; often they were out of stock. The X-ray showed that one bone was shattered. The bone splinters needed to be removed in the theatre. I hated the fact that this needed to be done under full anaesthesia and requested the doctor to allow my friend to be in the theatre during the operation. He had no objection although he did wonder why.

I was so grateful that he had accepted the request especially, when I saw a pussycat jump out of the open window of the theatre room, the moment I entered in for the surgery. I knew my friend would be able to make sure that they were not going to give me any blood and that they sterilised the instruments to be used during the surgery.

'Have I entered heaven?'

I woke up from the anaesthetic and had no idea where I was. People were singing and praying. I opened my eyes and saw familiar faces. I went back to sleep enjoying the African tunes, then I woke up again and realised that I was in the hospital, that I had survived death and that friends had come to encourage me and to pray for me.

With all the energy in me, I prayed a prayer and re-dedicated my life to Christ. I knew one thing: from now onwards I only wanted to live for Him for He had saved my life! I knew that I had survived for a reason. It dawned on me that it had been a very narrow escape, especially when we heard that the bullet had bounced back in between Irene and me; it could have caused so much more damage. We also learned from the doctor, that the chances of getting an infection were minimal because the bullet was fired from such a short range and therefore it was still very hot when it hit my arm.

Another thing we learned was that bullets are made off-centre. The further they travel, the bigger the circle they make and the greater the damage. Since they shot at me from such as short distance, it was only a hole; if it was fired further away I could have lost my forearm. What I thought was a very bad experience turned out to be best in the given situation.

When I'd regained consciousness, my friend told me that everything went fine in the theatre. They did not give me blood and all the instruments were sterilised and clean. She also told me that I had been singing during the whole surgery. I felt embarrassed. How could I sing and not know it? I felt too shy to ask her what I sang. When the doctor came he gave me the answer. He told me that the surgery went well, they had removed the bone splinters from the arm and then he said, "Ingrid, Ingrid, you were so busy praising your God during the surgery." I sighed with relief; at least I had not made a fool of myself in my unconscious state!

My arm was plastered from the hand to the shoulder. After the plaster had hardened they needed to cut a hole so that the wound could be cleaned. The medical assistant, who was helping me, went to a cupboard and from the bottom of a dusty box he picked out some instruments. My prayer became a plea against infection, *'How can he use a dirty saw to cut holes in the plaster?'* As I watched, fear for all kinds of infection overtook me but he did a good job. He cut a big hole on top of my arm and wanted to cut a second hole in the plaster. I asked him why he was doing that. I knew the bullet had skimmed off my arm. *'Why on earth does he want to make two holes?'*

I panicked and said to him, "What are you doing, why are you making two holes, who was there, you or I, don't you think I know what happened?" The medical assistant became very nervous because I lost my cool – I was not very polite. I could not hand over my medical state to the hospital staff. I wanted to be in control but I knew I was not; it was an unsettling situation.

He continued cutting the plaster but did not speak a word. It was a painful process. I became very dizzy and felt unable to walk back to the room. They brought a wheel chair and the medical assistant pushed me, as best as he could, back to the room. Every time the wheel rolled my arm shook, it was very uncomfortable and painful. Irene was waiting and when she saw my face she asked, "What is wrong with you?"

"Can't you see this wheel chair? If they cannot manage to put air in the tires, who tells me that they sterilise their instruments.

I want to leave this place!" Suddenly it had dawned on me that the medical care was so different compared to Europe and panic gripped me.

The doctor came and he was very upset; "How could you stop my assistant from cutting the plaster?" he asked. "This," he pointed underneath my arm, "is the place where the bullet entered your arm and here," he said, pointing at the hole on top, "is where the bullet left your arm."

I apologised for my arrogant attitude. It took some time for him to forgive me but in the days to come we became friends.

From Friday morning at 6.00am until Sunday evening at 5.00pm, a stream of people visited the hospital. Some street children worked the whole day to earn enough money to buy me a bottle of Coca-Cola. Paulo came and cried tears; the Police Commander came to take my statement and the women of the project stayed with me for many hours. Many of them contributed 10- dollar cents towards my medical bills. I was deeply touched by their love and concern and wondered why I had never realised that these people loved me so much.

'Was I so busy giving that I could not receive? Was it that I was still so task-oriented whilst these women were people oriented? Was it because this time it was I who was vulnerable instead of the people around me?' I did not know the reason but I felt loved and cherished by the people of Uganda. The expatriate community had made a schedule and every hour somebody came to take care of me in the hospital.

The second night a British lady insisted that she spent the night with me in the hospital. I wondered why, because we were not very close. I did not know her very well but it became a very special night. She confessed that she had played a very negative role in the problems I'd had with Paulo five years ago.

"I knew you had condemned me and I knew that, when I came

to Mbale to live and work in the school, I would not make any friends because you would have informed everybody about what I did to you. Over the years I realised that you had not talked to anybody. I really respected you for that but I did not have the courage to tell you. Will you please forgive me?" I forgave her and we prayed together; it became a wonderful time of reconciliation.

During much of my time in hospital, about fifteen women from the slum area stayed with me, seated on mats near my bed. Some talked softly, some cried and some just sat silently for hours. The door opened and a little girl from CRO entered the room. She was wearing her street clothes, torn and dirty. She cried loud, I could hear the pain in her voice. She found her way to my bed, squeezing herself through the groups of women that were seated on the floor. She knelt down, prayed in a language I did not understand, put two sticky sweets on my pillow, looked at me and said, "Bye, aunty," then she waved and walked out of the room. I was deeply touched when I realised how much the children loved me.

"There are these two men," the nurse said as she stuck her head in the room. "Do not allow them to enter your room, they are thieves." It was unsettling. Even in the hospital I needed to be on my guard. *'Was there a place on this earth where I could be safe?'*

Three men entered to see me. I did not know them and they did not say anything. They just stood there and stared at me for a few minutes. Panic gripped me and I just knew these were the people who shot at me. I had a deep conviction that they came to see if I was still alive. Later on I heard that this is a normal reaction after a traumatic experience and I probably judged the wrong people.

After three days in the hospital I longed to go home. It had been enough; I wanted to inform my family and friends in The Netherlands of what had happened. Irene asked the doctor if he could allow me to go home. "Ingrid can do whatever she wants," he replied. He clearly had not yet forgiven me completely, but we packed our little belongings and went home.

Some friends had baked a cake and the coffee was ready when we entered the house. It was a strange feeling. As much as the house was cleaned I could still see the faint marks of my blood on the concrete veranda. But it felt good to be home again. When we sat on the same veranda, with our coffee and cake the unforgettable happened: a beautiful, clear, huge rainbow appeared right in front of us. A sign that God was with us! We had a little spontaneous time of thanksgiving on the veranda and knew that He truly is Emmanuel, God with us.

Our South African friend offered to stay the first night with us in the house. He forsook his comfortable bed and his wife in order to sleep on the couch in the sitting room to help us overcome the fear. I was deeply grateful to everybody who stood with us. It was as if the whole town had been on our side during this traumatic experience.

After this experience Irene had to admit, "There is a God and I need Him in my life!"

The next morning, when I walked into my sitting room, my eye fell on the little sculpture with one arm and I looked at my own arm. *'Could this be a coincidence?'* I felt very uncomfortable. Suddenly the sculpture had lost its beauty. I asked some of my Ugandan pastor friends what they thought of this. They gave me a small lecture on African witchcraft. They warned me not to buy at the door. "Some people may even bring mats for you to sit on that are dedicated to gods," they warned.

Another pastor gave me a scripture ,which said, *"Do not make any gods to be alongside me."*[16] I had never seen this piece of wood as a god but now I understood that it was like an idol.

Immediately I decided to burn the sculpture. It smouldered but did not want to burn. At night I watched it from my bedroom

---

16 *Exodus 20:23*

window and saw its eyes lightening up by the fire but it had become very ugly to me. I had to admit, there is much more between heaven and earth that is not seen but that was influencing my life. I thanked God for the training He had given me months before that I have power over satan. It was very clear the power of Jesus had saved my life.

CHAPTER TWELVE ·

Dealing with the Wound

Early Monday morning I informed my family and friends of what had happened. It took two hours before I managed to get a phone connection with my parents. They were happy to hear the story from me, personally and suggested they come to Uganda to spend time with me. I told them I was doing fine and there was no need for them to travel all the way to Uganda.

The wound needed dressing daily. I had to line up for hours in the local hospital, between people with big infected wounds. I was concerned, *'Would this increase the chance that my arm would become septic?'* I asked the doctor if there was any other way I could receive treatment. I was relieved when he referred me to a private clinic.

I called a doctor in Kampala; almost daily for a second opinion about the treatment I was receiving in Mbale. He was a European and had lived in Uganda for a long time. Once family and friends in The Netherlands were informed of what had happened, the pressure to go The Netherlands increased. I called the doctor in Kampala, "My family is scared about the risk of HIV infection when I am treated here in Mbale. What do you think? Should I go to The Netherlands for better treatment?"

"HIV infection?" he asked, "Are you sleeping with the doctor?"

I did not appreciate his kind of humour. I was upset and felt that he was not taking me seriously. He continued, "This is just a small thing that happened to you, I used to treat bullet wounds on the back of a Landrover, and there is no need to go to The Netherlands." I did not appreciate this kind of pep talk, and lost my trust in this doctor.

Meanwhile my family insisted that the arm could be better treated in The Netherlands with more advanced techniques. I did not want to run away; I wanted people to know that I could not be scared out of Mbale. But after two weeks, I decided to move to Hans and Christine's place in Kampala for better treatment. One evening when we were sitting on their veranda, she reminded me of our conversation in June when I had given her my last words for family and friends. Once again it was so clear that God had prepared me for all of this. It was amazing; I was not dead but alive.

In the heat, my skin underneath the plaster became very itchy and I would try to ease the itching with long knitting needles. That's when I realised that treatment in The Netherlands would probably be better. I asked for a referral letter for the insurance company and the next day I booked my ticket to The Netherlands. Suddenly I longed to see my family and friends.

Irene was due to take some leave, so we travelled together. We had an overnight flight and were scheduled to arrive in Amsterdam early the next morning. My arm needed cleaning twice a day to avoid infection. We boarded the plane and waited for three hours to take off when the message came that there was a problem; we could not take off. An incident had happened at the Nairobi airport that had blocked the runway. At 2.00am everybody had to disembark again and we were taken to a hotel near the airport. Since my arm needed treatment the airline agreed to take us back to Kampala, to a hotel where there was a residential doctor who could treat my arm before the 10.00am flight the next morning.

At 3.30am we fell into bed, exhausted, only to wake up four hours later to look for the doctor. We asked around in the hotel but no one knew where he was until someone whispered that he usually had a hangover in the morning. It was better to look for another doctor. At 8.30am we went to a clinic in Kampala. The nurse rushed the treatment and we jumped in the taxi for the half an hour drive to the airport. When we entered the aircraft, the doors locked right behind us.

We had tried to phone from the aeroplane to inform our families that we were delayed but had not succeeded to get in contact with them. A large group of family and friends were waiting at Amsterdam Schiphol airport early in the morning. When we did not arrive, they panicked and went to find out what happened. All they were told was that there was a problem in Nairobi. For a few minutes they thought we had perished in an airplane crash until they were able to find out more details. They were told to go home and that the airline would take the responsibility of getting us to our final destinations.

We landed in Brussels late in the evening; the last flight to Amsterdam had already left. The airline booked a taxi and they took us to Utrecht where my family was waiting for us. It was past midnight when we finally hugged our family and friends. I had been a tiring 32-hour journey, full of uncertainty, but it was so good to be with them and to feel safe.

The following morning I went to the hospital. The doctor took another X-ray and removed the plaster. He explained that it was possible to get an external fixation, which was less heavy than the plaster and it gave me much more freedom to use my arm. I am right handed, so this proved helpful as it meant I could write again.

I was admitted to the hospital the same day. It was so good to have a room to myself. For the first time in more than two weeks I was on my own and I had a lot to work through and to discuss with God. It wasn't until I heard a familiar voice in the corridor that I found out why I had a room to myself. It was my sister but the nurse refused her entry because she had her young child with her. When I recognised her voice I opened the door and saw a big placard reading 'Quarantine'. I was isolated because of a bug that I could have carried from a Ugandan hospital. They tested me, and when I was 'bug-free' visitors were allowed in the room.

Late that same afternoon I was rolled into the theatre. It was heaven in comparison to the theatre in Uganda. There was no need for a full anaesthesia, they offered a monitor for me to follow the proceedings of the surgery, and I was offered my own choice of music on the headset. After the surgeon was finished, he gave me a mobile phone on the operation table to tell my sister that the operation had been carried out successfully. I told the doctor that I suspected he was showing off, knowing that I had come from Africa, but deep in my heart I really appreciated it.

The night was painful both physically and emotionally; I cried throughout the night. The nurse came and gave me a painkiller and, I guessed, a sedative too. It was finally time to let go of everything and to face all that was broken in me.

For a month after leaving hospital, I locked myself up in a peaceful little house and wrestled with God. The arm was healing well and it became clear to me that what had happened was part of the spiritual battle that I was involved in. Spearheading an organisation that brings children from the Kingdom of Darkness into the Kingdom of Light did not make satan happy. He tried everything to discontinue the programme. At the same time I knew with my head and through the Bible that nothing would happen to me without God's permission.

'If God is love, why had all of this happened?' My heart could not grasp it and heaven was silent.

'Am I so sinful that I had to be punished? Am I so rebellious that

God had to do these things so that I would stay close to Him? Is there no good in me at all?'

In the meantime Isobel had contacted the Ugandan ambassador to Canada. He came from Mbale and had been an influential leader. We had known each other quite well. Isobel told him that I had been shot and asked him if he could find out what had happened so that I could make a decision to return to Uganda or not.

Three days later he called me and said, "Ingrid, I am very sorry about what has happened. I have been in contact with Mbale and want to let you know that it is safe for you to return."

"How do I know?" I asked

"You have known me for many years, will you trust my word?"

It had become difficult for me to trust the word of a man. "Can you please give me the name of one person in the District that I can trust?" I asked.

"I will call you back," was his answer. Two days later he called and said, "Report to this office, as soon as you are back in Mbale." But, however important this man was, I needed to hear from God Himself.

I wanted to return to Uganda; no man or power could stop me from what God wanted me to accomplish in this life and He confirmed it with scriptures:

"You must go to everyone I send you to and say whatever I command you. Do not be afraid for I am with you and will rescue you."[17]

God continued, *"Get yourself ready! Stand up and say to them whatever I command you. Do not be terrified by them or I well terrify you before them. Today I have made you a fortified city, an iron pillar and a bronze wall to stand against the whole land, against the kings of Judah [Uganda], its officials, its princes, its priests. They will fight against you but will not overcome you, for I am with you*

---

17 *Jeremiah 1:7*

and will rescue you, declares the Lord."[18]

Someone rang me and said God had impressed a scripture on his heart for me, *"'No weapon forged against you will stand, and you will refute every tongue that accuses you. This is the inheritance of the servants of the Lord and this is their vindication from me' says the Lord."[19]*

My brother and his family had planned to stay with me in Uganda for Christmas. *'Would they have the courage to come right after this incident? Were they going to cancel their holiday?'* When I had rested for almost a month and I had learned how to administer treatment to my arm, I felt strong enough to return to Uganda. The mission committee of my church heard of my plans, and wrote a letter requesting that I send someone else to Uganda to pack my things and not to return to the country anymore.

I was discouraged. I had prayed and wrestled with God for a full month and it was pure obedience for me to return to Uganda. I was not suicidal. I phoned committee members individually and asked them if this letter was written based on concern or based on prayer.

They said that they honestly feared for my life and, out of concern, they had requested me to stay in The Netherlands. I shared my 'battle' with God and after my explanation they consented. When I rang the pastor he encouraged me even more and said, "Your return to Uganda is the greatest act of worship to God." I was happy that I could return to Uganda with the blessings of my home church.

The Ugandan sunshine felt so good after a cold November month in The Netherlands. I knew I had returned home. My bags were packed with sterilising medication to keep the external fixation in my arm as long as possible.

---

18 *Jeremiah 1:17-19*
19 *Isaiah 54: 17*

On my journey from the airport to Mbale some ambivalent feelings returned. *'Was God really going to protect me? What if they try to kill me again?'* The last 100 km was a long straight road. After a small bend in the road I could see Mbale town at the foot of Mount Elgon. But this time it was different. God answered my heart cry once again. I pulled over in the car and cried. What I saw, I had never seen before; a huge rainbow covered the whole town from the east to the west. God was telling me once again that He was with me and I continued my journey feeling strengthened. A huge party awaited me. The children sang welcome back songs; there were sodas and a huge cake. It was so good to be back in Uganda!

The day of my return, I reported to the Resident District Commissioner. He welcomed me back in Uganda and apologised for what had happened. He felt very sorry for me. I said, "Sir, I am in need of at least one person whom I can trust, and your name was given to me. I would like to ask you a very frank question: do you know this government official?" I gave him the name of the man. "Do you think that this government official could have hired people to kill me?" I continued.

He looked at me and said, "Madam, I cannot rule that out." It was an honest answer but not a very comforting one, because this man was still living in Mbale.

My brother and his family courageously chose not to change their plans after the attack. My contract in Mbale ended in six months and they still wanted to see CRO and share part of my life there.

Along with my own night watchman I now also had a policeman guarding my house at night. His gun fascinated my nephews. We had made a decision not to tell the children what had happened to me. We did not want to scare them. One evening I heard the familiar sound of the clicking of the gun. I ran outside and saw that the policeman was loading his gun with live bullets in front of the children. I lost my cool and told the policeman off. I over-reacted and it was clear that I had not yet completely healed from the experience.

One night the policeman was snoring so loud that he woke me up and once again I was wondering why I had an armed guard. I hated guns.

Despite the stress, I had a wonderful Christmas with my family and they loved Uganda. We spent a few days in my half-finished house in Jinja. My youngest nephew enjoyed the garden so much. Every morning he ran out of the house and shouted to the neighbour's children in Dutch, "Friend, let's go grasshopper hunting!" Half an hour later they would bring us grasshoppers for breakfast. I am still thankful for their courage to come. They made my Christmas time very special!

There were lots of rumours about who was involved in the attack. We were advised not to push the police to follow up the case to avoid confrontation and possible retaliation. Some of the rumours made sense. Months after I was back in Uganda, there was a prayer convention for all the Christians in Mbale. The different tribes and clans were asked to repent of their sins. One Christian from the same tribe as it was rumoured that the killers were, stood up and said, "We have a reputation of killing missionaries; the first missionaries in this part of the country were killed in our county." I felt the shivers along my spine. Was the rumour true?

I had not recovered yet from this shock when they called upon the missionaries in the room to repent of their sin. Since I was the only missionary present, they asked me to come forward. I was nervous, yes I could repent, but could I also forgive? Everybody knew what had happened to me. I repented of the 'know-best' attitude of the missionaries and for the atrocities done during the colonial reign and then, with tears in my eyes I forgave the people who had a history of killing missionaries. Publicly, with pain in my heart, I forgave the people who had tried to kill me.

After the meeting I drove home and passed by the house of the people who were suspected to have played a role in the attack. Their gate opened and a car drove out. My first impulse was to increase speed and ruin their vehicle. The second reaction was, "Ingrid, you just forgave the man in front of 250 people; what are you doing now?"

I realised that forgiveness and healing does not come instantly but is a process with multiple options to fail or to succeed along the path.

In February 1997, the time came to hand over the CRO project to the board and the staff. There was still three more months to go until I would leave for good. It had been a strange six months since my return from The Netherlands. I felt very ambivalent.

I loved the staff, children and the women. It was difficult knowing I would have to say goodbye, to hand over the work and I still did not know what God wanted me to do next. But I was also ready for a change, away from the high stress circumstances I had lived in. The CRO Board was talking about extending the services of CRO to other towns in Uganda but no conclusion had been reached. We needed to hear from God first.

One afternoon the Mayor of Mbale came to CRO and asked me how my surname is spelled. I asked him why and he said, "We have created a new road in this town and I want to propose to the council to name it after you." I just laughed and said that streets are only named after people who had died. I was still very much alive. I could not handle that kind of honour and the idea was cancelled.

There were many farewell parties when I left Mbale. One evening as I prepared to go to a party, the policeman guarding my house told me not to return via the same route. He had seen people watching the house and observing what was taking place. As much as I knew and felt I was an 'untouchable of the Lord' the continuous stress was tiring. I returned home via another route.

I started to pack my belongings and took them to Jinja to store them in my house until I knew what God wanted me to do in the next chapter of my life. A car stopped at my gate, it was the same car that I had wanted to run into. It was clear that someone was watching my movements. The man got out and asked my gardener where he was taking the flowers. In his wisdom the gardener told the man that he was taking the flowers to CRO. Fortunately, he did not reveal to the man that I was moving to Jinja.

My last Sunday in Mbale the pastor prayed for me and God once again gave me a word from His scriptures, *"Enlarge the place of your tent, stretch your tent curtains wide, do not hold back strengthen your cords, strengthen your stakes, for you will spread out to the right and to the left, Your descendants will dispossess nations and settle in their desolate cities."*[20] This was the same scripture God had given me two years before when I was praying about my future.

Another scripture that was given to me to hold on to was Isaiah 61:3, *"You will be called an oak of righteousness, a planting of the Lord for the display of His glory."* It was clear that God was not finished with me and I began looking forward to the next chapter of my life.

My friends told me not to inform anybody of the exact date and time of my move from Mbale. As quietly as possible I emptied the house and moved my things to Jinja, meanwhile praying that no person with wrong intentions would notice my departure from Mbale. I felt sad that after eight years of labouring and struggling, I had to leave the town so quietly as if I was the criminal.

The pressure had been so great and I knew it would be good

---

20 Isaiah 54:2

to go to The Netherlands for some time of rest and recuperation. The external fixation in my arm needed to be removed; that was reasons enough to go to The Netherlands. But in my heart I felt that I belonged in Uganda.

CHAPTER THIRTEEN

Time Out

I prayed and asked God to give me quiet place where I could rest, while I was back in The Netherlands, preferably a place with a typically Dutch view. I was so amazed when I heard that my sister had found a house with a million-dollar Dutch view in a multi-million dollar house. It overlooked meadows with lots of Dutch cows and one of the 'great rivers' of The Netherlands, the IJssel.

I would housesit while the owners were trying to sell it. The house was so big that I decided to use only two rooms. The answer to my prayer about the Dutch view exceeded my expectations, but I found it difficult to enjoy. I realised how stressful the last years had been and was thankful for a place where I could be on my own and sort my issues with myself and with God.

The external fixation was removed and the X-ray showed that the bone was not strong enough. The doctor considered a bone transplant, but we opted for physiotherapy first. I practised as often as I could with weights. When I was drinking coffee or on the phone, I constantly trained my arm as I dreaded undergoing more surgery. After six weeks, I had another X-ray and it showed that the bone had grown very strong. It amazed the doctor and I was dismissed from the hospital, declared healed.

I never had any nightmares or sleepless nights, the only memory I had about the attack was four pairs of arms up in the air. God really answered my cry in the car on the way to the hospital.

As soon as I was declared 'healed' by the doctor early in June 1997, Alma and I decided it was time for a relaxing holiday. We booked a hotel in Tunisia and I enjoyed the fact that I could swim again. In the quiet moments, on the balcony, overlooking the ocean, panic would engulf my heart as I asked God about my future. Every time I panicked, a thought came to me very clearly, *"See, I am going to do great and mighty things."* This thought kept coming back during my time in The Netherlands. I looked up Jeremiah 33:3, *"Call to me and I will answer you and tell you great and unsearchable things you do not know."* I claimed that promise for the future, not knowing what the future would bring.

Once back in my mansion in The Netherlands, my heart was too full to be able to enjoy life. I wanted to understand God but I could not. I saw glimpses of His love and care for me but I could not give up questioning Him. I locked myself in this beautiful house and became completely anti-social. I did not want to meet people; there were too many questions in my mind. I could not speak of them and felt no one would understand the pain, rejection and loneliness I had gone through. I tried to talk but could not. My heart was completely blocked. Many people showed their love and care for me but I was unable to receive it. Darkness had settled over my being.

My birthday was approaching and, since I was in The Netherlands, the right thing to do was to celebrate it. I had not celebrated my birthdays for many years, and even now I did not feel like partying. The day before the party I received the news that a close friend of mine had passed away in Uganda. I wanted to cry, but could not; I could not rejoice anymore and I could not mourn anymore. My emotions were numb and it scared me. I was supposed to be happy since I was alive but I wasn't. I felt a hypocrite and hated it, but couldn't express my heart. I had become a prisoner of my own heart.

Many question followed me wherever I went, *'Will disaster ever stop? Will it continue to follow me?'* I had seen death and been at funerals so many times in the past years. *'Was this ever going to stop? Was I meant to be alone in this world, since all my close friends were dying one by one? What in heaven was going on?'* I wanted to understand but I could not.

I cried out to God, *'If you are my friend why do you hide your plans from me? Are friends not supposed to know what they are doing? I do not know what You are doing with me, but I know You are my friend!'* I continued to pour out my heart, *'Will you ever show me your plan or do I have to accept that this is the cross that I have to bear for Christ and it is all part of dying to self? Is this the price I need to pay for what You have chosen me to do; does it mean that I need to continue to crucify my life? Is joy meant for everybody else except me?*

There was chaos in my thinking and chaos in my intense relationship with God. Answers were not coming and I tried to stop fighting situations and begin accepting them. It was a difficult process.

Here I was in The Netherlands; it was summer and there were lots of nice things to do and nice people to do them with but I just wanted to be on my own. I was locked in this beautiful palace with no space in my heart to enjoy the good things of life. So often I had complained that I lacked a social life and entertainment of any kind in Uganda; there were no concerts, cinema or theatre, there. Now that those were within reach, I could not enjoy them. I hid myself from people.

I did get visitors. A couple from my old church came to encourage me; they enjoyed the beautiful view one sunny afternoon. Before they left, they prayed with me. While praying, the woman saw a picture of an eagle that had built a nest. The bird was busy making the nest larger but it needed to go up for wisdom and energy, and the sun of righteousness shone upon the eagle. It was a new way of communicating. I had no experience in seeing pictures but I was deeply convinced that it was God speaking through this lady.

I was looking for someone who could understand me and who could understand all the questions I had. I needed answers but could not find them; so I decided to visit a friend who had lived in Jinja for many years. She had moved to Norway and I wanted to catch up with her in the hope that perhaps she would understand what I had been through. She was working every day so I had plenty of free time for myself. I looked through her bookshelves; Charles Swindall's book, '*Living Above the Level of Mediocrity*' captured my attention.

Every chapter described a different characteristic of an eagle and, for sure, after the picture about the eagle this was something close to my heart. I learned a lot about eagles and saw how applicable it was to my life and circumstances. I began to understand my Friend, God, a little bit better. The fact that eagles soar and not fly created a desire in me. I had fought so hard to fly, would it not be wonderful to just soar without struggle? I longed for that to happen.

I took lonely walks in the mountains and wrestled with God. I knew He wanted me to go back to Uganda, but how could I go back if there was no love for the people in my heart. Didn't the Bible say that anything done without love is like a clanging cymbal? I did not want to do a job; I wanted to make an impact for the Kingdom, a difference for the people around me. I knew that was not possible without love. How on earth could I return to Uganda without love in my heart? Yes, I had forgiven the people of Uganda but that had not brought love for them in my heart.

I decided not to share my deep internal struggles with my friend. It was a private, very personal struggle between God and me. One afternoon I was fishing with her neighbour. It was a beautiful afternoon and we caught one fish after the other. I feared getting the fish off the hooks, and he laughed at me, "You have lived for so many years in Uganda, and you fear to get a fish off the hook? What has been the most fearful situation you have been in?" he asked. I told him, briefly, the story of the attack. He knew nothing more than this; I did not share my problem of lack of love with him, I did not share all the questions of my heart with him.

That Sunday I attended the local church. The service was in Norwegian; I did not understand much until almost at the end of the service. Suddenly I heard a sentence in English. It was my friend's neighbour inviting me to come forward for prayer. He told the congregation that I had lived in Uganda, and that I was at crossroads in my life. He felt God telling him to pray for me. I walked forward and they prayed for me. After the church service a lady walked up to me. I had never seen or talked to her before but she had tears in her eyes. Through an interpreter she told me that when the pastor was praying for me she saw love flowing out from me, not only from my eyes but also from my heart. The only thing she saw was love. My eyes became wet too and I shared with her my struggles of the last week. I returned to The Netherlands knowing that God had put the love in my heart and that somehow it needed to come out.

On return in The Netherlands I began to share with people that I felt God wanted me to return to Uganda and mentioned the vision of the eagle and what had happened in the Norwegian church. Some people questioned me; how could I base my decision on what others had seen? Could God not talk to me personally?

These were new experiences for me too and I did not have the answers. I went to my pastor to ask him. He said, "God showed Moses His way and the people his deeds. Go ahead and let God show you the way, in a few years people will see His deeds."[21]

The Sunday after he walked up to me and said, "Did you find

---

21 *Psalm 103*

the scripture I gave you?" With a smile on his face he said, "I found it!" He gave me a beautiful card with the text printed on it. It was Psalm 103, which spoke of God's ways; it also spoke of the eagle in the first three verses. This was entitled 'Divine work'. It showed me once again that it was God who confirmed His word and His interest in the details of my life.

It was also the year that the song '*On Eagles Wings*', from Hillsong was new and in many meetings this song was part of the worship. It brought tears to my eyes every time I heard the tune. It became a very special song to me.

Just before I returned to Uganda, along with a number of women of my church, I attended a women's conference. The Spirit of God was so real in the conference that all I could do was cry. It was the first time that I experienced the fact that there was such a deep pain in me but I did not know what to do with it.

During the conference some people prayed for me. These were their prophetic words:

"The winter is passed, the spring is coming. God will place people around you and you will experience the power of God from the top of your head to the toes of your feet." The lady who gave this word then saw a picture of dry land where fountains were springing up.

God was surely teaching me that He uses others to speak into my situation through pictures! It was so new to me but everything was so much 'of Him'!

After the conference, back in my mansion, I took time to worship God for all He had done for me and suddenly I felt His physical presence in a way I had never felt before. I did not even know it was possible to feel His presence physically. I had asked people to pray and break the roots of unbelief about the work of the Holy Spirit but I had never experienced His presence so tangibly; I felt so close to God. It was the beginning of a new heartbeat. God's journey from my head to His heart had begun.

Before I went back to Uganda, the missions committee prayed with me and one of the members saw a picture of a bore hole full with living water and black children around it. It was a time in which God chose to speak to me through other people instead of through His word, as I was so used to. I was learning a new part of His character and a new way of communicating.

CHAPTER FOURTEEN

Jinja

Saying farewell was not very easy, especially for my parents. "Do you know that you are going back to a country where they tried to kill you?" My mother asked.

"Yes mum, I know, I just know that God wants me there, I am going back out of obedience. Trust me I am not suicidal."

That evening I was reflecting on what my mother had said on the phone. It made me think again. *'It is true, they tried to kill me. How can I go back?'* The different scenarios of what could happen to me passed through my mind and it scared me.

I picked up my Bible and said, "God, can You confirm once more that it is Your will for me to return to Uganda?"

He led me to a passage in Exodus where Moses asks God to send someone else to Egypt, he feared going back; God's answer to Moses was, *"Go back to Egypt, for all the men who wanted to kill you are dead."*[22] This was no coincidence; what God spoke to Moses, He spoke to me too. Immediately I called my parents again and told them how God had confirmed once more that it was right for me to go back to Uganda.

I had no idea what I was going back for, but I was happy to touch ground in Uganda again. There were 17 people waiting for me at the airport, it was a real homecoming. I felt the people in Uganda understood me better than the people in The Netherlands. They

---

22 *Exodus 4:19*

were a people who had also suffered in their lives and they had the ability to encourage me not to give up. Somehow their call to perseverance helped me better in my spiritual growth than the sympathy I received from the people in Europe. Sympathy did not help me much, but encouragement with the Truth of God was something I needed. Somehow the people in Uganda were teaching me to hold on and to be strong in the Lord. There is a more apparent need in Africa not to focus on the circumstances but on Jesus and to fight the enemy, I realised that even though life may be lonelier in Uganda, the circumstances to get the know God deeper were better. Hard times had driven me closer to God; in good times I often think I can manage my own life at that time I didn't know how many hard times were still to come.

My first night back in Uganda I stayed with Hans and Christine in Kampala. From there I picked up my car and drove to Jinja. I had promised my family and friends that I would not live in my 'self-made' house if I was scared. The house was built in a very remote area. There was only my house, my watchman's house and three dogs. No water, no electricity and only a few distant neighbours.

The journey had been pleasant. I loved the stretch through the forest; I stopped and bought fresh fruits and vegetables at the road site market. I had come home again! The music in my car made the journey even more pleasant. The moment I arrived at my gate, the 'eagles' song began to play. I looked up and I saw a huge eagle soaring over my home. I just knew God was communicating something to me; this was too much of a co-incidence.

I was so thankful and I enjoyed my homemade house to the full. I was also happy that the first mobile phones had arrived in Uganda; although they were still very expensive, I thought it wise to buy one. At least I could contact people if there was an emergency.

After a few weeks alone in my house I felt the need to know my neighbours so I invited the whole village for a party. I reckoned that if they knew me, they would offer help and protection in case I needed it. The watchman and I cooked food for 100 people and bought many crates of soda. I introduced myself to the villagers as one of their neighbours and told them that I wanted to be part of them; that they were welcome in my house, but that I had three dogs, and warned them that it would be wise to make an appointment before they entered the gate. I really struggled to find a way in which to communicate clearly that they were all welcome to my house but I also felt I had to protect my own privacy. My experience had been that day and night people could come to the house when they were in need of anything. The fierce dog that I had inherited from a friend was a good excuse to encourage the villagers to make an appointment.

The house had been dedicated to God before I left for The Netherlands. The whole CRO team had travelled all the way from Mbale to have a dedication service before I actually moved my things in. We all stayed the night, some in the unfinished house and others in tents. During the time of worship one of the staff began prophesying over the house. She gave us the scriptures of the dedication of the temple. *"I have heard the prayer and the plea you have made before me; I have consecrated this house which you have built, by putting my Name there forever. My eyes and my heart will always be there."* Tears rolled down my cheeks. God's heart would always be in this place; He would hear the prayers the people prayed here... I was so thankful.

I slept in a tent that night and, with a torch in my hand, I asked God, "Lord if this was Your word for my house, will you please confirm it by showing me where it is written in the Bible. I opened my Bible and it opened with the exact scripture. [23] I knew that this was God's promise for my house.

---

23 *1 Kings 9:3*

That night another prayer caught my attention. One of the staff members was praying for the foundation of the house. I asked him why he prayed for the foundation. He explained that many new houses in Uganda have a human skull or other sacrifices in the foundation of their houses to invoke a blessing from the gods. I was happy to know that it was my Dutch friend Johan who build the foundation. He was still too Dutch to believe in that.

The first night, alone in my own house was an experience. I kept hearing sounds I was not used to. At one point I woke up and realised that I was all alone in a remote area and started imagining what could happen to me. I needed to take these thoughts captive and remembered the eagle that had flown over my house the moment I arrived.

It was a great blessing to wake up in the morning and see the river flow. There were so many birds and insects in the garden giving me a private concert. I really enjoyed my home in the village.

What came next, for me, was a time of waiting. Waiting and patience were not my strength and apparently it was time for me to learn this lesson. I read and re-read Oswald Chambers' book *'My utmost for His highest'*. I loved his wisdom on waiting. He wrote, "We cannot attain to a vision, we must live in the inspiration of it until it accomplishes itself. Waiting for the vision that tarries is the test of our loyalty to God." I knew there was a vision in my heart, but I also knew that I could not start it without confirmation from God Himself.

During this time of waiting I had a lot of time for friends. Isobel came for a weekend and, as we sat down at the riverbank I asked her, "Did you know that there are demons in the river? The pastor in Mbale had said that the river is a place where demons live."

"No, I don't know anything about demons," she answered.

"If they are here, can we not just send them away in Jesus Name and declare that this land belongs to Jesus? What do you think?"

And that is what we did; we told the demons to go and invited Jesus to take over the land. We never thought about the demons anymore for a long time.

I knew it was right to wait but I was impatient too. I wanted something to do. I therefore began expanding my house. This was the time to make my house a home and work on the final touches. Friends and family offered all the help I needed in the house. My brother came and installed a solar light system. Alma came and helped me to decorate the house, and Irene came to assist in repairing a leaking roof. At one time we had five people all working on my house. I felt really blessed with family and friends and their willingness to help. It made the waiting so much easier!

There was a young lady who came to my house looking for a job. I needed someone to help me with laundry and cleaning of the house. I gave her the job and she came to live on the compound in one of the rooms I had built for the workers. She worked as my house girl. I also had a family living in the other room. The husband was helping me in the garden; he had worked for me, even when I was still in The Netherlands, guarding the place and looking after the compound.

I had given him the rooms to live there with his wife and children. Unfortunately not long after the house girl moved in, the quarrels began. They accused each other of visiting the witchdoctor in the village. The conversation went beyond my understanding of the local culture, so I asked the help of a Ugandan pastor. He came to settle the issues between the two parties. The house girl was accusing the family of visiting the witchdoctor and the family was accusing the lady of being a girlfriend to the witchdoctor. After a two hour discussion there was no breakthrough. Everybody was denying the accusations, so I had to make a decision.

I finally asked the man to leave. He already had received a warning before and since it was clear that he was hiding something from me I asked him to find another job. I gave his wife and children a week to pack their things and to find other accommodation. It was a painful decision. We were close and they had even named their daughter after me. Not knowing if I made the right decision, I told the house girl that if I ever heard anything negative about her, from someone else, she would also have to pack her bags.

When I took the pastor back to the town, a man at the corner of the road stopped the car.

"Madam, I need to talk to you," he said.

"Please go ahead," I encouraged him.

"Mum, it is confidential."

"Does it have anything to do with my compound?" He nodded his head so I encouraged him, "We have just spent the whole afternoon discussing issues at my compound so please go ahead it is okay for this man to hear what you have to say."

"Mum, your house girl is the girlfriend of the witchdoctor in this village. I am seeing her carrying food and drinks from your house to his house."

His final word to me was, "Ingrid, if you want to have an armed robbery in your house, keep the girl there, you have the danger within your gate."

That was all I needed to know to tell the girl to pack her bags and leave. She looked shocked. This was not what she had expected. The witchdoctor had given her local medicine to tie around her waist, so that I would not sack her. That same evening she moved in with the witchdoctor. I was now staying alone at the compound in a remote village. I did not like it but there was nothing I could do except to pray and trust that God would protect me.

The following morning Hans and Christine came with a youth group from their church in Kampala for a retreat. They spent their time praising and worshipping God in my garden; I loved

it and told God, *'This is what I want this compound to be used for.
Thank you very much!'*

I was still enjoying the thoughts of the garden being used for
worship when a panicked voice brought me back to the real world.

"We have lost a friend in the water."

'What?!' I did not want to believe it, *'Someone drowned in the
river at my compound?'*

I ran down to the river and saw a group of youth sitting together
in total silence. I went into the water to look for the body but
was not able to locate it. I had seen them playing with a ball and
wanted to warn them about the strong current. *'They are no longer
children, they know what they are doing,'* I had told myself just half
an hour before the accident. I felt guilty for not having warned the
youth and now it was too late. The group leader ran to the police
and I went as fast as I could to the fire brigade hoping that they
had divers to help us locate the body. There was nobody on the
compound to watch over the house. I felt terribly alone. I just had
to trust that no one would take advantage of this situation.

In the car on the way to the fire brigade, my phone rang. It was
my friend, from The Netherlands. She sounded so happy and just
wanted to chat. Suddenly the culture difference hit me as I heard
her happy voice. I briefly shared with her my struggle of finding a
way to get a dead body out of the water. I suddenly realised that
our worlds were incomparable; there was no happiness for me,
only struggle and the panic of that moment. I asked her to pray
because I was in a terrible mess.

The policeman at the fire brigade knew me and that was helpful;
they used to bring water to fill the water tanks in the dry season
and we had become friendly with one another. They did not have
divers but they were willing to come and see if they could be of
help. I thankfully accepted their offer. I knew they could not do
much but at least something was done. They drove the fire truck

as fast as they could with flashing lights and sirens. It was the first time I ever saw the car with flashing lights and sirens and knew it was useless, it could not change the situation. The fire truck caught the attention of the whole village and within minutes the compound was full of spectators. I tried to politely ask them to leave, but there is no privacy in Africa, so I gave up.

The fire brigade could not do much and advised me to go to the electricity board nearby as they had two divers. I went and they directed me to the house of one of the divers but warned me that since it was Saturday it was likely that he was drunk. I prayed as hard as I could, on my way to the house that he would not be drunk. I was relieved when I found him at home and sober. He agreed to come with me but there was no oxygen in his tank so he needed to fill that first and we also needed to talk money. I told him the money issue would be solved and forced him to hurry up and get the tanks filled.

At five in the afternoon the diver came, seven hours after the accident. I was desperate and upset that it had taken him so long to come. When he stepped into the water he told us that the water was now too cold. He could not dive since he did not have a diver's costume with him. I lost my cool and felt he was taking us for a ride. But he refused and said he would come back the following morning. By evening I was a complete wreck, so were Hans and Christine. They had sent the youth group back to Kampala to inform the parents of the eighteen-year-old student. Hans and Christine and a group of five young people stayed in my house. They all slept on the floor in the sitting room. A watchman was hired to stay near the river because of the threat of fisherman stealing the body. I had experienced that before, so I asked a village leader to keep watch.

That night a terrible storm came and we prayed that the body would not be swept away by the strong current. I could not sleep.

All I could do was remind myself that God was still good.

"Yes, God, You are still good. I know it because it is written in the Bible so I choose to believe it." My mouth spoke the truth but it had no power to reach my heart.

"Madam, madam," I heard a loud whisper at my bedroom window. Immediately I sat straight up in my bed. I lit the torch and saw that it was three in the morning. I recognised the voice of the village leader who was watching over the body in the river.

"Yes, what is the problem?"

"There are fishermen down at the river and they want to take the body. I need a strong light."

I gave him the strongest torch I had and he managed to scare the fisherman off. By 9.00 in the morning the diver came and by 10.00am he had found the body and retrieved it from the water.

An hour later the parents of the boy and the youth leaders came from Kampala. It was so hard to see the grief in the eyes of the parents. Hans went to buy a coffin and at 4 o'clock in the afternoon the group left for Kampala. What was supposed to be a great day had ended in tragedy that weekend.

I waved them goodbye and my heart broke as it hit me that there was a coffin in the car. Another young man's life lost. What was the purpose of this all?

It felt as if sin had entered my paradise; that the good was overtaken by evil. I began washing the dishes that were piled up from the whole weekend and by the time I had finished it was dark. Suddenly a panic gripped me; usually I was not scared but fear took over my whole being. I had learned to fight these kinds of battles and shouted on the top of my voice, "Satan, in the Name of Jesus, go!" Peace returned to my heart but questions remained. I began to wonder if there could be a link between the accident and the unmasking of the witchcraft on my compound.

CHAPTER FIFTEEN

Waiting

Not long after the accident it was my birthday. Since I had moved to Uganda I did not celebrate birthdays anymore. Not many people in Uganda celebrate them – some don't even know when they were born. I woke up that morning feeling lonely. There was no one who knew it was my birthday, no friends around, no one to congratulate me or give me a present.

As I lay there I said to God, "There is no-one who knows that it is my birthday here, there is no-one to give me a present. Will You give me a present? Will You give me Your eyes for one day?"

I really thought that I had asked for a wonderful present. I would see the world with the eyes of Jesus, which are the eyes of love. I expected a rosy day, all covered in love with little white soft clouds. I began looking forward to a day full of love. Little did I know about love...

Driving into town I saw a beautiful Muslim girl with her head veiled. She looked at me with her warm brown eyes. It was not the first time I'd seen this girl but this time it was different. I saw her beauty and suddenly it dawned on me that she was missing her destiny if no one shared Jesus' love with her. Pain filled my heart when I realised that she would miss God's plan for her life if no one reached out to her.

I also passed a garbage heap and saw the street kids searching for something to eat. I had worked with similar kids for so many years but suddenly this wave of compassion rolled over my heart. It hurt my heart and it brought tears to my eyes. I always encouraged the boys to be strong, to take charge over their lives, to control themselves and make sure they have a future. But Jesus' eyes looked with compassion. I realised for the first time that these children need a hug; they need to be loved back to life. Jesus' eyes were so different than my eyes. It took me by surprise, as I finally understood that the eyes are the mirror of the heart.

Was my heart so different than the heart of Jesus? Did I not do my best for Jesus in order to become like Him? I pondered these things. Driving home that day, I had only one prayer left to pray, *'Give me a heart like Jesus!'*

As I drove over the dusty road, I heard myself saying aloud, "What is this smoke coming from the village", I saw big black clouds from a distance and wondered if the whole village was on fire. When I arrived home I heard the story; three days ago a three-year-old child had gone missing. People had searched day and night and had not found him. Now they had found the body but it had been beheaded. The boy had been used for a sacrifice and the witchdoctor was arrested.

I felt nauseous. Yes, I had heard of stories like this before but I'd never expected that something as awful as this could happen in my own neighbourhood. The witchdoctor had told the police where he had hidden the head of the child while he awaited a large sum of money from the businessman who had ordered for it. Some people believe that if you cement a head of a child in the foundation of your business, your business will prosper.

The villagers were so upset with the witchdoctor that they had set his house on fire. The house and all his belongings were burned. A few weeks after the incident some of my village friends asked me, "Are you coming to watch the public execution?" I felt sick to the stomach.

"Public execution?" I asked, "Who is being executed?"

"The witchdoctor," my friends said "and we are all going to witness." I stayed at home and wondered what kind of justice was being practised in this country and how I could ever make a difference while I heard the bullets in the background.

The difference in culture and lifestyle kept amazing me. Death was so much a part of life and life therefore seemed to have less value than in Europe. I had lived in Jinja now for six months and it was still not clear yet what God wanted me to do; Heaven was silent. I so wanted to work again with the street children again but did not want to begin before I had a clear word from the Lord. As I continued to wait I had plenty of time to join a preparation meeting for a three-day prayer conference in Jinja. I entered the meeting room just when people were encouraged to trust God and pray for the needed funds to host the conference. The Pastor explained that everyone needed to repent for his or her debts; otherwise it would be a hindrance for God to provide for the conference. I sat and listened to the prayers of the people. People were shouting to God and praying loud prayers, while crying in repentance.

'I have no debts; I don't want debts; I have always made sure that I do not have debts, so what am I doing here?' I wondered to myself. Deep in my spirit I was criticising and judging, *'How can they expect You to give if they have debts everywhere?'* I silently asked God.

Everyone was deeply engaged in prayer and it seemed like everybody had debts. I just sat there and watched; I did not know how to pray until the leader said, "Those who have no debts do not sit in judgement but pray for those who have." He had read my thoughts, because I had just been asking God, *'Where will the money come from?'* When I focussed on God again, clear as a bell, I heard Him saying, "From you!"

'From me, Lord? You know I do not have a job, nor do I have a

regular income where do I get the money from?' In my mind God took me to a hidden corner in my house where I had kept a large sum of money to build my garage. I saw the envelope in my mind and I began arguing with God.

'Lord, this is money to build the garage and tomorrow the builders will begin I cannot give this money away.'

Immediately another instruction became clear in my mind, "I want to use you to answer the prayer of my people." I stood up and as fast as I could I drove home, went to the hidden corner, took the money, and drove back. I was so scared that I would rely on my common sense again. I did not want to delay being obedient. As soon as I delivered the envelope, peace returned to my heart. To my amazement, the garage was built without any delay or financial problem. God provided all that I needed and more!

God was teaching me lessons that I didn't realise I had to learn. I was contemplating all the things that had happened in this time of waiting, and still had no idea what God had in mind for me; I was feeling restless.

One day as I was wondering about the future, there was a knock on the gate. My former house girl had come to visit. We greeted one another, with the extensive Ugandan greetings, and I invited her in. It was very clear why she had come; she wanted her job back and had brought me a nice mat as a present. Immediately I remembered the story of people dedicating mats to their gods. "Thank you," I said, "That is very kind of you." We chatted for a few minutes before she had the courage to reveal the reason for her visit. I explained to her that I had appointed another lady to work for me and that her job was no longer available. She looked very disappointed.

After she left, the watchman walked up to me with a worried expression on his face and asked, "What are you going to do with that mat?" I gave it to him and said, "Please burn it!" He smiled, visibly relieved and said, "So, you already know!"

It was mid 1998 and my heart cried out to God to reveal to me what He had in mind for me. My impatience grew each day. I was ready for a new challenge and some action. I had been living in Jinja for the last eight months, and had not done any significant work. People all around me were suffering and all I had done was to keep myself busy with manual work in my house and in the garden. It just did not feel right. Other missionaries started to comment on my relaxed life style but they had no way of knowing the impatience in my heart. Some people started making fun of my redundancy but I just knew in my heart that I could not start a new project, unless it was cleared by heaven itself.

Although I was no longer involved in the day-to-day activities of CRO in Mbale, I was still a board member. In one of the board meetings it was decided that I would do a survey to see if it was viable to start another CRO branch in Jinja. When the board read the survey report, I was asked to write a project proposal. I was happy that I could be useful again. One person came immediately to my mind as a possible board member for the Jinja project.

I had come in contact with a loving 'mzee', a Swahili word for a respected old man. He was an engineer and had assisted me in the problems with my house. When I asked him to become part of CRO Jinja he told me that he needed to pray about it, before he could give me an answer. A few days later he came to me with a smile on his face. "I am accepting your offer to become a board member of CRO Jinja."

He shared with me that God had given him a dream in which He explained a number of reasons why the children were on the streets. The dream had ended by God saying to him, "Go ahead and do what Ingrid is asking you to do." He invited other people to join our board and soon after, the Board of Directors from Mbale came to inaugurate the Jinja Board in a joint prayer meeting.

God had finally broken His silence.

"You had to wait so long for me to clear the way and to remove the hindrances. I have laid the foundation, the work will be blessed."

God also said, *"My understanding is greater than yours, trust me, trust me, trust me!"*

My eyes became wet when I heard these words because God again showed me that He had been there all along. He once again had tested my faith in the wilderness.

CHAPTER SIXTEEN

CRO Jinja

It took eight months of waiting before God gave us the green light to start CRO Jinja. I did not want to run ahead of God; I wanted a clear confirmation that CRO Jinja was not my idea but His. A charity in The Netherlands, who had worked with us before in Mbale, was willing to be my sending agency and guaranteed my monthly income. I was happy about it; at least there would be no financial worries. Looking back I saw God's love in giving me the past months to work on my house and make it pleasantly habitable. By the time I began working full-time it was fully ready and furnished. Little did I know how much I would need that safe place in the years to come.

I found a small two-bedroom house in Jinja town that was available for rent and invited the street children to come. The CRO Board appointed a Manager and a Social worker and we would walk the streets of Jinja, inviting the children to come to our centre.

There was another project in Jinja working with street children. They were struggling to survive; their Chairperson had written a letter to us requesting CRO to take over the care of their children. Once we opened our centre, the workers of that project were upset and refused their children to come to CRO. This confusion made the children rebel. They tore their exercise books in pieces and burned them in front of our eyes. The children vowed never to leave the streets.

We organised a meeting between the local government and the other project to discuss the issue. As a result of that meeting the Probation Officer gave us the go-ahead to work with any child that we would find on the streets in Jinja.

On one occasion, when CRO Jinja had been operating for just one month, out of the blue all the children were arrested and locked up by the police. This had happened to CRO in Mbale many times as well and it had helped us in developing a good working relationship with the police. This time, our social workers went to the police to negotiate, but they were adamant. The children were in police custody and they were not going to be released. The situation was appalling. There were hardly any toilet facilities and no food. Many children were sleeping in one cell and they were treated like hard-core criminals. I was so disgusted when the children told me that they were drinking water from the dirty toilets. Fortunately the police allowed us to bring food for the children. Three times a day we visited them in the police cells where we were allowed to talk to them and counsel them.

After five days the children were loaded onto a vehicle and returned to their villages. Many of the children did not want to return home so they lied to the police about their place of origin. One child managed to get the police to take him to a town 200 km from Jinja when his home was only five kilometres from the police station! 60 children were taken back to their homes, after three weeks 55 children were back on the streets. It was clear that the problem of street children would not be solved overnight.

One morning Kato came to the project with a little pup. Kato was a much-neglected ten-year-old street boy; his whole family had rejected him.

"Why are you bringing this little dog to CRO?" one Social worker asked him.

"People may kill him when I am at school," he answered.

"How do you feed him?"

Kato said, "If I have food, I share it with him and if I do not have food, I let him sniff petrol, so that he does not feel hungry and he sleeps." I was so touched by this story. It never occurred to me in all these years that even the hardest and most rejected street child has a soft spot somewhere hidden in the heart. How I longed to be able to reach that deep place of the heart in the children. So often I felt that counselling was just not enough. I wondered, *'God, somehow You must have ways to reach the hearts of the children,'* but I had no idea how.

Daoudi was one of the most notorious street boys in Jinja. He could be found drunk on petrol or aviation fuel 24 hours a day. He looked like an 18 year old boy but it was difficult to guess his age, since, as young as he was, life on the streets had really aged him. During the rare times he was sober, he would come to CRO to bath and eat. We would take advantage of those moments to counsel him and to listen to his story.

He had a lonely past; his father died and his mother abandoned him when he was three years old. His grandmother raised him but she did not have the means to look after him. Six years ago, he decided to go to the streets to fend for himself. He was not very interested in education although we could see that he was an intelligent boy.

One afternoon, when I was working in my office, I heard commotion outside; people were shouting and yelling. I ran out of my office and saw Daoudi with a big sharp knife pointed at the project cook. I ran and grabbed his arm from behind, kept the knife away from the cook's neck and with my other hand I grabbed his T-shirt. As fast as he could he manoeuvred his body out of the T-shirt and ran. I felt funny; here I was with a knife in one hand and a T-shirt in the other but we were thankful that our cook survived without any injuries.

Half an hour later, I walked out of the project and saw a big group of children; they had climbed on the back of my pick-up truck. They loved jumping on the vehicle whenever I had to go into town. They could wait for hours in the hope to get a ride. Daoudi stood at a distance, watching them. I could see the loneliness all over him; he wanted to be involved but just could not.

The children loved my car and refused to get off when I left; I invited Daoudi to join them. He walked towards the car and said he did not want to sit in the back with the other children.

"Where do you want to sit?" I asked him. He pointed at the back seat.

"If you want to come, why don't you sit here?" I asked and I pointed at the front seat. He walked slowly towards the car, opened the front door and took the seat next to me. We had not spoken for a long time, when he suddenly commented on my broken windscreen. I pointed to other things in the car that were broken too. That was our only conversation, but it marked the beginning of long wavering friendship.

He kept coming to the project on and off. Sometimes he was great and very reliable; sometimes he was a nuisance to everybody in the project. Nobody knew how to interact with him, we had tried everything possible. He was an extremely wounded boy, not able to trust anybody. His will was law and he dealt aggressively with anyone who did not do what he wanted.

I did not want to give up on him. He was a boy with a lot of potential. I spent hours counselling him. For three weeks, every morning I would set time apart to sit with him but he refused to talk. I sat, prayed and waited to hear his voice, but it did not come. He would stare out of the window without uttering a word; I became desperate.

'Do I give up?' Something in me told me I could not give up on

this child. This was a wounded boy with a deep hidden treasure. After weeks of silence, while I was praying quietly, the word 'suicide' came into my mind. I asked him, "Perhaps you feel, 'life is worth nothing, there is no-one who loves me, it is better to kill myself'."

He did not answer but one big tear appeared in his eye and rolled down his cheek as he nodded his head. I prayed with him and the following day he began telling me some stories of his painful life. It took him many months to reveal the truth about his background. It was not always clear if he was telling the truth, but I was happy that he started trusting me enough to share.

Often he would disappear for weeks and would not inform us where he had been. Sometimes we met him in the capital city where he had run to again. The road to rehabilitation was a very bumpy one for Daoudi. After two years of working alongside him, he asked to go for a mechanics course. However, when some tools went missing from the workshop he felt people did not trust him so he disappeared again. We counselled Daoudi and explained that failure is an opportunity to try again. He would not trust anyone and refused to go back to the mechanics workshop.

After two months of intensive counselling he finally took an opportunity to go on a Christian camp organised by Teen Missions where he accepted Christ. There was a huge change in him and he confessed that he wanted to take hold of his life. He testified and prayed in public and I gave thanks to God. He asked us to pray for him because he wanted to become a missionary.

A few months later, however, he disappeared again. I was so disappointed and wondered if I had spent all this time with him in vain.

Soon the house we had rented was too small. The first six months we had worked with over 40 children and seven of them had already been resettled in their homes and were integrated in the formal education system. But the number of children attending the project grew fast. Within a year we were in need of a bigger place to use as our centre.

We found a house with eight rooms, big enough to carry out all CRO's activities. People knew there was a new organisation working with the street children and they saw a change in the town. A national newspaper reported on our successes and that is when the troubles began.

We heard rumours that the local authorities had a meeting during which they discussed closing CRO down. Since we did not hear anything ourselves, we continued the work. After a month of uncertainty an article appeared in the national newspaper, saying that CRO Jinja would be closed because the project was a security threat.

That same day a District Intelligence Officer, the person responsible for security in the district, came to the office to see what we were doing. I showed him around and he spoke to some of the street children. He was a born-again Christian and came to encourage us not to give up the good work we are doing. He told me that he was a neighbour to the driver in our project in Mbale and was fully aware of what CRO was doing with the children.

A few days later the man rang me at home and encouraged me with a scripture; I felt funny. *'Why would an intelligence officer ring me at night to encourage me with a part of the Bible?'* I got the feeling that it was becoming a personal rather than a work-related matter.

When one of our board members visited the Town Clerk my suspicions were confirmed; the man asked her, "How can you work with that woman from Mbale?" It was clear that the objections people were making about CRO were more to do with me as its leader than the project itself.

The following day the intelligence man rang me twice but I missed his calls. On a Saturday, early in the morning, he called me again; he actually woke me up. He asked me what I was doing that day and I told him that since it was a Saturday I was at home. He ended the conversation with the words; "I will read you on Monday." I was not sure what he meant by 'reading'; I assumed that he wanted to talk to me on Monday. I did not like the language, though, it sounded too military to me.

I felt very comfortable about it all. *'Why is he searching me out? What have I done?'* Many questions ran through my mind. I decided to pray about it and asked God what His thoughts were about this man. Although he was a brother in the Lord, I didn't like his behaviour towards me.

My devotion that morning read, *"Beware of wolves in sheep skin."*[24] I laid my Bible aside and thanked God for the warning He had given me.

Before I went to church that Sunday, I made a stop at the post office to check my mailbox. I got shivers down my spine when I saw the Intelligence Officer walking by. He greeted me and asked if I was going to church. I nodded.

"I am going to the same church as you are; can you give me a lift?"

I opened the door for him to enter my car but my mind started racing, *'This man has never been in my church, why is he here today?'*

He received a rousing welcome. People were so excited that an intelligence officer had made a choice to go to church. I was the only one who knew his real reason for being in the church; he was spying on me. I felt so disgusted, seeing him worship, knowing that he had come to the church with a hidden agenda. I cried out to God, *'Can I not even be safe in Your house?'* I felt deeply betrayed by this man, and by God, that He allowed this to happen. Fortunately I had nothing to hide so after the service I walked towards him and greeted him before I left.

He didn't contact me on Monday. The rest of the week was

---

24 *Matthew 7:15*

quiet until Thursday when he rang again. He was very upset and shouted, "Why are you hiding from me? Why did you not come to my office on Monday?"

I answered, "I saw you in church on Sunday and thought that you could have discussed with me there."

"There are certain things you do not discuss in church," he blasted.

I asked him if I should come to his office or if he wanted to come to my office. He answered, "Have you refused to come to my office?"

We made an appointment for the following morning for me to go to his office.

That night I had a special prayer meeting on my own and God really encouraged me with a number of scriptures. I went to his office, knowing that I needed to be bold and strong for the Lord was going to be with me.

We had a chat and he said that it was time for him to visit me at my home. I kindly requested him to wait until his wife was also in Jinja so that they could come together for a social visit. I had made up my mind; if he wanted to come alone he had to produce a search warrant.

On a number of occasions he came to the project to find out how we were doing. My standard answer to all his questions was, "God is in control!" Even at times when I felt God was no longer in control, my only answer to him was, "God is in control." I so longed for a letter from Heaven with instructions; I was so tired of guessing what was going on behind my back. After two weeks of regular visits, he stopped coming to the project.

However, the rumours that CRO was going to be closed increased. It was announced on TV and it appeared once again in the national papers. *'How can they close a successful project that has been in operation for one and a half years?'* I wondered, *'And why are they not telling us directly?'*

My brother was visiting me at that time. He loves Uganda and would frequently surprise me with his visits. I was so glad that he was with me at this trying time. At least there was someone I could talk to and who understood the pain and the struggles I was facing.

As the rumours increased we finally received a copy of the letter written by the Town Council stating that CRO Jinja had to be closed. We knew that the Bible says that we should submit to the leaders placed over us, but everything in me wanted to fight against this injustice. Would we have to send the children back to the streets? Again I felt like Habakkuk; I could only complain to God. It felt like injustice was surrounding me and it seemed like God was tolerating the wrong that was happening to us.

We showed the children the letter but they did not understand; another deep rejection took place in their lives. They had found a place of love and care and again it was taken from them.

'God have You forsaken the street children?' It didn't concern me anymore when people spoke badly of me, but refusing us to counsel, feed, treat and educate the children went beyond my understanding; I wrestled with God and wanted to argue with the authorities.

'Lord, let me be crucified once again, but not the children! Let people say about me what they want, but please, let the children not become victims. I know that You know my heart and that is more important to me than what people think about me. But Lord, the children do not yet understand this.'

The day we received the letter, directing CRO Jinja to close its operations in the town, my brother fell very sick. I decided to look after him first before letting the truth of the letter sink in. He could not eat, sleep and had to go to the toilet every 20 minutes. I saw him dying before my eyes and panicked. I called a doctor from Jinja. He came to my house but on entering it, it was clear that he was more interested in the view from my house than in my sick brother. He prescribed malaria treatment but I did not believe he had malaria; I've had malaria many times and almost died of it once but the symptoms my brother had were very different. I did not know what to do anymore. He was too weak to be taken to a doctor in Kampala and in Jinja he was receiving the wrong treatment. He had been put on drip in my house, but I saw him becoming weaker by the hour.

The following day he was supposed to return to The Netherlands but it was clear that he could not make the journey. I told him, "I cannot see you dying in this house; we are going to Kampala." I made a bed on the back seat of the car and I drove him as fast as I could over the bumpy roads to a clinic in Kampala, all the way praying that the journey would not be too much for him.

He was diagnosed with dysentery and, once he received the right treatment, he felt much stronger. We re-routed his ticket and after two more days of treatment he was able to travel. The insurance had arranged for a taxi to meet him at the airport; his wife was there too. She sent me an e-mail with the words, "I have never seen my husband so sick; it was as if he returned from a concentration camp."

Back in Jinja, that was exactly where I felt I still was, a concentration camp, where street children were denied their rights. I cried out to God, *'Your word says You are a Father to the fatherless, but where are You? I want to believe Your word but I don't see it.'* This became my heart cry and it was repeated many times in the months to come.

Because of all of the upheaval, the children rebelled and began throwing stones at us, spitting at us as they wrestled with yet another rejection in their lives. It was almost too much to bear.

We arranged an appointment with the Municipal Council; the

meeting was set for Thursday at 10.00am. The Board of Directors from our Mbale project were due to attend this meeting in an attempt to get the project re-opened. On Wednesday the CRO Jinja Chairman confirmed the date and time with the secretary of the Town Clerk and communicated it to the board in Mbale. I went to the Municipal Council as well on the same day in the afternoon and asked the secretary the exact date and time of the meeting.

"10.00am, sharp," she said. I did not like the sarcastic smile on her face.

At 9.55 on Thursday, a delegation of five board members of CRO arrived at the Town Hall. At exactly 10.00am we entered the office of the Secretary to the Mayor.

The same secretary looked at us and said, "You people are very late, the meeting was scheduled for 9 o'clock. The authorities are now unable to see you."

I was bursting out of my skin, but no one could see it because I stood behind the board members. Very politely the Chairman asked, "Can we please wait and greet the Mayor?"

"He is very busy and does not have time to see you."

We left the office and decided to go for a cup of tea, knowing that we had lost a battle but that we would not lose the war.

The Board of Directors took over the negotiation process with the local authorities and they did great job under difficult circumstances. During one of our board meetings, where we were discussing the problem, one member confronted me and said that she felt that there was something wrong with the early beginnings of CRO. She encouraged me to search my heart.

Inside I broke and cried deep within my heart, *'Lord I have done nothing but search my heart in the last months. Where else can I search? Reveal it to me!'*

It hurt me so much to know that even a board member queried my integrity. Tears were running down my cheeks. I tried to swallow them but they just kept appearing. I was ready to give up!

One of the people present in the meeting walked up to me and quietly said, "Ingrid, will you please stop manipulating the board members with your tears?"

I swallowed even harder and tried to keep the tears back. I made a decision in my heart: tears were no longer allowed. I had to be strong. The Chairman had noticed my pain and apologised a few days later. It was as healing oil to my wounded heart and I felt a little stronger.

One newspaper article after another appeared and the problem became even more personal; the allegations became even stronger. The core message in all the newspaper articles was, *'Jinja never had any street children, but this white lady was importing them into the town, to get more donor funding to enrich herself'*.

The stories were so bad, that people asked me; "Are you the Ingrid the authorities are talking about on the radio?"

Every day I went to the office and sat quietly at my desk. We had asked the staff to take their annual leave, while the Board of Directors negotiated with the Local Authorities. It was painful to see that the classroom, the medical room and the counselling rooms were all empty.

The project had been very successful. In the one and a half years of its existence 71 children had resettled back to their homes and 41 children were attending schools within the Municipal Council while there were another 50 children attending our rehabilitation school. The authorities had allowed us to continue the work with the reformed, school-going children who came to the project for lunch every day, but we were not to work with the children that were still on the streets.

We held daily prayer meetings each morning with the members of staff that were around. We continued to trust God and He continued to encourage us. The scripture that we held on to in faith was, *"See, I have placed before you an open door that no-one can shut."*[25] It was during this difficult time that I learned the power of worship.

It was so painful, almost impossible, to see the hungry street children at the gate and not be allowed to give them food. We needed to obey the authorities but when a street child was brought into the project with cuts all over his body I could no longer ignore the need so we treated his wounds. We could not let this child die on the pavement outside our gate.

Some of the children were already registered to go to a Christian camp not far outside Jinja. A week before Christmas we saw them off, hoping that God would touch their hearts now that we were no longer allowed to do it.

As it was approaching Christmas we had planned to hold a party but that was before we received the letter about the suspension of CRO's operations. Since we were not allowed to get in touch with the children, we asked a local church to host the party. We celebrated Christmas in a very modest way. To encourage the staff I had organised a staff party in my house. This turned into a prayer meeting and we were encouraged when God spoke and confirmed once again that He was on our side.

On Christmas day I was too exhausted to move, too lonely to take any initiative and completely empty. It was one of the most depressing Christmases I have ever had, knowing that the children were back on the streets with no one to care for them.

Some of my friends, however, had got together and raised funds for the street children in the days before Christmas; they played their instruments in the streets and people contributed towards a Christmas meal for them. I never realised it, I was too depressed and stayed in bed for the whole of Christmas. It was impossible for me to deal with this kind of injustice and I was wondering

---

25 *Revelation 3:8*

where God was in all of this.

"The righteous will live by faith and not by what they see."[26] I knew the truth but it was hard to put it into practice.

I was so desperate to see God move in my situation that I decided to go to an overnight prayer gathering in the hope that I would hear God speak.

At 9.00pm I went to the place where all the churches in Jinja gathered to pray and listen to the word. There were hundreds of believers; I was one of only a few white people. The first preacher came and began to prophesy, "Next year all of you will have built houses and you will drive big cars. God wants to bless you."

I listened to three more preachers and all of them except one were speaking about the same things. Cars, houses and riches were the main topics of the sermons. We were going to get material blessings from God. At 1.00 in the morning I left, feeling sad that God was only seen as someone to bless materially. I actually cried as I drove home, "Is that why we are in Christianity, only to receive things from You?"

I was still contemplating the preaching, when my phone rang early the next morning.

"Ingrid, your children are giving problems, can you come and solve them?" the leaders of the children's camp said.

I jumped in my car and while driving there, in my heart I complained, *'Why God? This is also my Christmas holiday; can I not have just one day for myself? These kids only call me when they need something from me or when they have a problem.'*

What God answered struck me deep in my heart.

"Ingrid, do you now know how I feel? My children only come to me when they have a problem or when they need something from me but they do not come for who I am."

I was dumbfounded and, in tears, repented in the car. This was

---

26 2 Corinthians 5:7

so true, I was seeking God only to solve my problems, but I was not seeking Him for who He is. I realised that the only relationship I had with God was crying out to Him in despair but now I was not even expecting an answer anymore.

I switched off my phone; I could not talk to anybody. I was exhausted from the fight against authorities. I put up the hammock and read a book to encourage myself. As I read, a part of Jamie Buckingham's book, *'Where Eagles Soar'* touched me deeply:

"Risky living puts you into a position where God will eventually take off your mask, peel back your layers and lay you bare for the world to see. However, if the process of inner healing has been thorough and complete those who look into your life from the outside will not see the nakedness but instead, through your transparency, will see the glory of the one in whose image you have been created."

I was amazed at how I found the right books on my shelf at the right time. There were times that I really worried about lagging behind with knowledge, since I do not have a TV, my radio has no clear reception and the only newspaper I read is a local Ugandan paper.

But once again God had known what I needed and used a book that had been on my shelf for many years. It was not the first time this happened and it proved to me that God knows my inner most need. I felt a little encouraged but not enough to take charge of my life. I needed more encouragement and found it in another book by Corry ten Boom:

"The closer you get to God, the less you understand Him, but the more you believe Him."

She goes on to say:

"If God gives you a dream be willing to wait, to be misunderstood, willing to work, willing for God to twist you until you are in the shape to contain your dream, and be willing for the dream to come to pass through somebody else!

Dreams live beyond man for the dreams coming from the heart of God are always bigger than the dreamer and bigger than those who try to stop them. God's promises are bigger than our comprehension. So, can we release our dreams to God to let them come to pass in His time and His way not ours?"

That was the question I needed an answer to for CRO Jinja there and then.

In my hammock I made a commitment, *'I had a dream, I have a dream and I will pursue the dream until God tells me to hand over.'* Deep inside I knew no one could stop the dream but I had to surrender the timing of the fulfilment of it to God.

God also gave me a strategy for CRO through Jamie Buckingham's book:

"He [or in my case, she] who ministers peace is the stronger warrior."

I gave up my fighting spirit, handed the problem over to the board and retreated. The problem had become too personal, and I was not the best person to minister peace. I was too full of pain and frustration.

On New Year's Day I received a resignation letter from our Manager, she could not handle the insecure situation the project was in and decided to leave. We were back to square one.

CHAPTER SEVENTEEN

More Pain and Loss

There were many people in Jinja who offered help to CRO or came to the office to encourage us. A big multi-national company offered us their legal advisor but the board refused the offer; they were ministering peace, while I had reached a stage of wanting to minister justice and I longed to take up the offer of legal assistance. I restrained myself and submitted to the decision of the board.

Ministers and influential business people went to the local authorities and pleaded on our behalf, but all in vain. I just did not understand the authorities and I did not understand God. That's when He led me to a scripture that helped me:

"Let not the wise man boast of his wisdom,

or the strong man boasts of his strength

or the rich man boast of his riches

but let him who boast, boast about this:

that he understands and knows me

that I am the Lord who exercises kindness,

justice and righteousness on earth

for in these I delight."[27]

I had to admit; I had been looking at the rich, the wise and the strong, to solve our problems. From that moment on I decided to

---

27 *Jeremiah 9:23-24*

tell everybody that God was going to intervene in His own time. I decided to boast in the fact that I know Him!

I did it in faith because what my eyes saw, and what my ears heard, was so contradictory to the scripture that I had embraced. I made a deliberate choice to fill my mind with the truth of the Word.

The negotiations with the Local Authorities were difficult; it took four months.

At the time I was so thankful to have support from a very good friend, but I had also come to realise that our friendship could not grow any further. I knew we had come to the season in the friendship that we either had to break our ties with one another or I had to marry him. I was on my guard because I did not want this friendship to be hindrance in my relationship with God. So I remained strong, fought any feelings of vulnerability and told myself that I could manage together with my God. I knew I needed a good friend, but I also knew that our lives, cultures and circumstances were so different that I would not be able to marry him. It was great having a good friend but not being able to share the deep emotional struggles of my heart, was difficult. My heart said, *'Surely in this season you need a friend,'* but my head said, *'Keep your distance.'* This battle between my head and my heart made me feel even lonelier.

I received an email message from my sending agency unexpectedly. It included a deadline; if the problems with CRO were not solved within two weeks, I had to wind down my involvement and return to The Netherlands. I felt so hurt by their cool interpretation of the situation in a time where the only thing I really needed was encouragement and emotional support.

Within the two-week deadline set by the agency, a breakthrough came; we received a letter from the Town Council that could be interpreted in two different ways and we choose to interpret it as saying that we were allowed to open the project again. We wasted no time and invited the street children to come back.

But the children had also lost confidence in us, after we had let them down for almost four months. It was difficult for them to overcome the rejection they had faced once again. Little by little they appeared in the project to test us out. It took two months before all the children had returned to the centre.

I was worn out and tired. I had been in the office alone for most of the past four months, conscientiously filling my mind with the promises of God but not seeing them come through. Fasting for many days and not seeing breakthroughs. Now that we were allowed to open the project I felt relieved but I also realised that the struggle had taken its toll on my emotional health. However, when I looked at the children and I heard them worshipping God, it gave me the energy to put aside my emotional pain and to concentrate on the task ahead of me.

Before the enforced closure, we had carried out night patrols once a month. As soon as we were allowed to re-open we resumed the night patrols. We looked for children who were new to the streets of Jinja so that we could resettle them before they became used to the hard street life. At the time we had a Dutch camera team with us who were making a documentary about CRO Jinja in order to raise funds for our own premises. On this particular night we'd had a long and shocking patrol on the streets; we'd found children everywhere: hidden in a maize field, in the trees and under plastic sheets; we'd had to have two policemen escorting us for security reasons.

By 3.00 in the morning we were finally in bed. Four hours later the phone woke me up. It was Christine, the Manager of CRO in Mbale. She informed me that one of our social workers had passed away. He had been sick and it broke my heart that he died so young.

'Why, Lord, are the righteous going and the wicked live?' I was starting to feel like a psalmist.

We finished the TV work as quick as we could, so that I could prepare to attend the funeral, deep in the village. I made the four-hour journey to the village where the burial was to be held – a long journey on dusty roads – and reached there just in time. I saw him lying in the coffin and asked God quietly, "Can't you raise him from the dead? He was such a blessing to so many street children; he was a model to them, Lord, can You please raise him?"

My hopes came to nothing. We buried him and I drove the long four-hour trip back home. I drove as fast as I could over the dirt roads thinking, *'No problem if I slide, heaven must be a much better place.'*

I was a wreck and just wanted to cry but could not. I realised that my heart had become numb and I was no longer able to feel any emotions. There was no love left in my heart. I had become a survivor.

I knew I could not continue like this but I also did not know how to change my situation. On a free Saturday afternoon, after the funeral, I went down to the river to calm my mind. It had been a good therapy in the past few months enjoying the beauty of the river Nile and letting the water and the wind take away the problems I was facing. As I sat there meditating and praying I heard God speaking to my heart,

"I just want to love you."

'God wanting to love me?' Yes, I needed to be loved; I so needed someone to take care of me. There was this deep loneliness in my heart.

In the days that had passed I had made a decision in obedience to God. It was a decision that went against all that I felt. With a lot of pain in my heart, I declined the expected marriage proposal from my good friend, the man who had been there for me through all my struggles. I had felt, for some time, that a proposal was going to come my way, but I also knew that God had given me a calling that I wanted to fulfil. I didn't see how these two things would work together.

I so needed someone to love and support me, but I had no peace about marrying this friend. Out of sheer obedience to God I refused his proposal and now God spoke to my heart, *"I just want to love you."*

I did not know how to receive His love. I even doubted if God still loved me, because everything He had asked of me had been so hard. I knew I needed a change of heart in order to receive what He had for me but I was also aware that I was unable to do it myself. I prayed and said, "Holy Spirit, search my heart and see where it needs change. I have searched and tried, I have prayed, worked and fasted; I am at the end of my rope and do not know how to continue, but I know that I love You!" My cry to God continued the whole afternoon.

I paced up and down in my room telling God, "It's all well and good; here I am ready to carry my cross for You as long as it shapes me into becoming more like Jesus, but what is happening to me now is having the opposite effect. Jesus is a people-person, and all I want to do is hide from people. Jesus loved people – I don't have love left for people; I find it difficult to trust people. Isn't it true that carrying my cross should make me more like You?"

I continued crying out to Him, "I do everything to please You, I try not to sin, read the Bible every day, I pray long and fast even more, don't You see that?" I had just finished forty days on only fruit and vegetables. I so badly needed a breakthrough.

"I love You and I have done everything possible to show You that I love You and I have no idea what more I can give You. I almost lost my life for Your sake, I have given You all the money I had, I have given up my family and friends, I have given up a marriage proposal, Lord what else can I do? You need to do something because I have done all I know to do. I have repented, I have searched my heart. I cannot find anything anymore that I need to deal with in my life. You need to reveal it to me. I just need you!"

I continued to pour out my heart, "I know Your word, and my life is not in line with it. Your word says 'Jesus has come to give us life and give it in abundance,' but here I am – I have life but I do not have it abundantly. I am struggling, fighting and surviving. There is no abundance. If this is all Christianity has to offer, I have seen it and done it, You can take me to heaven."

It gave me some relief to pour out my heart to God, but I was still desperate to hear His reply. At the time, though, I was too full of my own struggles to receive God's answers.

CHAPTER EIGHTEEN

Friends

It was nearing the end of 1999 and, now that CRO Jinja was fully operational again, the chairman, Joseph and I were invited to attend a workshop in the capital city. It was a workshop on Servant hood in leadership and was led by one of the overseers of the denomination that had expelled me from the church in Mbale. I had forgiven the pastor who had told me not to attend his church anymore, but somehow I did not feel free towards his overseer.

'What did he think of me? Who had he believed? Why had he never acted when things were so painful? Did he now value my contribution or would he still be thinking that I am the devil's agent?'

On our way to the Kampala, I discussed the issue with Joseph and shared all the accusations and stories that had surrounded me.

Joseph said, "Ingrid, that is one of the reasons why I joined CRO. When you came to Jinja some brethren were saying that you were a witchdoctor and I decided to find out. Some people went ahead and reported you to the police, warning them that you were planning a mass suicide of 1000 people. I reckoned that if you were a cult leader, you needed Christ. I was determined to lead you to Christ if the rumours were true. With a small group we started praying for you, every Saturday afternoon. But the more we worked and interacted together the more I saw that all these stories were lies."

When we arrived in the city, he said, "Ingrid, I need to ask you for forgiveness for what my people have done to you."

Tears filled my eyes. This was exactly what my wounded soul needed. It was the first time a Ugandan friend and brother took responsibility for what his fellow Christians had put me through. I was deeply touched.

Whilst we were in Kampala for the course I went to the overseer and asked him if he had any doubts about my integrity. He did not understand the reasons behind my question. After I'd explained the history, he made a point of investigating the source of these rumours. Over time we became good friends and working partners and I was thankful that the leadership of the denomination cleared this issue of expulsion from the church.

I was very grateful for two other good friends in Jinja; Ferne was an American missionary who had lived her whole life in Africa and was one of the most beautiful elderly ladies I ever met and Rakesh was an Asian, born in Uganda.

Ferne had been widowed at an early age, when her husband died in an airplane crash in Congo. Now she used her healed past to encourage and assist widows in Uganda. She worked for six months in America, raising funds for the widows, and the other six months she would work in Uganda. She did not have a home on her own. She was happy to housesit any of the houses of missionaries that went on leave. Wherever she stayed she put her own tablecloth, flower vase and candle on the table and made it a place of her own. When she celebrated her 65th birthday with us in Jinja, we enjoyed a special treat – her amazing home baked cake. We were good friends.

Rakesh was a businessman in Jinja. A mutual Irish friend who had moved back to Europe introduced me to him. It was so good to have at least two people living in Jinja where I could walk in and out without knocking on the door and where I would always find a listening ear.

To celebrate our birthdays, Ferne, Rakesh and I had taken a wonderful safari to one of the game parks in Uganda during which we spent lots of time talking and sharing about our faith. Rakesh was a Hindu but he showed a lot of respect for our Christian faith.

I had given him a Bible and some other Christian books. He would often encourage me to have more faith in God during my times of trouble. He wished me God's blessings when I passed through hardships and he praised God when I shared my victories. It was a friendship based on respect for each other and I had made a commitment to pray for his salvation every day.

Not long after our great but short safari, I realised I needed a real break. I'd had two years of intense struggle and I had not taken any holidays for a long time. Because of the situation CRO had been in, I had not allowed myself to take time off. Now that the situation had calmed down, I decided to take a long leave. This time it worked out perfectly, since Ferne was in Uganda during that period; she would stay in my house while I was on leave.

She moved her things in, in preparation for her stay and on the last evening before I left we had a great night, catching up on each other's lives. I was happy that she had an opportunity to enjoy my house and the beauty of the river Nile. She showed me a little wound on her foot that had refused to heal, but it did not look too serious.

After I said my farewell to her I sat on the plane, pondering all the plans I had for my leave. It would be good to have time with family and friends. I was looking forward to going to Iran for a wedding of a good friend of mine. And on the way back to Uganda I would meet up with my brother in Dubai and we would tour the United Arab Emirates. I was looking forward to doing a lot of fun things. Life had been so heavy these past years.

My family and friends tried their best to make my time in The Netherlands wonderful, but I could not enjoy it. Many people commented on the wonderful work I was doing with the street children but I could only look at them and politely say, "Thank you." All I could think was, *'I am so aware of what it says in 1 Corinthians 13, 'If we do anything without love it is useless, like a clinging symbol.' What I am doing is useless in the eyes of God because I have no love left, but I cannot tell you because you are supporting me.'* I felt like a terrible hypocrite, giving the outward appearance of a life that people admired but having an inner-life that was a mess.

My heart was too heavy. I tried to enjoy life, but I failed. I wondered, asking God silently, *'Is this the life I was supposed to get, I want to hide from people but I know that is not what You want. You want me to be with people and make an impact wherever I go.'*

I just knew there was something wrong in me but could not find the answer.

"Ingrid," Ferne's voice sounded weak on the phone. My heart skipped a beat. *What was wrong?* I had been in The Netherlands for a month when I received her call. *'Why would she be calling?'*

"Ingrid, I need to tell you that this morning Rakesh passed away," I could not believe my ears.

I opened my e-mail and found a message from his office. *"I regret to inform you that Rakesh has passed away."*

'Another close friend has died?' I struggled with the fact that so many of my close friends were passing away. I called his friends in Uganda and they all confirmed the news. He'd had a stroke and died within three hours on his way to the hospital in Kampala.

I contacted our mutual friend in Ireland and told her what had happened. She knew Rakesh's family well and arranged for me to attend the cremation in the United Kingdom. I did not know the family except for his nephew who had visited Uganda and we had gone on a rafting trip together.

The same day I rang, Rakesh's brother in England and asked if I could attend the cremation.

"Rakesh's friends are our friends, you are welcome to come. Please stay with us in the house, do not look for a hotel."

It would be so difficult to face the family. I just did not have any words but I knew that it was right to attend the cremation. I arrived early in England and needed a place to get myself together before I could go to the family. Tears rolled down my cheeks; I felt so lost. I went to Westminster Abbey and asked the cashier if there was a place where I could pray. I did not need to see the cathedral, I just needed a place to be quiet, cry and pray. She directed me to the back entrance and when the watchman at the gate saw me he directed me to the chapel, without asking any questions; grief was written all over my face.

I emptied my heart before the Lord and cried, "I do not understand, I have prayed and believed for his salvation every day."

I lived in faith, believing that God would answer my prayer but now he had died. Was it too late? I just needed to know if it was well with him. I was determined not to leave the church before I knew. If I did not know that Rakesh was in heaven, how could I face the family? I did not want to add a burden to them during these difficult days, especially because they were so welcoming to me, opening their home for me. I wanted to be an encouragement for them even though I did not know them. I needed strength and I needed to hear from God.

I opened my Bible and my eyes fell on a scripture in James. Through my tears one verse jumped off the page, *"The prayers of the righteous are powerful and effective."*[28]

I knew I had prayed for him every day, was God telling me that my prayer had been effective? How is that possible if Rakesh never confessed his belief in Jesus Christ to me? I re-read the whole chapter of James five. This time verse 11 stood out to me, *"The Lord is full of compassion and mercy."* I meditated on these

---

28 *James 5:16*

two scriptures. *'If the Lord is full of compassion and my prayers are effective, something must have happened with Rakesh, even if I do not understand it and even if he had not shared anything with me.'*

A memory came back to my mind: Alma and I had gone to Papua New Guinea on a working trip in 1987; we were making TV programmes about Dutch missionary children growing up in different cultures. We had arrived from Japan and seen the Hindu temples, we had been to Thailand where Buddhism is the most important faith and we had travelled to Muslim Indonesia. We had just arrived in Papua New Guinea and had learned about the animistic beliefs of the people. It troubled me, *'If the Bible says that Jesus is victorious, and no one would be saved except through Jesus, what happens to all these people from other faiths?'* I was confused.

One evening as I walked along the beautiful beach questioning God about the issue of salvation, I saw on one side, the bright blue ocean and on the other side a beautiful lagoon. I remembered stopping and enjoying the lush green in the lagoon. I began counting the different colours of green but lost track. I asked God, "If you are so creative, why did you only create one way to heaven?"

As clear as anything a scripture came to mind, *"I am the Way, the Truth, and the Life; no-one comes to the Father except through me."* Immediately God continued, *"That is your only responsibility!"*

I had shared the way, the truth, and the life with Rakesh and I had fulfilled my responsibility. I wiped my tears and, when I looked up I saw a beautiful carving on the wall of a man lying in Jesus' arms. I did not understand it with my head but in my heart I had received a confirmation: Rakesh was safe with Jesus. I felt much stronger when I took the Underground to his brother's house. Rakesh's nephew, picked me from the station. We hugged but had no words.

I shook hands with Rakesh's brother when I arrived at his house, and asked him how he was doing. He told me that he was very distressed but that he was doing better now since he had seen Rakesh's body this morning.

"There is such a determination on his face, I just know that he is where he is supposed to be. The only one who has a problem with him now is God."

He explained to me that in his culture, people pray for a number of days to accompany the spirit of the deceased but he just knew that Rakesh had already reached his destination. He had cancelled the prayers. Rakes spirit was no longer wandering around. Despite the pain in my heart, I rejoiced in this second confirmation.

The house was full of Rakesh's relatives and they made me feel at home as much as they could; I was amazed at their hospitality. We all had our own memories of him and shared them together. I had never met this family before, but they were very open and warm to me.

In my interactions with Rakesh in Uganda, I had never noticed the difference in culture. But now, suddenly, I felt that I had entered a different world. Every evening in this time of grief family and friends came to support the family. They were a community in mourning and I could see that it brought encouragement to the family.

Rakesh's niece had sacrificed her bedroom for me. I was so thankful to have a place on my own to retreat to and get courage for the funeral the following day.

"This is going to be a difficult day but I do not want to see emotions," Rakesh's brother said when I came out of the bedroom.

I swallowed and prayed, "God give me the strength. I do not want to be a burden to this family – they have been so good to me – but I feel the need to cry."

When his body was brought in the house, I broke down. I tried to hide my tears but failed; I tried to stop it from showing in my voice but failed. This was my friend and he was no longer with us. I walked out of the room, sat down in the kitchen and wept.

The priest came and the service began. There were many people; family members came to the kitchen, took me by the hand and led me into the sitting room. The whole ceremony was so foreign to me. Flowers were strewn all over the body, people gave the body water to drink and a coconut was put in the coffin. They asked me if I wanted to give the body something to drink, but I could not. I had brought my own farewell card for him but kept it in my bag. I looked in the coffin and swallowed my tears. How I had needed friends and how cruel it was that I would not see him again, in this world. At the crematorium, I said my final farewell to a good friend.

I left for The Netherlands early the following morning. My sister and brother-in-law were at the airport. It touched my heart; they had travelled many miles to be at the airport to help me work through this intensely painful experience. I had gone through so many trials in Uganda but had not experienced people who went the extra mile to comfort me, like I was experiencing now. I suddenly realised what I had missed in the past years.

It was just three weeks after Rakesh's death that I had planned to go to Iran with a group of friends to celebrate the wedding of one of them to an Iranian. What was supposed to be a great trip was overshadowed by the death of a good friend.

After my two-week visit to Iran I met up with my brother to tour Dubai and the Emirates. We had looked forward to it, and anticipated a lot of fun. But the fun and the joy of discovering new places did not reach my heart. I told myself to enjoy it but I did not feel it. A few days into our trip my brother received a phone call that his father in law had passed away. His trip was cut short and I flew back to Uganda, tired of death.

Ferne was there to welcome me back but she did not look well.

It turned out that she had stayed in my house for only two weeks. She'd had so much pain in her back that she couldn't travel the bumpy road to my house, so she had found another place to live.

Her foot had not healed and she told me that she had consulted a doctor in Kampala, who said that there was nothing wrong. But now, after almost three months it still wasn't right. The following day she decided to go to the doctor in Kampala again and when she returned she told me, "The doctor was shocked when he looked in my file. 'What!' he asked, 'Did they not call you to inform you that the wound on your foot is malignant. You have cancer and need to go back to the States immediately'"

I took her to the airport as tears rolled down my cheeks. I felt that this was my final goodbye to her and I could not handle losing two of my closest friends in less than four months. A few weeks later, as I was driving along the road to my house, I was thinking about Ferne, *'I can imagine this road would be bad if you are sick.'* Even I was feeling pain in some parts of my body. It had only been three weeks since I had said goodbye to her, but was already missing her.

At home I discovered the pain I'd been experiencing was a problem with my breast, but didn't want to think about it. I pushed it away. It was a Friday afternoon and Christine and Hans were coming for the weekend; we were going to make it a fun weekend. I had gone through enough heavy stuff. But it did not leave my mind and finally I had the courage to share it with Christine. She told me to take it seriously and go to the doctor. I laughed it off choosing not to believe her. I decided to look it up in a medical handbook especially designed for the tropics and it said to, "radio call for help." I realised the urgency of my situation and, on Monday, I drove the same bumpy road back to the capital city to see a doctor.

The sermon I had heard in church that Sunday spoke about how satan wants to steal our future and our visions. I felt that he was exactly doing that right now. The doctor called me into her office and I realised that she knew me. "Ingrid, it has been a long time since we met. What can I do for you?"

I shared the problem with her and she took a puncture to be tested in the lab. After a few minutes she came back and said, "There is no infection."

"Good!" I answered and stood up to leave.

Her face changed, "Not good," she said, "You need to go for further tests. There is a possibility that you have breast cancer."

My whole life ran though my mind, *'Breast cancer? Dying of cancer? Never!*

I shall not die but live! Enough is enough! I have seen death and tasted it but I shall not die.' A fighting spirit rose up within me.

I rang the travel agent to book my flight for the following day and I rang a number of friends in The Netherlands and asked them to pray. I was determined not to die. That favour I would not grant to satan.

I felt so mad; not even a month ago I'd come back from The Netherlands and now I had to pack my bags again? I had just arrived and now I had to leave again. What kind of timing was this? I felt that satan had taken over control of my life and that I was nothing more than a football being kicked around wherever he pleased. He was out to destroy me and I refused to be destroyed!

I rang my prayer partner in Jinja and she organised a prayer meeting for that night. A number of colleagues and missionary friends came together, they anointed me with oil, and we all felt that God was going to heal me. We also prayed for the manager of CRO who had to lead the project during my absence. Two people felt God saying that the mantel from Elijah had to be given to Elisha. I knew I had to hand over my responsibilities some day and it was comforting to hear that God was going to raise up local leadership for CRO Jinja as well.

As I slept that night I heard these words:

"This sickness does not lead to death but is to glorify me!"

'Did I hear that right? Where had that voice come from in my sleep?' As I realised that it was God's voice, I calmed down and felt reassured. *'I am not going to die but I will glorify God. I am coming back to Uganda. I may be away for a week, a month or a year, but I am going to live and glorify God!'*

CHAPTER NINETEEN

The Beginning of the Inward Journey

The first tests were done in the Dutch hospital. Within half an hour the doctor gave me the results. I was so surprised when he said that he was 90% sure that there was nothing wrong with my breast. Other tests needed to be done but he already wanted to encourage me.

I felt stupid. I'd come all the way from Uganda and in just half an hour the diagnoses was 'healthy'. I decided to go for a thorough medical check in a hospital specialised in tropical diseases and found out that my body was completely healthy. There was no medical problem.

After the doctor heard a few of the things that I had been through he prescribed some rest. It made me wonder, *'If I am physically fit, why did I have to come to The Netherlands? There must be a reason for it. Nothing happens without a reason.'*

I wanted to know. I went to my pastor and asked him and his wife to pray with me to find out why I'd had to return to The Netherlands. I also wanted to know why so many problems came my way. It was overwhelming and nothing seemed to be 'normal'. I had reached a point where my spiritual life had become a struggle instead of a joy.

The pastor looked at me and gave *his* diagnosis, "It looks as if the 'good' has become the enemy of the 'best' in your life," and that is exactly what I felt. I had been doing a lot of good things but I was not enjoying God's best for me. Whatever 'the best' might be, I was yet to discover.

We had times of prayer and waiting upon the Lord. The word 'pain' came up and they asked me if there was anything that was causing me pain. There had been many things but I thought that I had worked them through. I could not really tell exactly what caused the pain; I wasn't even aware that there was pain. They asked me, if I was ready, to allow God to let me feel whatever pain there was in my heart. I was desperate for change and so the following day I went for a long walk on the beach and finally I had the courage to ask God.

"If there is any pain in my life, please reveal it to me and let me feel it."

Instantly I felt a heavy block on my heart; I found it difficult to walk. A heaviness that I had never experienced before embraced me and I could hardly move. I made my way home pondering my situation and asking God to reveal the cause of this deep hidden pain. And, over time, He did.

The heaviness and the pain remained for the whole time I was in The Netherlands. I was wondering how I could ever get rid of it. I just didn't know what to do, but I knew I could not go back to Uganda with this heaviness in my chest. I did not want to become an even greater hypocrite. I struggled with it but did not know the way out.

One morning I woke up with a strong sense that God was performing 'open-heart' surgery on me. With a surgeon's knife He cut out my heart, held it in His hands and replaced it with His heart. It was a new experience for me, I had never received such a clear picture from God but it reassured me that He was in the business of changing me!

It wasn't long after, that Alma invited me to a Christian conference, with John and Carol Arnott of the Toronto Airport Fellowship, in Amsterdam. I had heard so many different stories about this Toronto Church and did not know what to think about it. Some people loved the meetings where God would show up in unexpected and unexplained ways, while others believed strongly that those manifestations were from the enemy of God.

She tried to persuade me to stay a week longer, but I had already spent a month in The Netherlands; I just wanted to go back. I felt responsible for CRO. I had been away long enough and I longed to be back in Uganda, to postpone my ticket just for a church service felt a bit too much to ask.

My phone rang. It was Hans, my long-time friend.

"Ingrid, you have been in The Netherlands and we have not seen each other. I have air miles, would you like to go skiing for a weekend in Switzerland?"

I just could not refuse that offer; I loved skiing and I loved catching up with my friend and so I postponed my flight. We had a wonderful weekend in the fresh snow and beautiful sun, but I realised that I could not fully enjoy it. The pain in my heart and the heaviness was constantly present. It was so deep that I could not even share it with my friend.

Since I was still in The Netherlands I had a chance to attend the conference with John and Carol Arnott. It was the first time in my life that I went forward for prayer during a conference. I just needed to get rid of the pain and the heaviness. All I could do during the service was cry. When they prayed for me, I felt a tingling feeling in my right arm. This sensation became stronger and stronger until it left through my fingers. When we drove home, I realised that the heaviness from my heart had lifted. I could return to Uganda without carrying this load with me. God again had answered my prayer, but I knew that this was only the beginning of a process.

The day I returned to Uganda, with a clean bill of health, I received the message that my friend Ferne had passed away. Even as I mourned her, I knew that I had started on an inward journey towards healing. I slowly began to believe that perhaps there is an answer to pain.

As the weight of this huge block was lifted from my heart, it created a deep desire in me to learn more about God's freeing love. I read in a magazine about a worship conference, taking place in Toronto five months later and I just knew I had to be there. I sent my brother-in-law an e-mail and asked if he felt like going with me to Toronto. Without any hesitation he said yes!

Not long before I was due to leave for Toronto, I opened another mail; it was from my sending agency. I had also informed them that I wanted to go to Toronto, since I still had a lot of leave days that I had not used. The email read, *"If you are coming through Holland again, we want you to see a psychologist. You are not allowed to go back to Uganda until we have a psychological report on you."*

I was so upset, *'A psychologist? Now that I am finally finding a solution to the things I have struggled with for all these years I need to see a psychologist?'*

I had worked as an Assistant Child Psychologist for five years before I came to Uganda and had helped people to find ways of dealing with their problems. But I no longer wanted to deal with problems I wanted to be free of them.

I rang the agency and explained that I was very disappointed that they had made this decision without involving me or even asking me how I was doing. I did not commit to going. I felt betrayed; all those years that I had been struggling on my own, there had been no support. Now that I found my way out of the problems, suddenly I would not be allowed to return to Uganda without a psychological assessment?

My tone of voice had not been very nice, I was angry and I pondered about it on my way to Toronto. During the flight I picked up a book that someone had given me minutes before I left, it was about the Toronto Church. I opened it, looked at the index, and saw that the author had a negative mind-set about this church. I immediately closed the book. I had seen enough negativity in my life. I knew it was God who brought me to this place and I was not going to be influenced by other people's opinions.

We arrived a day early for the conference and went to visit Niagara Falls. With a cold drink in the early spring sun God convicted me about my wrong attitude towards the sending agency. That evening I rang them and asked them to make the appointment with the psychologist.

I said to God, "You work everything for good, for those who love You. I love You so please work this thing out for my good, also."

I walked into the church and knew that I was expected. Although I could not experience His presence as others could, when I looked up and saw all the flags from the nations that had been to the church, I saw the Ugandan flag hanging right next to the Dutch flag. It was as if God welcomed me personally to the church.

I was amazed at the level of freedom people expressed in their worship, but it was also very strange to me. It was so different than what I was used to in Uganda and even in The Netherlands. I sat at the back of the church observing what was happening, not ready to jump in. The manifestations at times scared me and at other times excited me. My brother-in-law was up at the front; he joined in as if this was his daily activity. *'How different people are,'* I thought.

It was as if everybody used his or her own unique gift to worship God. I needed time to look around and see what was happening and how God's Spirit was touching people. Some people were laughing, others were crying. There was shouting going on and some people just rolled over the floor. I had never seen anything like that in my whole life and it was very stretching for my faith. It was strange but it was good, there was peace in my heart being in this controversial church.

It took a number of days before I was able to concentrate because what I saw was so new to me. I did not understand it but it was clear that it was God's Spirit touching people. I heard people shout, "I see Jesus, high and lifted up." Quietly I walked to that corner and looked up but could not see anything. Then someone shouted, "I smell Jesus," so I went to that corner and smelled; I could not smell anything. It made me upset and angry that so many people were experiencing the presence of God in so many different ways and I could not.

When the offering bag came everyone was encouraged to ask God how much to put in. I asked God and He said, "You don't have to give anything, you have come to receive."

I put back the money that was already in my hand, wanting to obey but not understanding it, *'Is it not a normal thing to put at least something in the offering bag?'* All that I thought of as normal was suddenly not normal anymore.

One evening as I listened to the words of *'The Father's Love-letter'*, by Barry Adams a deep voice spoke through the auditorium, "I am for you not against you."

Instantly my heart broke. I had known that with my head, I had told myself many times during my problems but I hadn't been able to grasp it with my heart. Now the truth penetrated my heart and broke it. What I had known with my head suddenly was revealed to my heart and all the pain from deep within came to the surface. I could hardly walk. Could it really be true that God is for me?

I cried throughout the night, not just crying but shaking all over my body. What I had seen happening with others was now, unwillingly, happening to me. All I could do was to surrender to it; it was overwhelming. The next day I was too tired to worship, to raise my hands or even to open my Bible; I was a wreck.

"There is no use in me sitting in this service. What else can I do to show you that I love you? I feel so useless," I cried out to God. Tears flooded down my cheeks. People around me were all happy but I felt no joy whatsoever, there were only questions and a deep pain.

Deep inside, I heard a voice, *"He gives His beloved sleep. Go and sleep."*[29]

I wrestled with this, *'Can I please God by sleeping? I have come to worship Him, how can I just go and sleep? That's not normal! God, do You mean I just need to sleep; can't I do anything to get the joy?'*

Again I heard the same scripture spoken to my heart and I decided to walk out. I lay in the early spring sunshine in the garden and slept. I don't know how long I slept, but when I opened my eyes a big white bird flew overhead. It was as if God said, *"I will do it, not you. Depend on my Spirit! Your Christianity has been about what you have done for me, but Christianity is what I have done for you!"*

This was a huge paradigm-shift in my thinking. I had given all that I had to God; I had given up my family and friends, my career, my money, my life but had never learned how to receive from Him. The truth that I can only love because He first loved me hit my heart. It dawned on me that He was willing to give love but that I was unable to receive it, that I had been so busy for Him and had not spent time with Him to receive what He has for me.

I had been the kind of person who looked over my shoulder and said, "Jesus, can You manage my speed, I am really going fast for you."

---

29 *Psalm 127:2*

He wanted me to learn that I was in need to receive before I gave. The real truth was that He loved me first. He was the initiator of love. I could only love because He first loved me. And He loved me for who I was and not for what I did for Him.

A few days later, in the car at a traffic light in downtown Toronto, I lowered the mirror to see if my eyes were not too swollen to be seen in public – I had cried so much. When I looked at my reflection, suddenly I saw something different. There was a twinkle in my eyes that I had not seen before. The light had been switched on!

The worship week created a deep hunger in my heart for more of God. One night, His presence filled my room in a special way after which He asked me a question, *"Are you willing to give CRO to me in order to receive more of me?"*

I willingly gave CRO to God knowing that it was ultimately His programme, not mine. I had a great need to experience more of Him in my life.

At the end of the conference, on my way out of the church I had picked up a leaflet about a one- month leaders' school; I knew I needed to be there. The answers to my struggles were on the way and I knew I needed more of God in my life. I was tired of struggling and surviving. God had broken through, now I needed to give Him space to go deeper. It was time for resurrection power to be manifested in my life.

When I looked at the costs of the school, I hesitated. It was so much money and together with the cost of airplane ticket the amount could feed all the CRO kids for many months. But in that one week in Toronto I had seen enough of the power of God's love to realise that I had aligned my thinking with that of the enemy of God and that there was a great need to begin to see the world from God's perspective. I needed to see Africa from His heart of love, with His eyes.

'Is it responsible to spend so much money on myself?' I struggled

with this question. In my heart I knew that I wanted to go but my head questioned the large amount of money involved. I had never spent so much money for my personal benefit alone; it was a great dilemma. Not knowing what to do, I randomly opened my Bible and found the answer in Proverbs, *"Though it costs you all you have, get understanding."*[30]

The following day my application for the leaders' school was on its way and I was on my way back to Uganda!

I had hoped to see the psychologist the day after I arrived from the worship conference, but I was disappointed to find out that she was too busy. I had to wait for another two weeks in The Netherlands in order for an appointment with her. It was necessary to postpone my connecting flight to Uganda. It annoyed me; all those years of struggle the agency was not there to help me and now that I was finding the answers, I needed a psychological test to see if I was fit enough to return to Uganda.

"What do you think about this appointment?" the psychologist asked.

"What do *you* think of this appointment? It is not my choice to be here," I answered rebelliously.

She smiled and admitted that some serious procedure mistakes were made.

I explained to her that I was searching for a better connection between the head and the heart. I told her that my work was not influenced negatively by my personal search because our street children programme was still one of the most successful programmes in the country. I shared with her that I had been surviving and that it was now time to begin living. The psychologist felt that my search for a better connection between my head and my heart was a legitimate search and she concluded our hour together with the words, "What you want is what all of us want. I

---

30 *Proverbs 4:7*

do not see any reason for you not to return to Uganda."

I asked her if she could recommend the leadership school to my sending agency, since I had set my mind on attending the school. I knew that a journey into my heart had begun and I was determined to continue the search for freedom and spiritual abundance.

She wrote a recommendation and the sending agency allowed me one month's unpaid leave to attend the school and paid for half of the tuition fees! God had indeed worked it out for good!

I travelled back to Uganda. Relieved that answers were on the way, relieved that, after all, God had come through for me.

CHAPTER TWENTY

Freeing Truth

"I will repay you for the years the locusts have eaten."[31] In the six weeks ahead of the school, I heard this scripture at least five times and every time I knew it was especially preached for me.

We were warmly welcomed at the leadership school. I knew that this was going to be my time with God. I did not know anyone else in the school and I was happy about that. There were about 60 people from many different nations in the world but I had no interest in getting to know them; it was my time with God. The mornings were filled with worship and teaching with ministry times; in the afternoon there was 'soaking' prayer. Soaking prayer is a receiving and meditative prayer; a time to be in the presence of God when one allows the Holy Spirit to do what He needs to in each one's life. God surely needed to do a lot in my life!

It was a completely new form of prayer for me. I had heard people say that it was a New Age practice but the environment I was in was so full of God that I readily surrendered. I had no experience with it but it brought a lot of peace to my heart.

I thought I knew God, because I had seen His power during the attack but I realised that I had not experienced His love. His presence made me want to cry and I found I just could not stop crying. Out of the four weeks, I cried three full weeks day and night; it was as if God stood at a distance with a loving smile on

---

31 Joel 2:25a

His face and said, *"My child, you have been so strong, but now, in your weakness you will experience my strength."*

It was so good to have a safe place where I could be vulnerable. Love and acceptance flowed everywhere; it was really a time between God and me. I did not socialise with other students, and no one minded about it. There was a freedom that I hadn't seen in any other church anywhere else. I could be who I was, just a wounded little girl; I no longer needed to be the strong person who had it all together; I could be honest with myself and with God.

People prayed for me and I was relieved that I did not need to explain anything. I did not have to use my head to formulate sentences but I could allow my heart to cry freely. During these times God revealed to the people what they needed to know in order to pray effectively.

While lying on the floor, crying my eyes out, somebody shared a picture God had given her, "I see a picture of a nail bomb and it has gone off near you. Your body is full of nails. It's painful but I see Jesus and He is removing all the nails, one by one, smearing oil on the wounds and you are healing really quickly." I knew deep from within that healing had begun and I was so thankful!

I knew that, *"weeping may remain for a night, but rejoicing comes in the morning."*[32] My morning was on the way! We were encouraged to ask God to show us pictures; He showed me that the scar tissue from the nail bomb became as soft as a peach skin. I knew that He was going to turn my sorrow into laughter and my pain into joy! I was on my way out of misery and loneliness. It would not be by some kind of supernatural intervention but on a journey where Jesus would take me by the hand and lead me through my own heart on the way to the Father's heart. I had known the scripture that Jesus is the Way to the Father so well, but I never knew that it was going to be a journey of discovery into my own heart.

---

32 *Psalm 30:5*

As I laid my heart bare before God, all the accusations, the stress, the arrest, the attack, the loneliness and the pain I had endured passed through my mind as in a film and the pain hit my heart. I had never allowed myself to feel the pain, as it had been too difficult to admit that there had been people in this world that wanted me dead. I had never wanted to feel the pain of being called a witchdoctor or cult leader, but God's loving presence enabled me to feel the pain so that I could forgive the people from my heart and be comforted by Him as my Father, just as Jesus spoke the words, *"Father forgive them for they do not know what they are doing"* through his pain as He hung on the cross.

Since I was young girl, I had known that Jesus died for my sins, but now He showed me that He had also died for my pain, disappointments and anger. God did not want me to struggle on my own any longer; He showed me that Jesus died for all the disappointments and negativity that I had been through and that He would carry me through life.

I learned how to hear God's voice. We were taught how to listen to God and how to commune with Him, how to distinguish between your own thoughts, God's thoughts and satan's thoughts. I just could not get enough of God's voice speaking to me; it was revolutionary. He was so loving and so positive! I was very shocked that I had believed so many things that were actually not of God. I discovered many negative patterns in my thinking that had led me into bondage and hindered me from living out the positive words of God.

Yes, I had heard God's voice before, but never more than a few words. Now God spoke whole sentences to me, many pages full. I finally received the letter from heaven I had wanted for so long.

I noticed that there was a significant difference in what I heard from God and what other people received from Him. God continued to speak to me of how grateful He was for the work I had been doing for Him, while other people in the class received wonderful love letters or even poems. It worried me and I showed my journal to the teacher.

"Why is there such a difference in my journal compared to the love songs other people receive?" I asked.

"Your emotions must be very deeply hidden," he concluded, "so deep that you cannot receive any emotional, loving words from your Father but only work-related encouragements."

I asked God to begin healing my emotions, because I was desperate for encounters with His love. I wanted to be able to experience Him as I had seen other people experience Him.

I asked Him, "Why did I have to go through so many struggles Lord?"

"I was shaping you for the future, for a life full of joy. I wanted you to know me for who I really am. I have seen your tears and I had kept them as a symbol of your love for me. Each one I have kept even the once that were not shed. I counted them like I counted all your hairs, not one of them is wasted. I am bringing you complete healing and I am doing a perfect work."

God assured me that He had been with me and that He had a purpose for all the things I had gone through. I listened and wrote as the truth of His words to my heart began to set me free. It made my relationship with Him alive; I could ask and He would share; I could ask for more and He would share more. It was an exciting journey that I had started.

I received a wonderful prophecy that started with the words, "The night is over." In my heart I rejoiced; that was what I needed to hear. It continued, "God will take away everything from you." At that point I broke down and did not hear the rest of the prophecy; I was too upset with God. What else could He take away from me? I felt there was nothing left for Him to take. I began to cry again and missed the rest of the words spoken over my life.

It wasn't until much later on, that I listened to the tape and realised that God, at that moment, had laid out His future plan for my life in a very precise and accurate way, but I was still too wounded to receive it.

It was clearly not the time for the prophecy to be fulfilled. God's priority was on healing my heart so that I could be united with Him. He faithfully showed me where He had been in my times of loneliness and struggles.

"I am proud of you because you continued to seek me. I will be found by you. We will spend lots of times together because I want you to know my thoughts. I have seen your loneliness and I will be found by you.

My plan for you is special and I will show it to you, step by step. I have given you a specially designed training school but from now on you will hear my voice and know that I am with you. I long for a time to come where we will continue together, hand in hand.

Don't look back, I am going to do a new thing and it will bring you joy, things that will amaze you.

There is a season for everything and your season of joy has come. I, your Father, will personally take care of you. I will make sure that no hair on your head is damaged. I will protect you and I will fight for you.

Be still and know that I am God.

It is in the stillness of your heart that I can speak to you. I have seen all your works; my heart wanted to reach yours but your heart was so often too busy. The pain has built a wall and your stillness was partial. Now I want to give you a whole heart that can be still and commune with me. Your times with me will be full of joy because I am removing your preconceived ideas and filling you with my thoughts.

I want to heal your eyes so that you can see me face to face, so that you can enjoy my smile when I look at you. I want you to see how colourful I have made your life. I want you to see that I am always with you, even at the moments that you felt that I was not there. I will open your eyes so that you can see."

"Lord, what if I see the pain and the suffering?" I asked.

"The pain and the suffering will be seen through the cross. My hope and love will blend through the pain and will enable you to see the solution instead of the problem."

Although the promise was there, the reality was different. I received an e-mail that CRO had again received a letter from the local authorities saying that the project had another six months to wind up the activities and to close its operations. It was too much, even in the centre of God's love, the enemy still managed to discourage me.

People prayed for me, encouraged me and one of them gave a scripture that she felt God had put on her heart, *"I will plant Israel (CRO) in their own land, never again to be uprooted from the land I have given them."*[33]

God also encouraged me personally, *"I am in control and I was in control but you could not experience it because you felt that you needed to be in control."*

Convicted of the sin of control, I repented and gave CRO back to God and claimed the promise that a mind controlled by the Spirit of God will bring life and peace.

We went through a week of inner healing and I discovered that all the things I held so dear, my reasoning capacity, my analytical thinking, my intellectualism and my need to understand God were holding me back from seeing who God really is.

I asked God, "Why are these things linked with unbelief?"

It was so helpful to be able to tune in to His voice, *"My daughter, my world is the invisible world, and if you want to reason, analyse and understand me you are missing out on my world. I want you to come to a level where you cannot understand me because I am God*

---

33 *Amos 9:15*

and I am so much bigger than you are. I want to move you to a higher level, a level of trust in me and not of understanding with your brain. It is a level in which you are able to test the spirits and know who has to submit to my Name.

"*Your reasoning has been a hindrance to receiving from me. Lay down your own capacity of reason and move to a level of trusting me, knowing that I only have good things for you. I am preparing you for greater works and the enemy will have to submit to you because I am living in you. Therefore, my child, trust in me and do only those things that I tell you to do.*"

It made sense and I repented of the deep-rooted unbelief in my heart. In the night that followed, for the first time in my life, I had a dream in which God called me to pray for the peace of Jerusalem. I was amazed; I had never before had a dream right from God's heart. *'How faithful He is if I am ready to deal with the issues of my heart,'* I marvelled.

"What is the significance of this dream Lord?" I asked.

"*Jerusalem is my chosen city. It is special to my heart. Israel is my people and I am longing to bring peace to the nation. If you want revival, pray for the peace of Jerusalem. I have set my people as an example for many, so pray that my will be done.*"

It was early morning and I was still in bed when God asked me a question, "*Ingrid, do you want to remove all the walls around your heart so that my love can brake forth out of you?*"

I panicked and said, "Oh no, don't You know what I have been through? Don't You know that I have been like a football that everybody has kicked around all the corners? I am sorry God, but I can't!" There was no response from God as I contemplated the question.

The following day when I woke up God asked the same question, "*Ingrid, will you remove all the walls around your heart so that my love can brake forth out of you?*"

Again I said to God, "I am so sorry, but I cannot. I am too hurt; I cannot trust people anymore, I have no idea what will happen to me if I no longer protect my own heart."

God remained silent on the subject until the third morning when He asked the same question, *"Ingrid, will you remove all the walls around your heart so that my love can brake forth out of you?"*

I became desperate; I so wanted to be obedient but I could not. The pain was too much. Finally I managed to answer Him:

"God," I cried out, "I want to be obedient but I feel I cannot."

As soon as I said the words, 'I want to be obedient', God immediately spoke to my heart and said, *"From now on Ingrid, will you believe that my love is stronger than all evil?"*

I strongly protested, "Lord, don't you see the wars in Africa, the AIDS and the hunger?"

God simply replied, *"My love is stronger than all evil."*

Here was another paradigm-shift taking place. I had seen so much death, suffering and pain; could it be true that love is stronger than all the things I had been through personally and everything I had seen happening around me? Thoughts raced through my mind and the only response I could make was, "Please, make me a person that can receive as much of your love as my heart can contain so that I will always win. Expand my heart with your love, Father!"

To this day I am still praying that prayer because I found out that His love is unending and there is always more.

I received new insights about myself, my background and character as well as insights into how God desired to be my Father. I had become a strong fighter – a survivor – but He showed me His desire to fight and provide for me. I came to realise that I had opened the doors of my heart for satan to enter and 'kill, steal and destroy' whenever I locked pain and disappointment away in my heart instead of giving it to Jesus, who had already paid the price for it. By carrying it hidden in my heart I was actually living my life as if Jesus never died for me. It was a shocking revelation.

He showed me how I had forgiven people with my head but that I had not dared to go to my heart and forgive them from the place where the pain was hidden. I had struggled on my own, accused God for leaving me and judged Him for allowing so many struggles in my life. I began to see that I had directed my accusations to the wrong person; it was satan who was the source of my struggles and not God. God only has good plans for my life but my heart was incapable of receiving it. This truth hit my heart: it was not God who was at fault; it was the condition of my own heart that had given access to satan. With tears, I repented of my silent accusations and questions of God.

My thoughts had become clouded by the experiences and the circumstances I had gone through. They were more aligned with the thoughts of the enemy than with God's thoughts. My thinking-patterns and the negative expectations that they brought about came from satan and not from God; the enemy had gained access to my heart and in return gave me exactly what I had come to expect.

The negative things I had experienced and my confrontations with death had made me believe, subconsciously, more in the works of satan, whose role it is to kill, steal and destroy, than in the work of Christ who wanted to give me life in abundance. God showed me that my belief system was based on my experiences and not on the truth of His Word. I had believed so many lies about myself, other people and even about the character of God. Every time I discovered a lie, I repented of it and in the process the truth continued to set my heart free.

I received deep revelation that everything God had allowed, He'd allowed because He loved me and He wanted me to find His love. He wanted to be my Father and for me to simply be His child. He wanted to use these experiences for me to seek Him and know Him for who He really is. I had known about Him in my head but now I had received an encounter, which brought a deep revelation about His nature to my heart. God *is* love and He is the Perfect Father.

It was still difficult to comprehend that God's only motivation in doing things or allowing things to happen to His children, is love. I had to work through two days of anger towards God. It was much easier for me to blame satan for the pain and disappointments I had gone through than to realise that God actually allowed it to happen.

One day someone gave me a scripture, she felt it was especially for me, *"For I am going to do something in your days that you would not believe even if you were told."* I looked it up and found it in Habakkuk.[34] It was God's answer to Habakkuk's complaints; how much had I identified with Habakkuk over the years! Once again God showed me that He knew the deep hidden things in my heart, that He was concerned and that He had not forgotten about them.

God had answered me like He did Habakkuk. Tears came to my eyes when I realised that nothing is wasted in the Kingdom of God. That He was going to restore what the enemy had taken and that was a lot in my life. If Father God was going to give me back double, then this could only mean that my future was bright!

He showed me that He is not a distant God, but a Father who knows every thought that I think and hears every word that I speak and He counts every hair on my head. He showed me that He had been with me in every situation but that my heart was so full with pain that I could not experience His presence. I saw how I had worked with orphans for so many years but that my thinking and my behaviour had been just like theirs. I might have

---

34 *Habakkuk 1:5*

been a bit more civilised but I had also become a fighter trying to survive, begging for food, striving to be the best, comparing myself with others, being as independent as possible, feeling homeless, lonely and abandoned.

It shocked me to realise that I, who wanted to love orphans had worked all these years with the same state of heart as the children who had been orphaned. The hidden issues and motives of our hearts were very similar. My eyes opened when I realised that I had lived my whole Christian life as a spiritual orphan. It hurt me when I saw that Father God had been waiting for me with His arms open wide to run into His love in my time of struggle, but that instead I had hardened my heart, believing that I needed to solve my own problems. It no longer surprised me that I had run out of love; I had never known that a fresh outpouring of His love was available to me at any time. Now God was inviting me to the other side of the cross, the side of victory, right into His heart where I could freely receive His love and live in intimacy with Him.

I had been 'religiously' active but my heart had not been in it. All those years I had complained in my heart, "God, don't I deserve better?" I had been so obedient and tried so hard to please God, I had lived a life of striving, competition, struggle and this heart-attitude had reflected on the relationships I had with people. I had become a good professional but had no intimate, heart-to-heart relationships with the people around me. I was shocked to realise that my whole life had become a sin against love. It dawned on me that I could not earn God's love but that Father God had already given me every blessing in his loving Son, Jesus. It was a free gift for me to enjoy.

In doing good for God, I had missed the best: His loving presence in my life; that is what He wanted me to have. He was after a heart-to-heart relationship with me. *'How could I have missed that point for so many years?'* It suddenly made so much sense; my pastor in The Netherlands had got it right; the good had blocked the best.

All Father God was after was my heart – everything – the good and the bad. He wanted the good in my heart to make it better and the bad to make it the best. He wanted all of me without reservation. I was His daughter and nothing could separate me from my Father's love. How could I have been so blind for so many years? Jack Frost, one of the teachers on the course, in one of his lessons said, "Intimacy means 'into me you see'". All God wanted was to see into my heart and reveal what is there, so that I could take what is not of Him to the cross. Could Christianity really be that simple?

God not only touched my heart, He also touched my body. It was strange, I never expected myself to have physical manifestations of the Holy Spirit at work like I had seen with others. One time I was shaking on the ground and experiencing strong contractions as if I was giving birth. I felt so embarrassed and asked a ministry worker who was praying over me, "Have you ever seen this before? I really feel awkward."

"Just allow God to do what He wants to do," she answered. "No-one is watching; it is between you and God."

As I was on the floor 'giving birth', God spoke to my heart, *"I am leading you into a new birth with all the birthing pains. The pain you are feeling now will be turned to joy."*

So often I had watched people having a physical response to God's presence these last weeks and I did not know what to think about it. Now I was lying there giving birth to something I had no clue about, except that it was of God. I asked God about it:

"Do not worry about the manifestations they are a sign that I am at work in you. Just submit to my power and rest in my love and you will see that I am doing a perfect work."

I smiled and made a decision to allow God to do what He wanted to do not minding how it would look like and not minding about the other people around me.

Every session in the school showed me points where I had allowed the enemy of God to infiltrate my thinking, my words and my actions. It was so freeing to know that the power of the Cross is so much stronger than the power of the enemy. It was a completely new discovery for me.

As these issues had been identified and repented of, the time came for them to be dealt with during a deliverance session. Throughout this session I was shocked to see so many demons leaving my heart. Whenever the name of Jesus was used I felt that there was a real battle going on. I noticed a change in my heartbeat, I felt hot and cold at the same time and sometimes I literally coughed out these oppressive forces. I had never been in a session like this and I just laughed when I looked at myself. Who had ever thought that I would respond so strongly to the invisible world? Even though it was new and strange to me, there was no fear. On the contrary with every prayer I prayed, I felt freedom being restored to my heart. The core teaching that morning was, 'Bad things out and good things in'. It certainly felt that there was a divine exchange taking place, pain and fear were taken out of my heart, while healing and love were poured in.

It became very clear to me that demons not only live in the water. They were in my heart too. Satan had killed, stolen and destroyed a lot in my heart, but Jesus had come to claim back the territory the enemy had occupied and fill it with His love and presence. He'd begun to unfold His blessings in my heart; it was going to be an exciting and sometimes very painful, inward journey. But I knew that whatever darkness He found hidden in my heart would be expelled by His light and it would not influence His amazing love and acceptance of me.

God rewarded my seeking; He broke through the ceiling of my mind and reached into my heart to join it to His heart. He not only wanted to reveal His heart for me but also for the deeply broken world around me.

I was constantly surprised by the different ways that God demonstrated His presence amongst us. One night His presence was so real that a number of people had gold dust on their hands. I felt like a doubting Thomas when I asked, "Can I touch it?" I tried to remove some of the gold dust but could not.

But then, in another of the sessions people ran up to me and said, "There is gold dust all over your cheeks." It was His special way of showing me that I was worthy of carrying His glory and His presence as His beloved daughter. Later I asked Him, "What about the gold dust, Father?"

"I sent gold dust from heaven as a sign of my glory that you will behold; a sign that I want to share what I have; a sign that I am concerned about you and a sign that I love you."

How I had longed for those 'greater works' than Jesus had done, for the supernatural to come in the natural. How often I had tried to achieve them by working harder, praying more and fasting longer.

I now knew I was called for the 'greater works' but it was such a relief to discover that they could only be given by the One who prepared them. It was not something I could work myself up to. It would come by grace, and grace alone. It was easy to proclaim these truths in a safe setting like Toronto, but how would it work in the harshness of Africa? Could I allow my heart to be open to grace, even if someone might step on it again? If someone mistreated me again, would I be able to turn my other cheek? There were still many questions lingering in my mind but they did not worry me anymore.

"You have persevered in faith, now I want you to persevere in love with a joy overflowing. You will experience that where I am there

will be love, hope and joy."

I had come to the realisation that it's not about me; it's all about Him. The journey to become rooted in love was going to be His journey with me not my journey with Him. It was not about my effort, it was His gift. It was no longer I that lived but Christ who lives in me.[35] And where my life was still about 'me', again and again He had given me the opportunity to repent and hand it over to Him. I had given Him my heart, my body and my soul so that He could claim all the territory in my life that was not yet His.

All I asked Him was to do it fast. In His love He answered, *"Where I want to take you and where you are now is too big a step, it is a journey of intimacy that needs to be lived.*

"The higher level of intimacy will not be understood by everybody therefore spend much time with me so that you can learn to trust the ways I am taking you on."

I left Toronto full of God, full of His love and His promises. I knew that a bright future was ahead of me, one of restoration. I returned to Uganda knowing that I was no longer alone but that my perfect Father had made His home in my heart. From that point on I knew I was a child of the King of the Universe and no longer a football to be kicked around, a person with an identity as His daughter, with His authority and His abundance inside me.

With these words, Father sent me back into the big wide world, *"I am taking you on ways you have not gone before; you will enjoy every step because I your Father will hold your hand and help you with every new discovery. Remember, I have not given you the go-ahead to minister. The last instruction I gave you was to sleep and rest and let me do what I have to do in your heart. I am not asking you to do anything for me because you did what you could; now I want to do what I can for you. You persevered for me and I will do the same for you. I will come to you with my love that is overwhelming."*

---

35 *Galatians 2:20*

CHAPTER TWENTY-ONE

Living out of Love

My heart had changed, and therefore my eyes saw things differently. My compound looked so much more beautiful, the flowers were more colourful, the sky bluer, the river wider, the birds sang louder, I had a different outlook to life. What I also saw was that my house needed serious maintenance. It had been a place where I would come to sleep, but now it had to become a home where I could 'be'.

Life was good and I was a happy person. When people asked, "What do you want to eat?" I no longer said, "Anything," I could say, wholeheartedly, "Today I want pizza!" They looked like small things but they made a huge difference. People looked at me and asked, "What has happened to you? You look so much younger." I felt born again, again.

A month after my return from Toronto, I looked over the mighty River Nile from the veranda of my house and my heart was filled with worship. Truly God had been faithful and He has shown me the way out. The way out of my misery was the way into His heart of unconditional love for me. All He wanted of me is to seek His presence, receive what He wants me to do and do it. It sounded almost too simple.

As I sat, I read what God has spoken when I left Toronto, *"You have shown yourself faithful to me and allowed your will to be broken by my love. That is what I did this month. I broke your strong will, independence and self sufficiency and replaced it with my love. You are broken and filled. Remember you do not belong to yourself anymore but to me. You are mine; do not walk away from me but stay with me, so that I can instruct you in the way to go. I will whisper in your ear and you will know. Stay in my heart, stay in my love."*

It was so good to be back in Uganda. I was full of new life and energy; full of faith in the good plans that God had for me and for CRO. I re-read the prophecy I had received, typed it out. Still with some unbelief in my heart, I tried to hold on to the words I had received. I looked at my circumstances and, though they had not changed I knew I had. My perspective on life began to align itself with His heart, *"I am turning evil to good. I am the Winner. In the misery there is peace, in the poverty people can be rich and in weakness there is strength. My Kingdom is so different than the kingdom of the world. Learn to see with my eyes and you will only see hope. Learn to hear with my ears and you will only hear encouragement, for I am love and all that I am involved with is rooted in my love."*

The day I returned to the office, full of joy and new revelation, I found a note on my desk. *'Dr. Okello wants to see you,'* it read. I had met Dr. Okello once before when he had moved to Jinja three months before. I was impressed by his attitude and knowledge about street children. It was a pleasure to go and see him. My interest increased when he showed me an e-mail from an American charismatic foundation saying they had US$ 130,000 available to be used for a street children programme. *'Could we use this money?'* I was thrilled, *'Was God fulfilling some of His promises so fast? Was He already showing me that time for begging was over?'* I was very excited that God was immediately fulfilling some of the promises of abundance He had given to me.

We discussed, planned, wrote proposals, shared and prayed together. I was intrigued by the fact that he was missing three fingers on his left hand but did not have the courage to ask what had caused it. His wife and son were also in Jinja and we had fellowship and meals together. I rejoiced in my newfound Ugandan friends. On several occasions he stressed the fact that evangelism needed to be part of the proposal as he was an active member of a church in Jinja. We met almost daily for planning purposes.

I introduced him to the board members and took him to our project in Mbale. I wanted him to understand properly what we are doing and how we were doing it. He had a lot of contacts and knew about the problems CRO were facing with the local authorities. He pledged to help us out with these problems. I laughed when he suggested a trip to the USA to meet with the donors myself. One night he rang me with the flight details and the programme. The Foundation would pay for my ticket if I did not mind staying with Christians in their homes. I could not believe my ears.

"Please prepare for a fundraising dinner with Bill Gates so bring a gala dress. A plate will cost US$5,000." I laughed it off, thinking, "I will pack my bag when I have the ticket. This sounds too good to be true, but God is a God of impossibilities! You can never know!"

Once Dr. Okello had received copies of all the proposals I had written, he went to a lawyer to have the contract made between CRO and the charismatic foundation.

Being the 'bush girl' I was, in faith I looked around for a gala dress among my business friends in Jinja. Dr. Okello also suggested that he help us with an appointment to see the Minister of Local Government about the problems CRO was still facing with the authorities. He knew the Minister personally. We arranged a date and time to travel to Kampala to meet with him.

Two days before the meeting Dr. Okello rang and asked if I could see him in the office. I went to his office and he explained his problem: he supported a project in Congo and the pastor from

Congo had come and needed to travel back the following day, but the money for his project had not yet arrived in the bank. He asked if I could assist him by providing US$ 4,000. I told him that I could not use any project funds but I would see how much I had personally in the bank. That afternoon I scratched together all my money and brought US$ 1,000 as an advance for the Pastors in Congo. It was all the money I had in the bank. He took it but his comment irritated me terribly, "I am so sorry that you cannot give me US$ 4,000."

I thought to myself, *'I am so sorry that you cannot say thank you for U$1,000!'*

The following day he rang to check if I had informed all the board members who were to travel to meet the Minister the next day. All of us were ready by 9.00 in the morning to set off to Kampala. The only man missing was Dr. Okello. I called his mobile phone, but there was no reply, I rang the home number but there was also no reply. I finally decided to drive to his home and found that the gate was locked. There were two other people outside the gate looking for him and wondering where he had gone until it dawned on us that the bird had flown. Everything about him and the donors had been fake. I felt badly cheated! I trusted the man, cared for him and his family and now he had packed his bags and had left with my proposals and my money. I could not believe it. I rang the office of the Minister and the secretary was not aware of any meeting with us. The Minister was actually out of the country.

'Was that perhaps the reason that he had lost the three fingers on his hand? Had he tried to do the same in a Muslim country and they cut his hand?' I thought sarcastically and wished that I had asked him. I decided to journal about it and asked God how on earth it was possible that I was so badly cheated.

God said, *"I am not looking at what he did to you but what you did to him. It is important that you showed him my love. Don't stop loving people who cheat you, for my love will change them. My love will soften the hardest heart."*

God surely had interesting ways of teaching me. To this day, we've not seen or heard from Dr. Okello.

The date that CRO was to stop its operations in Jinja was approaching fast. The 1st January 2002 was the date given for the project to close down. We continued to trust God for a miracle but by Christmas time there was still no solution. I reminded God of the promises that He had given to me while in Toronto that He will not uproot CRO from the land He had given them.

We had invited a representative of the President to be our special guest during the Christmas party and the children sang, danced and gave speeches. One child suddenly said, "Sir, we are very sad because we have no idea how we will go to school come January; how we will eat and how we will live when CRO is no longer there."

The man leaned over to me and said, "What is this child talking about, are you stopping your project in Jinja?" I explained the order we had received from the Jinja Municipal Council to close down the project. "Please give me all the correspondence with the Town Council and I will handle the matter," was his reply.

On Christmas day the man went to his office, wrote a letter to the Mayor of the town and ordered him not to disturb CRO any longer. I was amazed at God's goodness when I opened the national newspaper on the 27th December and read an article that CRO was allowed to continue its operations in Jinja. At the last minute God had rescued us again.

Daoudi, the bright street boy was doing very well and he was happy to see me back from Canada. He had returned to CRO and was attending primary school. He was about 16 years and the eldest in the school, but also the number one in his class. I felt really proud of him. How we had struggled with him and now it was so good to see the boy develop his potential. One day, he did not come for lunch to the project and we really missed him. The following day he was also missing. We inquired from the school and they confirmed that he had not been there for the last two days. We asked around. Had anybody seen Daoudi? No one knew where he was.

After a few days, information started seeping in that he had returned to Kampala. Somebody had seen him on the garbage heap just outside the post office. I felt so bad. Here was a boy with so much potential and again he was losing it. Everything in me shouted, *'Get in the car and bring him back!'* Suddenly I remembered the story that had impacted me so much in Toronto, the story of the prodigal son; the Father never followed the son. When I asked God, "Why, if You love Your son did You not stop him or follow him? Why did You give the son money which enabled him to waste his life, contract HIV/AIDS and make a fool of himself?"

God answered to my heart, *"Love is a free choice; love cannot be forced."* And I knew I had to wait until Daoudi would come to his senses and choose for himself to come back.

It was a long wait. When my friends travelled to Kampala, I asked them to tell Daoudi that I was waiting for him. When I was there myself and I saw him on the rubbish pit, I waved at him and drove on with pain in my heart.

I asked God, "Will you please make me this waiting mother, like You were the waiting Father so that I can love him when he comes back. I don't want to judge him but I want to love him." It took three months for him to come back. One afternoon I heard a familiar voice. My heart jumped. This was Daoudi but he did not sound very repentant. I did not mind, I was just excited to hear him.

"If you don't allow me to go to Ingrid then I throw this hot porridge in your face." It was Daoudi's angry voice, shouting at the Social Worker. I was working in my office when I overheard this conversation from a distance. I stood up and ran outside, grabbed his hand with the hot porridge still in it, looked him in the eye and said, "Who are you to shout at social workers?"

He looked me in the eye and that is when I realised that, as the only person who had ever loved him in his life, I had now rejected him. His eyes were full of anger and he lost his temper. He kicked, shouted, spit and fought. It was terrible to see how his anger was destroying him and the people around him. All that we could do was to take him to a counselling room, to cool down. Together with a Social Worker they spent an hour trying to calm him down.

I went to my office, left the door open and sat behind my desk, with my head in my hands, feeling bad. Here I was, wanting to be this loving, waiting mother and now I had spoiled it. I had seen the hatred and the rejection in his eyes and knew that I had failed in loving the unlovable.

I asked God to forgive me and teach me to become a person who is free to love unconditionally. As I was still having my heart to heart conversation with God, a pair of black eyes peeped into my office. If looks could kill, I would no longer be alive; it was Daoudi and he was still very angry. Slowly he walked into my office and approached my desk. I saw that he was carrying a big metal bar in his right hand and when his left hand became visible I saw a huge knife. He moved towards my desk with his hands full of weapons and his eyes full of murder.

Quietly I stood up, walked slowly towards him and said, "Daoudi, welcome back, I have waited for you to come back. I have waited for this day to see you here again and I am so happy that you have decided to come back!"

As he heard my words he stopped, his mouth dropped open; the knife fell out of his left hand and the iron bar dropped out of his right hand, then he turned around and ran away. God proved

Himself faithful again and showed me very clearly that love is stronger than evil.

Two days later he came to apologise and asked for another chance. Soon after, he went back to school. Although there were still a number of ups and downs in his life, he is now settled with his brother and works in his carpentry workshop in Kampala.

I was coming to realise more and more that God wanted me to live out of love, not out of duty or law. He valued relationships more than me being right and He gave me many opportunities to practice the principals of love.

One quiet Sunday morning I was on my way to church. It had rained in the night and the road was narrow and slippery. The only other person on the road was a man on his bicycle carrying a big bag of maize. We passed each other very carefully, making sure that we would not knock each other. Unfortunately the mirror of my car touched the man's arm. I watched in my mirror to see if he was doing fine and what I saw shocked me, he threw his bicycle on the ground and started shouting that I had knocked him down. Everything in me said, *'He is a liar, he just touched my mirror and I saw him throwing his bicycle.'* Still thinking about the principal of relationship over righteousness I made a deliberate choice to go for relationship, especially because the incident took place in my own village. I stopped the car and walked over to the man; his shouting attracted the whole village.

Many people gathered and it was very clear that the man wanted a big sum of money from me. Everybody started talking over each other and it became a loud fight of words in a language that I did not understand. I was the centre of attention but could not understand one word of what was said.

The leaders of the village were called and I was accused of causing an accident. I was summoned to go and meet with them. Kindly, I asked them if I could go to church first and meet with them afterwards. I did not only want to go to church but I also did not want a meeting with the whole village interfering and voicing their opinions.

We agreed to meet in the afternoon at the home of the Secretary for Defence in our village. At 2 o'clock the man was already there and he had brought his bicycle as evidence. There was no damage on the bicycle except for the stand that was bent because he had thrown his bicycle down. After a long meeting it was finally decided that I would straighten the stand of the bicycle and buy the rider a bottle of soda to overcome the stress. I walked away from the meeting seeing that relationships are more important than being right but they also come at a cost. The meeting had taken my whole Sunday afternoon.

Time and again I learned that walking in love is a process and not a one-time event. Six months after I came back from Toronto, I recognised God's presence in my room one morning when I woke up early. God spoke to my heart, *"I want you to bless the people who have blessed you."* I knew this was God and I knew He meant the church in Toronto. I had received such healing, freedom and blessings from them. His voice continued and he gave me the specific amount I had to give. This amount exceeded far beyond anything I had ever given to anyone and far beyond the teaching of tithing that I had heard so often. I had to dig deep into the savings for my future. I laughed and was shocked at the same time. *'Had God not said to me that I did not need to give because I had come to receive? Why should I give it to a rich western church, and not to a poor suffering church or project in Africa?'* It didn't make sense!

God repeated the words, *"I want you to bless the people who blessed you!"* I knew myself well enough to obey immediately because all the excuses not to give this money, were already lining up in my mind. I arranged the transfer as fast as I could; it was the next step in trusting Father God to be my sole provider, and He showed me that love does not always make sense.

CHAPTER TWENTY-TWO

Winette

Jinja is the second biggest town in Uganda but it is still small enough for locals to know one another. The town borders Lake Victoria and often you can feel a nice breeze on the lakeshore. There are a few little restaurants in Jinja where they serve good food.

One afternoon in February 2002, I was having a drink and a little chat with the owner of one of the eating-places in town. She was an elderly lady with a Dutch heritage. We had come to Jinja at about the same time and so now and then we would catch up with one another. I shared with her my life changing experience of encountering the Father's love.

At the table next to me I heard people saying to each other quietly, "Yes, she resembles the woman in the picture." They spoke English with a slight Dutch accent. I was wondering if they were talking about me, because I was writing columns in a Dutch women's magazine and every month they printed the same picture with the columns.

"Are you Ingrid?" I had not seen the lady walk up to me.

She introduced herself as Winette and shared that she has been in Jinja for a year working with a church. We had not met each other before but discovered that indeed we were both from The Netherlands. She shared that she did not have much to do since the church she was with was more interested in money, which she did not have, than in what she as a person had to offer. She sounded frustrated and was openly wondering what her purpose of being in Jinja was. We made an appointment to meet and soon began sharing our hearts with one another. She had been trained as a nurse and specialised in heart diseases. The last four years she had worked in youth hostels in Amsterdam, sharing the gospel with tourists visiting the Dutch Capital. She had lived in Israel and had a real passion for that country.

"How did you end up in Uganda?" I asked her.

"I was in Uganda two years ago but did not like it," she told me. "There are already so many Christians in this country so why should I go to a place where there are enough people who can share the gospel with their own people. They really do not need me. I also felt that the spirit of religion is so strong in Uganda; it reminded me of the legalistic church I came from and did not want to have anything to do with it any more. When I applied to go to Africa, I told Africa Inland Mission, I am willing to go anywhere but not to Uganda.

"The AIM leadership felt strongly that Uganda was the right place for me and in obedience I have come but there is nothing for me to do. I am walking through Jinja not knowing what to do; I feel bored and have asked God to give me something to do with the poorest of the poor."

'Great,' I thought. 'Our women's programme in the slum can do with some strengthening'.

The following week Winette began a discipleship class with the street boys and she assisted the social workers in sharing the gospel with the less fortunate women in the slums. It was not a full-time job, so she had time for other things as well. It was clear that she was searching for more of God. I gave her all the books, notes and tapes that I brought from Toronto and she read and listened to them all.

God had already revealed areas in her heart that He wanted to work on. After reading the books I had given her and listening to the tapes of the leaders' school teaching, her desire to get to know God as a Father grew. I saw God breaking her in front of my eyes. As she listened to the Father-heart teachings on the tapes, her own childhood pain started to surface. It was difficult to see her going through her deep personal struggles. There was pain and frustration pushed away safely in her heart, but God started to draw hurts from the deepest parts of her heart and I witnessed her go through much of what I had experienced myself – one loss after the other. There was no longer a job, no ministry, little money, lack of friends and, by the time her wedding plans were cancelled, her heart was completely broken. It was a very painful process to watch.

At a time where she felt she had nothing more to give and to live for, the same leader's school from Toronto came to Kenya. I was on the ministry team and encouraged Winette to apply to attend the school.

"School of ministry?" she said sarcastically. "I need ministry myself!"

"Then ask if you can attend, even if you are not an African leader."

With the last bit of energy that she had within her she wrote an email and applied for the school. Although she was not an African leader she was warmly welcomed. From day one God touched her pain with His love. I watched her and almost saw a repetition of what had happened to me – pain, tears, questions – she was broken by His love and immediately Father God started to put the pieces back together but now His way. In the first week God gave her a picture when she asked Him to reveal Himself as a Father to her.

She saw a baby on a cushion and saw that it was in her baby room. She recognised it from the pictures in her family's photo album. The baby had black hair and since she is the only baby in the family with black hair, she knew it was herself on the cushion in her baby room. A man in white robes walked in and picked her up. He turned her around and when she saw his eyes she knew these were the eyes of Jesus. Jesus spoke to her, *"Today is your day to be born, and I am so happy for you. I have planned this day for you and your life is going to be beautiful because I am your Father."* This touched her deepest pain, which had been the need of a loving Father in her life.

She broke down and cried for days. Even though there was so much pain coming out of her heart, my heart rejoiced because I knew her freedom was on the way! She came back from Kenya a transformed person. She now knew with her head and her heart that she was a beloved child of God and that He is her Perfect Father. All other things were no longer important for her. The truth had really set her free. When she came back from Kenya she still had no work, no husband and no idea what her future would hold, but what she did know was that she had a Father who has everything under His control.

CHAPTER TWENTY-THREE

New Commissioning

Towards the end of 2002 my sending agency had informed me that my contract would not be extended beyond one year. It was time to prepare the organisation and myself for my departure. I was happy that CRO's existence in the town was now secured, but still it was a very ambivalent feeling to let go of the organisation I had started and worked for over the past 12 years. God had spoken, and asked me to let go of CRO and I had consented, but I did not realise that it would come so soon. It was as if I had to let go of my baby. I was struggling with it because in my heart I had seen myself like the Mother Theresa of Uganda; all that I was and all that I had was connected to what I did. My work had become my identity.

"Your identity has been in what you did but I want you to know that your identity is in who you are. You are my child". God encouraged me with these words for many days, every time I struggled with handing over CRO.

We had just finalised a survey in Masaka, a town in Western Uganda and were planning to begin a new CRO branch there. *'Could I not be involved with one more project?'* I bargained with God but the decision was final. My contract was due to come to an end in July 2003 and I needed to work on letting go of the organisation. Once again, God was asking me to let go of the things I loved to do so much. I had poured everything I had into the development of CRO. People, who knew me, saw CRO in me. It was so hard to leave my friends in the projects behind, the children and the women.

We had many meetings and discussions with the board and they also agreed that they were able to take on the organisation without further input from me. I wondered, *'What is the next thing You have for me Father?'*

I began distancing myself from the operations in order to phase out gradually and to allow myself to feel the pain of letting go. It was difficult but surprisingly it was not as much of a struggle as I had anticipated. I knew I was a child of God and that His plan for my life was ready. I only needed to do the good works that He had in mind for me. That was new to me. I had always asked God to bless the works of *my* hands and had not realised that I only needed to receive the works He already prepared for me in advance to do.

My heart became expectant for the new things God had for me. I desired to see what He would do if I let go of the people I cared for and the things that had filled my life. Very lovingly, my Heavenly Father removed me from the operations and future planning of CRO. I felt very ambivalent; on the one hand I wanted to continue what I was doing. I had a deep desire to lead everyone involved in CRO into the freeing revelation of the Father's love. I still liked to participate in expanding CRO in Uganda but on the other hand I was also very curious about Father God's plans for my own future.

'If God is telling me to let go of CRO what could He have in mind?' I had no clue and all I could do was trust my future in His hands, knowing that it was going to be good because He is my perfect Father.

People came to my office, telling me it was too early for me to leave. Others cried, because I was leaving and that made me cry too, but I had to be obedient and I knew my Heavenly Father well enough now, that He would honour that. Looking back, I was thankful that I had made a difference in the lives of hundreds of street children and I prayed that one day the revelation of God's Father-heart would also change the hearts of the street children I had been working with. I left trusting that the seeds I had sown in the hearts of the children would germinate and bear lots of fruit.

I said my goodbyes and looked forward to the new things ahead of me. I had a sense that God wanted to use my land for the next chapter of my life and I asked Him about this. He comforted me and confirmed His plans with these words, *"The land I have given you is in the first place a place where you will find rest and peace, for my eyes are on this place. My Spirit is there and He will bring many people to a deeper understanding of who I am. He will bring healing to the broken hearted. It is a place where my Spirit dwells and where my Spirit is, there is always change for the better."*

With no job and no idea what God wanted me to do I was open to anything that came my way. One of these things was an invitation to do a seminar about traumatised children in Eastern Congo. Missionaries from Africa Inland Mission had heard about the change God had brought to my heart and my desire to see more people healed from within, not just experience an improvement in their outward circumstances. They were working in Congo, a country that had experienced a long civil war. Almost everyone in the country is traumatised so I sought to share Father's love as a solution to trauma.

I was soaring in the sky. A small bush plane had picked me up in Entebbe and we flew over the African landscape. My heart raced and I fully enjoyed the trip. This was my continent; Africa:

a continent of hope created and loved by God. I knew that God's heart was to restore it with His love; to give back double of what the enemy, or literally the locusts, had taken in this land.[36] A joy and excitement welled up in my heart; I was going to be part of bringing God's heart of love and restoration to a small village in the bush of Congo.

25 people were waiting for me in a small primary school. One man had ridden his bicycle for five days in order to attend. He had slept in the open or found shelter in the homes of people he did not know. I felt so humbled. This man had travelled such a long distance to hear the good news of Father's love. I almost begged Father God, "Please, will You show up with Your love and not disappoint this man. He has travelled five days to be here and he needs to cycle five days to get back home."

Father did not disappoint – He showed up with His loving presence. At the end of the seminar one pastor stood up and spoke in French. I asked the translator, "What is he saying?"

"He thanks God for the war in Congo."

"Why?" I asked him – the man had lost everything he had in the war, his wife, children family and church.

The pastor went on to explain, "If the war in Congo had not taken place I would not have been displaced and would not have received the love of God in my heart and I would not have met Him as my perfect Father." He stood there, crying like a little child, and I stood there, crying like a little child. God brought back to my memory what he had spoken in Toronto, *"My love is stronger than all evil."*

At that moment I knew that this is what I would love to do the rest of my life – bringing healing to broken hearts and leading people to the heart of God, the perfect Father, seeing God's Kingdom come down to earth and creation restored. It felt like I

---

36 *Joel 2:25*

was receiving my new commissioning.

God's timing is often very different than ours and that was one of the next lesson I had to learn. However much I expected God to make it clear to me what His detailed plan for my future was, it did not happen as fast as I would have liked.

It took one and a half years before God opened the door to a new venture.

It was a big test on my patience.

Often I would ask, "What do you have for the future?" and His answer would be, *"My presence can only be experienced in the now, I want a relationship with you, my name is I Am and not I Will Be."*

I was a good planner and organiser and knew all the details for tomorrow and next week in my head. I was a fast thinker and I knew how I wanted things done and when they had to be done. My mind could race from Uganda to Holland, to east and west in one minute. Sometimes it made me tired but overall I had a pretty good control over my life.

This was the season where God began to teach me that a mind controlled by the Spirit of God brings life and peace. I had to let go so that He could lead me, not in the future but in the 'now'. I was so used to working that it was strange for me to wake up and not know what to do. I wanted to be active and achieve something and when I asked God about it all He would say was, *"I have seen your works, but I am not interested in your works, I am interested in your heart."*

God also revealed to me that I had been very good at giving to Him but very bad in receiving from Him. He wanted me to know that He is the Giver, He is the Initiator. He wanted me to live out of the revelation that I am loved for who I am and not for what I do and that, like Jesus, I only needed to do the things He would show me to do. I'd understood this truth long ago with my head but now it was time to receive that revelation in my heart.

CHAPTER TWENTY-FOUR

The Process

Since there was nothing that I was committed to do, I was able to spend a lot of time in God's presence. The experience in Toronto had given me such an encounter with God's love that I knew it was His plan for me to find His heart and that He would lead me on. I realised that all I had to do was open my heart to His presence and He would change me, soften me and heal me. Tears would flow in His presence as memories came back to me of times when I had hurt people and others had hurt me.

I forgave and was forgiven. God began to expand the tent pegs of my heart and I started to understand one of the meanings of this scripture from Isaiah 54, which I had received so many times in the past years – God was increasing my capacity to receive His love and expand my heart so that I could love others like He loves me.

"Ingrid, do you remember all the 'whys' you asked me?" God's tender voice spoke to my heart.

"Yes, for sure there were many, Father."

"My daughter, every time you asked why, you were holding me accountable, but I am not accountable to you, you are accountable to me."

Suddenly the veil fell from my eyes, *'Who was I that I expected the Creator of the Universe to report to me?'* I felt ashamed at the arrogance of heart that I had had towards my Father. I had tried so hard to understand Him with my brain, as if my brain was big enough to contain the wisdom of the King. Suddenly, I grasped how much I had diminished God by wanting to fit Him in my box, wanting to understand Him with my simple mind. I recognised the need for Him to make His home in my heart, the place of revelation, and not in my head, the place of knowledge. Deep from within, I asked God to forgive me for all the 'whys' I ever asked.

At times what God revealed was very painful but His tender touch softened my heart. It was a long and sometimes tiring process. He kept encouraging me amidst my tears, *"I will use your past to shape your future, so trust in me. I will work things out in my special way. I want to use all your experiences in a unique way because you walked a unique path. Trust your future to me and learn to walk day by day in my presence and I will give you rest."*

One day I asked God, "Can you not heal the rest supernaturally. I am tired of the process."

His response was, *"My daughter, supernatural interventions don't build relationships, all I want is a relationship with you."*

All I could do in response was surrender to His process and allow Him deeper and deeper into my heart. Lots more tears followed. The more the light of God's love shone in my heart, the more darkness was exposed. The change could be seen in my eyes; the dark brown colour was lightening up with every touch of His love.

A memory came back to me of an instance where I had not treated a former employer very well. My attitude had been one of standing on the law and righteousness, not love. God challenged me to write him a letter of apology about this situation that had happened almost 15 years ago. In the letter, I shared with him how God had shown me that I had not represented His love to him but that I had judged him.

Two weeks later, I received a handwritten letter back; I recognised his handwriting. Full of anticipation I opened the letter but I was so disappointed by its contents. He wrote that my letter had opened the darkest period in his life again and that he wished I had never written the letter. He was still angry and upset and concluded the letter saying perhaps he should go to the same school that I had been to. I was troubled by his reaction to my honest attempt to put things right with him. The pain in his reply disturbed me so I asked my Father, "I wrote this letter in obedience but it has not brought reconciliation. What do I do with it?"

"You cannot be responsible for somebody else's heart. You can only be responsible for your own heart," He responded.

With my heart at peace, I emailed the address of the school to him.

Almost a year had passed since I'd left CRO. In my quiet times with Father God, I received an ever-deeper revelation that I am a child of God; that He loves me, His daughter, with an unconditional love. I had struggled to live my life independently and had prided myself on the fact that I could handle my problems on my own; I did not need anyone to help me. I discovered how much I had hurt Father God with my self-sufficient attitude when His open arms had always been there to love me, protect me and provide for me. Instead of allowing Him to meet my needs, I had kept Him out of my heart. I had actually lived my life as an orphan, as if I did not have a Father. I also discovered the freedom that comes from living under the authority of someone who loved me unconditionally and wanted the best for me; this concept of 'sonship', a theme repeated in the Bible, was finally becoming real for me. My experiences with spiritual authority had not been very positive. I was reading Jack Frost's book about spiritual sonship and was struck by this quote:

"The heart of Sonship is a heart that has learned to honour all people. Whenever we do not have a heart attitude of honour to those in authority, we are dishonouring God."[37]

It was if an arrow hit my heart when God spoke, *"Ingrid, you have not honoured this pastor in Mbale."* I knew immediately that God was referring to the pastor in Mbale who had believed all these lies about me and had expelled me from his church.

'Had I not honoured him?' My first reaction was to argue with God. *'Wasn't it him who had made life so difficult for me? He had sent me out of his church and accused me falsely, spreading stories about me.'* Everything in me said that he should be the one to apologise to me.

'At least I had brought him food and I had visited his house. What else could I have done?' But deep inside I knew what God meant. The matter had to be settled at heart level, not only at head level. I had done all these things out of sheer obedience but they had not come from my heart; they had not been rooted in love. I had to admit, there had been some rebellion hidden underneath my 'good deeds'.

"You need to go to him and tell him that you have not honoured him as your spiritual authority."

I swallowed and hesitated, *'Had I really heard this right? Did I have to go and apologise to the man who created so many problems for me?'* I felt very ambivalent about it but in sheer obedience, I looked for his phone number because I knew I could easily postpone this. He had moved to Kampala. I searched for his office number and, when I called, they told me that he was out of the country and gave me the date when he would be back. I waited for a week so that he could settle back before I met him. I reckoned that if I saw him after his church service it could be done in five minutes. I did not have to make it a long speech.

I travelled to Kampala and went to his church, but the service

---

37 *From Spiritual Slavery to Spiritual Sonship, Jack Frost, Page 159*

had already ended and there were only a few people were left in the building by the time I arrived. *'The services are no longer taking five hours,'* I thought to myself! The only other thing I could do was to call him. I dialled his number and he was surprised to hear my voice. I asked to meet with him but he hesitated, "Tomorrow is my first day in the office, after my trip to the USA. I am very busy; I may not have time to see you."

I insisted, "It does not need to take long, I just need five minutes of your time. Could you please spare me five minutes?" He finally agreed that we would meet at 10.00am the following morning.

We arrived at the same time at the church and when I got out of my car, I was thankful for the long Ugandan greetings, 'How are you? How is the family? How is the church? How is the sickness? How was the journey?' Usually I did not have time for long greetings but in this case I did not mind, because I was not sure how I would explain the reason for my visit. We walked to his office and, in my heart I prayed a short prayer for help. As soon as we both sat down I started to say, "The reason why I have come to see you…" and immediately I saw a dark cloud cover his face; I needed extra courage to continue. "I want to share my spiritual journey of healing with you and how God has revealed to me that *He* is my perfect Father and if I want Him to be my Father I need to learn to honour authority.

"I have come to apologise. I am sorry that I did not honour you as my spiritual leader."

His face relaxed. He stood up and with a big smile on his face he walked towards me. He threw his arms around me and said, "Ingrid this all happened in my first church, I wanted a perfect church and you just did not fit in my picture of a perfect church member. Will you please also forgive me?"

We embraced, laughed and thanked God together for the gift of forgiveness.

With a heart of thankfulness I drove back home. Happy that reconciliation had taken place; very happy that another unresolved issue in my life had been dealt with at heart-level.

God continued to work on my heart and exposed lies that had kept me in bondage. During my quiet times with Him he brought back many memories but this was a very specific one:

I was about ten years when I had a confrontation with my art teacher. I did not like art and struggled with it. One day she came over to my desk, bent over me and shouted, "You, you don't know how to cut, you don't know how to paste, you don't know how to draw, you don't know how to hold a pencil, you don't know how to hold a needle." She went on and on. Her words penetrated my heart and I believed everything she said about me. When I did my exams in secondary school, the art teacher came to my parents and asked, "What has happened to this girl?"

"Why are you asking?" My parents replied.

"She is functioning at the level of a six year old child."

The moment the teacher had spoken the words I had believed them and something had died in my heart. I now knew the steps to get free. I asked God to forgive the teacher for speaking those words over my life, I asked God to forgive me for believing those lies and living my life based on them and in Jesus' Name I broke the power of her words over my life.

The next time Christine came from Kampala, she entered my house while I was sewing a button on my blouse. "What on earth are you doing?" she asked. "I have never seen you with a needle."

I looked at her, smiled and said, "I guess God is healing me up."

I listened to Father God every day and heard Him speak affirmation to me. He promised to lead me on in love and peace, step-by-step one day at a time. I realised how much easier it was to wait this time, in comparison with five years ago. There was no loneliness now but a peace and a rest in the full assurance that my future was safe in His hands, that I had a Father who cared and knew the desires in my heart.

There was a foundation in my heart that could no longer be shaken as it had been before. His love that was poured in did not leak out, like it used to do. I knew I was in the centre of His will. There was such a change in me; the world had become a different place after my one month of forgiving, repenting and crying in the loving presence of my Father. He assured me that He was building His house in me and that He was placing His heart in me. I had never felt so secure in His love, in spite of my circumstances being so unsure.

CHAPTER TWENTY-FIVE

New Beginnings

From the moment I bought the land on the Nile I knew that I did not have that place for myself, I always knew that God was going to use it for something specific. The location is so unique, very close to the source of the mighty River Nile. I was still in the season of waiting and had no idea what my future would hold. Since I believed that God was going to do something on my land, I decided to build so that at least I could have people to stay there. I had no commitments outside my compound so I felt I could begin a small building project. I had found a local builder who was a great support to me and he took charge of the whole building process.

During the month when I had seen Winette receive healing from the pain in her heart and experience the truth of God as her perfect Father, I suddenly began to see that this is what Uganda needed. There were so many broken families, so many orphans and abusive fathers. Suddenly my eyes were opened to the deepest need and wound this country has– the need for a Father. I asked Winette if she would pray and think about starting a retreat centre with me to share Father's love with Ugandans and to bring healing to the hearts of the wounded orphans. Her first reaction was, "Oh no, I am just beginning to receive healing myself," but the thought did not let her go. She still did not have a full-time job and had no clarity about what her future would bring either.

So I asked her if she wanted to stay in my house during my leave in The Netherlands and, in the meantime, supervise the building activities on the land. She loved staying in my house but had not supervised any building projects before. However, she was willing to do it and I was happy that she would be there to keep an eye on the work taking place at the compound.

Because I did not have any obligations in Uganda I was able to spend the last three months of the 2003 in The Netherlands. I had a growing desire to share my newfound understanding of God's Father-heart with my family and friends back home. I wanted to be sure that there were no unresolved heart-issues in my family and with friends following my discovery that I had lived my life as a spiritual orphan.

During my leave Irene called Winette. Irene was working with World Vision and had asked if I wanted to do a few days programme with peace and reconciliation workers from Rwanda; they were helping people to reach a place of forgiveness following the horrible genocide that had taken place in Rwanda nine years before, but they were now feeling burnt-out themselves. They were coming to a hotel in Jinja for a rest and Irene wanted some spiritual input for them. Winette told her, "Sorry, but Ingrid is in The Netherlands, so she cannot do it."

Irene replied, "But have you not done the same school? Can you not do it?"

Winette gave her a good religious answer, "I'll pray about it," but she never did!

Some days later Irene rang again, "Have you prayed about it?" she asked.

"Uh, no," Winette said, fully convinced that she was not going to do it.

"You better pray because they are on the way," was Irene's answer.

"Give me a few minutes," Winette said, "and this time I will pray!"

In that moment, Winette turned her heart to Father God and He said, *"Just give away what you have received from me and come back for more."* She called Irene and said, "It's okay, I am doing it."

God moved the hearts of these burnt-out Rwandans deeply with His love. The group left refreshed, knowing that God is their perfect Father and that His love is stronger than the horrible genocide they had been through. That was also the moment Winette received her calling to step out and give away Father's love… So when I came back from The Netherlands she shared that she felt it was right to begin a retreat centre together. I was excited that God's purpose for me and for the land He had given me had become clear.

We wanted to create a safe place; a place where God's healing presence would be welcome and where people could receive forgiveness, healing and freedom – to help Ugandans to see that Jesus is the way to the Father. There were still a few hiccups, though. Winette worked in Uganda through Africa Inland Mission. As a mission agency, AIM was not working with new initiatives. Since this was a brand new initiative, we were not sure if they could allow her to work with me. When she shared it with her leaders, they affirmed her step by saying, "If God opens a door, we are not going to close it," and they gave her permission to work together with me for 50% of her time while the other 50% she was to work with an organisation in Kampala.

Three months after I had handed over CRO, I began building the African style huts (commonly called 'bandas'), even though I had no idea what they would be used for. The first two round huts were already complete before it finally became clear that I actually was building a retreat centre; I had built them in faith! Winette moved into one of them and we began working together.

Evening after evening we would brainstorm about names for the centre and board members that were needed. We spent time in the presence of God together and He would give us ideas on how to design the centre. We had a lot of faith that God would make His will and His ideas very clear to us; this venture was all about Him and we wanted to recognise Him in the small details of our lives and the work we were beginning.

We brainstormed about a name that would reflect what we are doing and one that would also be understandable for most Africans. We decided on Mto Moyoni, which, in Swahili, means 'river in the heart'. How applicable that name was; our centre is located right by the River Nile, just one kilometre from the source, surrounded by the constant sound of flowing water which soothes the soul. It was a place for the heart, not for the head.

One morning Winette woke up, feeling very low, wishing she could skip the day. All of a sudden she realised that there was something unusual happening but it was hard to tell what it was. She walked outside and heard a lot of excited voices. Looking down she saw that the river had dried up. The mighty River Nile was reduced to just a small stream. Something had blocked the dam and had stopped the water from flowing freely.

People from the villages enjoyed the dry riverbeds; they picked plenty of fish, dried them on their roofs and ate from it for days. I quickly organised a few people to carry rocks out of the river for the foundation of the new banda we were building at that time. Everybody tried to benefit from a dry river.

Winette went back inside her house and said to God, "Why do I feel so rotten? Why would I want to skip this day? I know You want to do something new every day, so if I don't want to live this day, I will miss out what You want to do."

"*Go outside again,*" came the reply. In obedience she went outside not knowing what to expect.

"*Look at the river,*" God continued. "*I have created this river to carry lots and lots of water, but today you only see a little stream in the back. So it is with your heart. I have created you to carry lots and lots of living water but you are content with only a little stream. I am not content with it. I want to show you what is blocking the river of life from flowing from your heart.*" That is exactly what we wanted the centre to be about – creating an environment where people would be so safe that they could willingly open their hearts to God and He, in turn, would show them what was hindering the river of living water from flowing within them. The river in my heart had been blocked for many years and what a joy it was that it now began to overflow.

We needed board members and did not know whom we should ask. What we wanted to do was so new and so different from what other ministries were doing. Isobel suggested that we met with the new Anglican Archbishop, Dr. Henry Orombi, to share our vision and get his ideas. It was amazing that we were able to get a meeting with him within a week and it was one of the most divine and encouraging meetings we'd had.

We entered his office and he shared some of the problems he faced in the church in general. It was so easy for me to chip in and share some of my problems but more importantly, also the solution that God had given us – the revelation of His unconditional love. I knew deep within that His love was the answer to all problems in this country, whether economical, spiritual or emotional, even for problems in marriages and families. Father's love had been the huge missing piece of the puzzle in all the years that I had done development work in Uganda.

Winette and I shared our testimonies and all he said was, "What can I do for you?"

We asked him if he would be willing to be our spiritual cover in Uganda and if he wanted to be part of our advisory committee.

He willingly accepted and before we left he asked us to bless him in his new office as spiritual leader of the nation. We left his office so encouraged, knowing that God was on our side.

We needed to get our paperwork in order – the organisation needed to be registered as an NGO and my work permit needed renewal. I dreaded the thought of going back to the Immigration Office again. I made my mind up and applied for a resident permit again. I was entitled to it since I had worked in Uganda for more than fifteen years. Three years ago I had tried but at that time I only got a work permit for a specified period. I was hugely disappointed when I went to the Immigration Office this time and found out that my application had been denied for a second time.

One of my Ugandan friends was very upset about it. She knew some people at the immigration department. One day she went in and asked them, "Why did you refuse my friend, Ingrid, a resident permit?"

The answer was brief, "Don't you know she is a satanist and we don't want satanists in this country. She will never get a resident permit"

I was disturbed by it and said to God, "I am now leaving this whole immigration process in your hands; if I am supposed to be in this country, then it is Your business. I am not going to struggle with it any more. I am not going to fight for it anymore. You are my Father and I trust that you will do it."

In full assurance I gave the whole work permit business back to my perfect Father. Not long after that He acted in a very surprising way; we were visiting the Chairman of the Evangelical Fellowship in Uganda to share the vision of Mto Moyoni. Out of the blue he asked me, "You have been so long in this country; do you have your resident permit?" Since he knew about the problems I had been through I told him honestly that the immigration department believed that I was a satanist and that they assured me that I was never going to get it.

"Give me your application," he said, "I am praying with the Minister of Internal Affairs every Friday morning and I will give your papers to her."

After two weeks I received a letter from the Minister herself telling me that I qualified for a resident permit and that I could pick it up from the immigration department. It was a clear sign that my time in Uganda was far from over.

Some of my friends in The Netherlands had noticed a great change in me after my time in Toronto. They commented that I looked so much younger, so much more at peace and at rest; it made them curious and that gave me a great opportunity to share with them my 'born again, again' experience. Now that we wanted to give away what we had received, they immediately offered to become our support group in The Netherlands. Four months after Mto Moyoni was born, the 'Friends of Mto Moyoni' also came into being.

Two months after Mto Moyoni was established, I woke up to a beautiful morning. The sun was bright, the birds were singing and the smell of fresh coffee filled my nostrils. I enjoyed the early morning when the air was still fresh; this was my time with God. I was so thankful about the meeting with the Archbishop and the fact that I now had my resident permit and we had friends in The Netherlands who were supporting us. I was counting my blessings with a thankful heart. As soon as I opened my journal to hear from God, He spoke, *"Ingrid, today I want to spend time with you."*

My heart leaped – I felt I had won the lot in the lottery, *'God wanting to spend time with me? Of all the people in the world, He had chosen me to spend time with today!'* I felt so special and immediately decided to cancel my programme for the day. I took my Bible, journal and music down to the river in great anticipation of what my Father would share with me.

The river was beautiful, the birds amazing, with such a variety! A fish would jump right at my feet and the monitor lizards swam around me. I felt like Adam in the garden and felt sorry that all the animals were already named. It would have been so much fun to name animals! I thanked God for the beauty of His creation and began to listen to what special message He would have for me. I waited, listened, soaked in his presence but to my amazement God did not speak at all. I asked Him, and He was silent.

I read the blue-marked scriptures in my Bible and saw how faithfully I had obeyed them in the years past but how the letter of the law had kept me in bondage. How liberating was it now to enjoy the freedom of the Spirit of God! I loved what I had heard Bill Johnson, a Pastor from California, say one day, *"Are you married to the principals or to the Presence?"* For sure the principals had bound me and they had suppressed His presence in my heart. I smiled as I remembered a time when I had been cutting cake for my night watchman. I had cut two pieces and when I put his piece on the plate, it was smaller than my piece.

'Oh no, the word of God says, value the other person's interest more than your own.' I had walked back and replaced the cake with the bigger piece all the while wondering why Christianity had to be so complicated. I had lived my life according to the letter and it had killed my joy. All that I needed to learn now was to recognise His presence and be obedient to what He asked me to do. How liberating!

By 4 o'clock in the afternoon it was still quiet. I had read the word, opened my heart to hear and chosen to seek His presence for the last seven hours and it was only quiet.

"Father, here I am for you, I changed my whole programme for the day to be with You but You are not saying anything. What is happening?" I complained. A memory came back to my mind of something that had happened sometime previously. We had been to Kampala to see a government minister in his office regarding the registration of Mto Moyoni. As so often, you need to wait for important people.

That's when God spoke to me, *"Ingrid, you have waited for me the whole day, you have shown to me how important I am for you, Thank you!"* That one sentence made my day. The King of the Universe had said 'thank you' to me. I felt so honoured by Him when, in the evening sun, I climbed my way back to the house.

CHAPTER TWENTY-SIX

Sharing Father's love

After five months Winette and I felt strongly that we had Father's go-ahead to begin with the ministry. We decided to do our first 'Healing of the heart' seminar and invited a number of friends who had shown interest in our stories of a changed heart. We were encouraged that five of our friends were willing to set a week apart to be with God.

I was waiting impatiently in the stationary shop one hot and humid day. I'd come out to buy some materials for our first seminar. There were two people in front of me but time is no issue in Uganda. A Ugandan friend of mine, when he'd seen my impatience one time, had said with a huge smile on his face, "You Europeans have the watch, but we have the time!" After so many years in Uganda I still found it hard to wait.

My hand was resting on a photocopy machine as I played, absentmindedly, with a small piece of paper. After a moment, I wondered to myself, *'Why are my fingers so sticky?'* I looked at my index finger and saw blood dripping out. I looked at the photocopy machine and to my shock there was a used razor blade lying idle on the machine. I'd cut myself with a used razor blade!

Everyone who works in Uganda is aware that used razor blades can be a cause of infection with HIV. I asked the lady what the razor blade was used for. She felt very embarrassed and said she did not know as it was not hers. I quickly bought my things and rushed home to call a nurse, who specialised in HIV/AIDS.

"You need to know what they have done with the razor blade and you need to know the HIV status of the person who used the blade. If the person is HIV positive, you need to come to Kampala immediately. There is a treatment that you can take, within 24 hours of the possible infection but it is a very strong medication that can only be administered to you under doctor's care."

I jumped in my car and drove back to the shop. As I drove back to town my memory went to another time when I feared being infected with the HIV virus. It had been on a very deserted road in the middle of nowhere. I was driving fast, when suddenly far away I saw a big group of people standing in the middle of the road. When I approached a soldier stopped me, waving with his gun.

'I am not taking soldiers with guns,' I told myself. When I got closer I saw a badly wounded lady lying on the dirt road. As fast as I could I stopped the car and jumped out. The soldier told me the story; his mother had been sitting on the back of a pickup truck and when the car hit a pothole, she fell off the car. Her clothes were torn and her whole body was covered in blood.

"Let's get her in the car and I'll take you to the hospital." Together we lifted the lady on the backseat and I drove as fast as I could to save her life.

As I drove, I looked from my hands to the glove compartment, *'Silly and stupid; why did I not think about it?'* I kept rubber cloves there; just in case I needed them and now that I did need them I had completely forgotten about them. I looked at my hands and prayed a prayer against an infection with HIV/AIDS.

I arrived back at the shop. "Can I please ask you an embarrass-ing question," I asked the lady, as she walked with me out of the shop – I did not want anyone to hear our conversation. She looked at me, not saying anything. "I need to know who used the razor blade, what it was used for and I am sorry to ask but I also need to know the HIV status of the person who used the blade."

"Let me call the man who used the razor blade." She left and came back with a healthy looking gentleman.

"Sir, I cut myself with a used razor blade in your shop. I am sorry to ask you a very personal question. What did you use it for and have you been tested for HIV? If you are HIV positive, I need to rush to Kampala now for treatment."

He looked at me, showed me his hands and said, "Madam, I cut my fingernails with the razor blade." His fingernails looked very clean and short as if they were just cut. I quickly checked if he had not cut his finger in the process.

"I have been tested for HIV three times and all the tests were negative. I can go home and show you my medical card, if you want."

I hesitated, *'If he's offering for me to look at his card, most probably he speaks the truth,'* I thought to myself.

"No, it's okay, I choose to believe you." In my heart I prayed another prayer for protection and remembered what God had told me, *"Love is stronger than evil."* I had responded in love and respect to the man, so now I chose to believe that God's love would protect me also.

Before we did our first 'Healing of the heart' seminar, we had asked permission from the Toronto Church if we could use their materials. They happily agreed to it. We saw it as another green light to continue. Once God said 'yes', we were going for it.

We conducted the seminars in an open hut in the compound and cooked the food in my kitchen. The builders were still constructing the centre around us and painters were busy painting, but we could not wait any longer. We were so eager to share the new revelations we had received. When Irene heard about our vision and about our first seminar, she spontaneously donated a banda for our centre. It was another great encouragement.

We taught about generational sins, lies that we believe and the inner vows that we make and shared from our own experiences how unresolved issues and broken relationships can hold us in bondage. Our teaching focussed on revealing God's amazing Father-heart to them and explaining that we are all born by His will. We shared what we'd learnt about Father God sending Jesus to be the way back to His heart and how He desires to take us on a journey through our own hearts to discover what is hidden there; the things that hinder us from receiving the fullness that Jesus came to bring by leading us to His Father's heart. We were helping people to see God's amazing dream for each of their lives and how He longed to use His children to bring restoration to the whole of creation. God moved deeply in the five people that were present and it was beautiful to see how He healed the broken hearted.

We were surprised to hear some people comment on our pro-grammes, "Why healing, do you think we are sick?" When we re-named the same programme 'Transformation of the heart', the interest in the programme suddenly increased significantly.

News that a new organisation had begun travelled fast. After our first seminar, a man named John was sitting in our office; he was looking for a job. I had met him before when he was working for a hotel in Jinja. We had realised, as we talked, that we were both Christians. When he came to Mto Moyoni, he had just lost his job and was looking for a job with us. When he shared what happened in his former job I strongly felt that he needed to make things right with his employer before we could even continue talking about a job with us. I heard Father God say, *"I am taking him on a journey. Encourage him but do not interfere in my process with him."*

John visibly struggled with my suggestion. Asking for forgive-ness is a huge thing. I knew it from experience. He wouldn't look at me, and his eyes suggested he was not sure if he was able to go back to his former employer.

"Please, give me money for transport and I will go," he said, "God will really bless you when you give me the money."

"I am sorry" I said, "I can't give you money" He sat down, said nothing and after a few minutes he left the office. As he was walking out he said again, "Please, you give me the money for transport and I will go. God will really bless you for giving me the money."

"John, all I want is to be obedient to God and He just told me that this is His process with you and that I should not interfere. If I give you money now, I will not be blessed because I would be disobeying God". At the gate I prayed a blessing over his life and asked Father to give him a spirit of courage to face the unresolved issues in his life.

His eyes were filled with unbelief, when he walked out of the gate, still undecided if he would make it to his former employer. I walked back to the office, feeling so relieved. How often had I given money to people, even when my heart did not want to give? I had always felt guilty when I did not give the money when asked. Often I'd felt manipulated to give, but did not have the courage to say no. How much easier it was now that I could hear Father God speak. I realised that He truly is alive in my heart, and that it is okay to follow my heart even if people around me think differently. It was a great discovery that my head no longer ruled over God's heart in me.

The relationships with the pastors in Jinja were still very fragile. So now and then I still heard rumours about myself but they did not hurt me anymore. I knew who I was in Christ, so I had learned to run back to my Father if someone said something bad about me, cry in His presence and allow Him to comfort me. I did not want my heart to be hardened again.

I had introduced Mto Moyoni to the Jinja Elders' Fellowship, a fellowship of all the pastors in Jinja. The chairman suggested that I give a brief introduction of the new ministry to a group of 350 pastors who came together for leadership training. I marvelled at this opportunity. I asked Father what I should share; He told me simply, *"Be as open as possible and share all your pain and struggles. Do not hold back."*

In five minutes I shared how God was healing me from the pain of being falsely accused. How people had believed that I was a witchdoctor, a cult leader, a rebel leader, training youth against the government, and how I was arrested and shot at. I shared how thankful I was to God for showing me His unconditional love and how God's love had healed my heart; how He had revealed Himself as a perfect Father to me.

As I sat down, the pastor of one of our CRO workers rose from his chair and shouted through the hall, "Who has given this women permission to speak? These allegations are very serious! Does anybody know her? Who tells us that these allegations are not true? How can we be invited to a place that we don't know of?"

I sat in my chair and my spirit rose up within me. In a flash the first line of the prophecy came back to me, *"The night is over..."* In my heart I rebuked the spirit in this man, *'Not again! In the Name of Jesus I stop this man from accusing me!'*

At that moment the chairman of the day grabbed the microphone and said, "This sister spoke her heart and no-one is to judge her." I sighed with relief – finally, for the first time in so many years of accusation, there was a Ugandan leader that publicly protected me. That in itself was healing for my soul. During the coffee break a number of pastors came and shared that they could identify with my suffering as each of them had been through similar situations and accusations; they all said they would love to come to our centre to receive healing.

However, the Jinja leaders felt that they had to put up an inquiry about me and asked if they could come to see what we were doing. Three days after this confrontation we welcomed them to Mto Moyoni and sat in an open hut in the garden when we shared our vision with them. There was little readiness to listen; they had come with their own agenda. They fired their questions at me: how long had I been a Christian, when did I get saved, how often had I backslidden? Winette's face turned from white to red. She was sitting on the side, listening to the questions and I noticed that she was clearly embarrassed by this crossfire of questions. I was happy that they did not involve her in the questioning; I answered all the queries as accurately as possible and was relieved when they left. Ten minutes later one pastor rang and said that they had had a meeting together at the end of the road and decided that we had passed the test.

While so many people were blessed during our programmes, we felt sorry that the Jinja Christians were missing out on God's touch in our place. It took a long time before one of them dared to set foot on our land. Immediately God arrested her with His love. After the first session this lady handed me a small note, which read, *'I am very sorry for I believed false accusations towards you by the time you were working with CRO, forgive me.'*

My heart jumped with joy, complete vindication was on its way.

CHAPTER TWENTY-SEVEN

Ministry Dogs

Things moved on slowly but surely. Building works continued and we carried cement and had sand delivered almost daily to build more rooms. We worked on the designs and landscaping; it was fun to see the centre taking shape. Every time we found people interested in one of our programmes we conducted a seminar and witnessed God's love healing deep wounds. It took time for people to get to know about us; God had said that He would bring everybody and everything we needed, so we decided not to advertise.

It was a slow start. One morning, after almost a year of building and only a few seminars, I was complaining to God that it was going so slow. He spoke to my heart, *"Ingrid you are despising the small beginnings."* I realised that this was a scripture so I looked it up in my Dutch Bible and I was so pleasantly surprised when I read, *"Despise not the small beginnings because the Lord is happy that the work has begun."*[38] I smiled – that was just the encouragement I needed at that time.

'At the start we decided there was no need for a conference room, or so we'd thought – we were just two ladies sharing God's love – but as soon as the rainy season started we knew we surely needed a conference room when we found ourselves all shivering in the rain in our small open hut in the compound. And so we

---

38 *Zechariah 4:10*

added another building to our plans.

The centre expanded before our eyes. In the space of one and a half years, we had built three round huts and were able to accommodate 12 people. Mto Moyoni was a quiet place; all cottages had a private view over the river. It was a joy to live so near to the Nile – to hear the birds sing and watch the river flow.

The nights were dark; there was no electricity and when there was no moon, it was difficult to see your own hand. One night I woke up at 1.00am, *'Am I hearing things? Is someone trying to enter my house?'* I knew there was no one else on the compound besides Winette and the workers who lived in their own rooms. *'Who could this be?'* I heard somebody trying to open the door and slowly, with shaking legs, I got out of my bed to see what was happening. In my heart I heard Father God say, *"Fear not, I am your protector,"* and again one phrase from the prophecy came to my mind; I claimed the promise *'the night is over'*. Strengthened by this assurance I walked to the door, opened the curtain and saw two men dressed in defence uniform, they were carrying guns. I asked them what they wanted.

"We are on a night patrol and we need to know who is in your house. Open the door," They shouted.

I asked them, "Where is my night watchman?" They left and I assumed that they were bringing my night watchman. I quickly dressed and got my mobile phone. I knew I did not have any money on it to make a call, but I could try the emergency numbers. I dialled 112 and when they answered the police told me there were no official night patrols in my village. I told them, "Then I have a big problem, you need to come." They promised to come. I dialled Winette's number and was so surprised that I managed to get through to her since there was no money on my phone to make a call. She was still living in the first banda. The commotion in the garden had woken her up. "Stay low," I said on the phone, "they may not know that you are also in the compound."

The men came back but not with the night watchman, they returned with a third armed man. They saw me on the phone and shouted, "Who are you calling?" I told them I was calling the police to check their story. They left shouting, "Let them come!" I waited nervously for the police. After twenty minutes I heard a car coming and ran to the gate to open it, in faith that the thugs had left and they would not shoot at me. The police searched the compound and found out that the thugs had bolted all the doors of the people living in the compound. They searched the garden and found the night watchman tied to a tree. He was not injured but completely in shock.

We made a cup of tea for everyone to calm our nerves down and to share our experiences. That's when I heard that Winette's phone battery was empty and I'd already known that I did not have money on my phone to ring her but in spite of both these things we still were able to connect. It had been a divine intervention! I was at peace and realised that God allowed it to happen to show me how much healing I had already undergone.

"Would you like to have a dog on the compound?" Winette called me from Kampala; she was attending an AIM meeting there. "My team leaders have a beautiful female German Shepherd puppy and they want to give it to me as a gift." A dog – I had never liked dogs; there had been a few in the compound but I really did not have any affinity with them. As far as I was concerned they were good for security purposes only. Whenever I said 'go' to them they would come and that annoyed me – I was not known as a dog lover! Those dogs had died and I never thought about getting another one. But it would be good for security reasons to have a dog again. I was quickly weighing the pros and the cons when I said, "It's fine, as long as you keep it in your house and care for her." I figured the compound would be big enough for her to enjoy and as long as I did not have to keep her in my house it would be okay.

As soon as the three-month-old puppy got out of the car she stole my heart! With her faithful eyes she would watch Winette wherever she went. Snif became her personal bodyguard, as young as she was, and when Winette was not around I had a bodyguard who would follow me all the way up to the bathroom and wait until I was ready. I was surprised at how quickly Snif had stolen my heart.

We'd had Snif for six months when one afternoon, a kayaker came running up the hill in our compound holding something in his hand. It was a little animal, the umbilical cord was still attached and it had been screaming. He'd stopped his boat and found this little creature barely alive. It made a sound like a duck but it looked like an otter. She had two little wounds in her neck. It looked as though a bird might have caught it and dropped it on our peninsula when it discovered that it was not a rat. We couldn't think of any other way that a one-day-old baby animal could have landed on the peninsula.

The vet had just come to treat Snif and he immediately saw that it was a little puppy. The eyes were still closed. Winette began feeding this mini dog from a bottle. Seeing this day-old puppy grow softened my heart completely and my aversion against dogs melted away like snow in the sun. We called her 'Droppie', an apt name since she was dropped on our peninsula. Drop also means liquorice in Dutch, a black sweet that is very popular in The Netherlands. Droppie became a little bundle of joyful aggression. Since she was a small puppy we were not concerned about her aggressiveness, we could still handle her and discipline her, though her little teeth were very sharp.

One day Winette used Droppie as a teaching aid, during one of our seminars. She explained that trust is developed by positive touches, eye contact and tone of voice. After her teaching she gave Droppie to me. I said to God, "Father, this is a place for healing, we cannot have an aggressive dog; we need a dog that loves people." Suddenly Droppie's whole body started shaking and rolling, her eyes moved and closed and rolled. "Winette," I said. "Look at Droppie, I only asked God to give us a dog that loves people!"

She looked and exclaimed, "She is dead!"

When Droppie came back around all her aggression was gone. She was instantly delivered. Never did I know that dogs could be possessed. *'Where is that in the Bible? Swines okay, but dogs?'* But however we looked at it, her aggression was gone; now all she would do was play and instead of biting Droppie would only lick.

One day I asked God, "How does it feel to be fully alive?"

"Look at Droppie," was His answer. As I looked at her, I saw a little bundle of joy and happiness, enjoying the garden; playing with anything she could get hold of with all her senses alive.

Very soon she was promoted to become Mto Moyoni's first ministry dog. She would lay with people when they were in tears and she showed them Father's love by comforting them. During a soaking prayer session one day, we saw Droppie going to a very neat English man who lay on his mat enjoying God's presence. She put her paw on his arm. Thinking that it was one of us who had come to pray for him, he kept his eyes closed and continued to receive God's love. After fifteen minutes he thought to himself, "These ladies are really praying over me for a long time." He opened his eyes and saw that Droppie had ministered to him. We all had so much fun when we saw it unfolding before our eyes.

During another seminar a lady asked God, "How do you want to show me your love today?"

"Today I have a very unique way of showing you my love," God said to her.

As she was waiting to hear what the unique way was, Droppie walked up from behind and gave her a huge lick on her cheek. She burst out laughing and shared with all of us God's unique way in showing her His love!

In their free time the monkeys in the garden entertained our ministry dogs. But one day the entertainment turned into an attack; Snif was chasing the monkeys through the garden and had cornered a huge one. The monkey tried to jump out of the compound but the fence was bending over it and it bounced back on the ground. Feeling threatened the monkey jumped on Snif and threw her on her back. I had seen the chase but my attention was on the book I was reading, until I heard Snif cry instead of bark. I ran to see, what had happened and in my shock I saw that the monkey had his teeth already in Snif's throat. I had heard of monkeys killing dogs but had never seen anything like it. I ran and fell, sliding on my back down the hill. By some miracle my foot ended up exactly where the monkey was and as hard as I could, I kicked it off Snif's neck. The animal flew through the air, landed and looked at me. My mind raced, "What can I do in case the monkey attacks me now?" But a moment later she turned and ran away.

Snif was completely in shock; she could not walk and did not eat the whole night. All she did was hide in the corner. I decided to keep her inside my house for the night and leave the door to my bedroom open. I wanted to be able to hear her if there was any problem. At three in the morning, she woke me up with her paw on my arm as if to say, "Thank you, I am fine now."

CHAPTER TWENTY-EIGHT

Orphans No More

A young man named Fred came to visit us; he had a question on his mind. We had been to his church 15 km outside Jinja two weeks before to share the message of God's desire to be a Father to us. We had explained that so often we live our lives as if we do not have a Father.

Fred was struggling; his biological father had passed away and his mother was poor and could not afford his school fees. At 13 years old, his biggest desire was to study. Fred loved school and wanted to continue with his education but there was no money. The only solution he could think of was to visit us and ask us to give him money for his school fees.

He had walked the 15 kilometres in the heat of the day. As he drank a cold drink, we asked him what had brought him to us. His brown eyes smiled when he answered, "What I wanted to ask you, I no longer need to ask you anymore. I am in need of school fees but as soon as I entered the gate at Mto Moyoni, Father God spoke to my heart that He is going to provide for my school fees. He said that I am His son and that He is my perfect Father. I wanted you to help me but I now know that Father God is going to do it."

He left the compound happy, knowing in faith that his problem was solved. Not only was he happy but we too were happy - there had been so many times that people came to us asking for money. Often I had felt like a walking bank; how exciting it was for us to witness God showing them to refocus from the 'mzungu' as their source of provision to Himself! When Fred arrived home, the headmaster of his school was waiting for him. He was one of the best athletes the school had and they did not want to lose him, so the school had decided to sponsor him!

Three years after Mto Moyoni began, CRO Jinja asked us to pray with the street children once a week. I was so excited; I had asked Father to give us opportunities to minister alongside CRO again and introduce His heart to the street children. I realised that I had set up the organisation with my own orphan-heart so I asked God for entry points to bring the truth of His Father-heart to the staff and children of CRO. Winette introduced soaking prayer to the street children connecting them with Father God's loving presence.

There were times that I joined Winette to share Father God's love with the children and on this occasion an amazing thing happened; just before the worship music began to play, Tabu walked in. I still remembered him. He had been living on the streets for many years; he was a real hard-core street child.

This time he staggered in, completely drunk on aviation fuel. All the other children started laughing when he said he wanted to pray with us. We invited him to sit in the circle with the other children and invited Father's love to come and touch our hearts. Soon he was deep asleep. We put our arms around him and asked Father to arrest this boy with His love. After thirty minutes, when the music stopped, we asked if anybody wanted to share what Jesus had said to them.

Tabu stood up and stammered, "Jesus said that I need to get saved."

We asked him, "Do you want to get saved?"

"Yes," he said.

Right there and then we prayed a sinner's prayer with a street child high on fuel. Three months later, the CRO staff told us that he was home with his parents and that he was doing very well.

I was so amazed. For 12 years I laboured to get children of the streets and the Father's love was changing hearts within hours. His love is truly the answer to a suffering world.

One afternoon, as Winette walked through the slum area with a few visitors she met one of CRO's children, Monday, a ten-year-old girl who had lived on the streets for many years. Monday had been taken on by CRO and was doing well in primary school. She had accepted Jesus in her life and her circumstances had changed for the better. Her mother had also opened her heart for Jesus and instead of buying booze; her mum now spend money on food. But today she was crying and looked very unhappy. Winette asked her what the problem was, "My step father has come back and had chased my mother away. I don't know where my mother is and I am also scared of my stepfather." That night, her stepfather came home late and chased Monday from her home too. She had no-where to go except to the old tree where she used to sleep while she was still on the streets. It was a dark and cold night. She felt very lonely and scared.

Winette was asked by CRO to take the girl to Kampala, to look for her mother. In the car she began to share her story, "When I was so scared in that tree at night, I remembered that you told us that we could invite Father God to come very close to us. I asked Him and then I received a vision. In the vision I saw a very important, big man, He was sitting on a big throne and He called me with his hand. I feared coming close to Him and asked Him, 'I cannot see Your face, who are You?' He said, *'I cannot show you my face, but I will show you the hands of my Son.'* I saw blood dripping from the hands and knew that these were the hands of Jesus." She described how she then dared to walk up to the throne and, when she was near, Father God stooped low and lifted her on

His lap. "I slept very well that night," she told Winette.

"The following day the neighbours told me that it was not safe to sleep in the tree," she went on, "so they invited me to sleep in their home. But the home was also not a safe place. People were drinking and shouting. On my mat in the corner I invited Father God again into my situation. I fell asleep and got a dream. In the dream a huge angel came and carried me from the mat back to Father God's lap."

The girl was in tears when she told Winette the story. Winette was in tears when she heard the story and I was in tears when Winette shared it with me! This was the answer to a question I had asked God for all the years that I had worked with street children, "God your word says that You are a Father to the father-less, but I am not seeing it. There are thousands of people working with orphans but there are thousands of orphans who have no one to care for them. Where are You?" God used this ten-year-old girl to show me that He has made His home in the hearts of His children but that the pain and circumstances of life had hidden His loving presence. He showed me through Monday's story that it has always been His desire to be a loving Father and that He is available for everyone who asks. Surely we can approach His throne of grace with boldness.

Three weeks after her encounter with Father's love, CRO were welcoming some visitors and Monday shared her testimony with them. When they heard her story, they felt strongly that the slum area was not a safe place for a young girl so they decided to sponsor her in one of the best boarding school in Uganda. She was now sharing her class with children of government ministers and big business people. At times that was very intimidating for her but in her heart she knew that she was a child of the King of the Universe. Her friends were receiving gifts from their parents but she did not have any one to give her a gift. When Christmas approached she complained to God and said, "I also want a new dress for Christmas like my friends and I need soap and toothpaste but there is no-one to give it to me."

That night she had a dream. In the dream she walked through a beautiful garden. The garden had dresses, soap and toothpaste in it. All the things she so desired. God spoke to her and said, *"This is your garden, pick what you want."*

"I picked so many things, my arms were full. When the dream ended, the garden was still full," she told us, full of amazement. Days later when she came to CRO, there was a large parcel for her and in it was a new dress, soap and toothpaste among many other things. A few months later, when she was given the microphone to share her testimony at a children's conference that Mto Moyoni was hosting, all she shouted was, "Children, listen! Children listen! You are not orphans, you are not orphans; you have a Father in heaven who wants to care for you!"

The Northern part of Uganda had suffered twenty years of civil war. The Lord's Resistance Army had been fighting in the villages and abducted many young children for recruitment in their rebel army. There has been immense suffering and I found it a constant challenge. God had spoken that His love is stronger than evil, and I so desired to see more of it. We asked God for an entry point into this suffering area of the country.

A few months after my silent prayer about an entry point to Northern Uganda, early in 2008, Irene called one day. She was working in Gulu, the biggest town in Northern Uganda. "Ingrid, there is a lady who has just escaped from the rebels, can she come to Mto Moyoni and you pray with her?" she asked me.

This young lady had been abducted from her school when she was 14 and had escaped from the rebels when she was 23; nine long years in captivity. She was the only Christian believer among the rebels. She had not been allowed to have a Bible; all she had was a living relationship with her Father in Heaven. Every day she asked Him, "When is my day to escape?"

For nine years He said, *"Wait, not yet."* It was a life of agony, pain, suffering, humiliation and distress. She was given to a rebel commander to be his wife, as young as she was. We cried as we listened to her stories.

"One day I was baking pancakes for the commander," she told us. "I was so hungry and secretly ate one. I knew I could be killed if he found out that I had eaten his food. That night I had a terrible dream of a snake following me and almost biting me. The following night I dreamed the same dream. God was telling me, through these dreams that I had to repent to the commander for eating his pancake. I feared because the man could kill me for it."

She went on, "I confessed and to my big surprise, nothing happened. That night I received the same dream but this time I had a stick in my hand and killed the snake. This is how God showed me that disobedience is an entry point for satan to steal, kill and destroy in my life."

"We had to pass through rivers," she continued, "Everybody was told to put some water on their heads before crossing the river to be protected from drowning. I knew this is witchcraft and I did not want to have anything to do with it. But one day I was weak, and I also put water on my head before crossing the river. When I had crossed to the other side, I stood under a tree and something fell on me. In the hours that followed I became very sick. I knew a demon had entered my life. I was so sick that they carried me to my hut. People came to see me and sympathised with me. They heard a voice coming out of my mouth, 'We want to get out of this girl because she has a praying mother'."

The demons that had entered her wanted to get out because they could not stand the prayers her mother prayed for her in a distant land. "They took me to a cleansing place and put a red hot metal into my mouth to cleanse me from all the demons." She continued as we listened in disbelief, "When people came to see me they could see no scar; I had no pain and was of sound mind".

"After nine years, God spoke to my heart saying, *'Today is your day; today you will be free.'*

"I whispered to a friend, 'My God has told me that today I will be free, are you going with me?'

"'Are you stupid?' my friend asked, 'This is the worse day you can choose. The bullets are flying everywhere; you will be killed if you try to escape now.'

"'My God has told me so I am going,' I replied."

The young woman brought her story to its conclusion, "That night, after a difficult day of escape, I slept at the UN base in Southern Sudan, safe from the rebels and the guns. A few days later I was welcomed back home by my praying mother in Gulu."

Winette and I listened to her amazing testimony of God's faithfulness. Her spirit was alive, but her soul and her body were wounded. We rejoiced that God had kept her alive, but she came out of the war beaten, wounded and with HIV in her body. We shared Father God's heart of unconditional love for her, and invited Him to bring healing to her heart and body. For the first time in nine years, tears came to her eyes when she experienced Father God's tender embrace that touched her wounded heart and body.

"It does not matter that I have HIV anymore, I know I have a Father who loves me and wants the best for my future," she said as she left our compound.

Through this faithful young lady, we were introduced to the overwhelming suffering of the people of Northern Uganda and, a few months later we made our first trip to Gulu to do a Father-heart encounter for pastors there. During that time God spoke to my heart, saying, *"My children in Gulu have fought, prayed and fasted but I am after their hearts. I love each one of them individually and I am not looking at their collective efforts but I am looking at the individual's heart. I am ready to bless the land but the hearts of the people are far from me. Their hearts are full of questions and they have lost sight of me as their loving Father.*

"My daughters, speak about my nature, my character and my desire to bless them. I do not need aggressive religious striving, what I am looking for is a love relationship with my people. I have seen their cries for peace but my desire is to give them peace amidst the storm. A peace amidst the storm is stronger than a peace without a battle. It is my desire to give peace but the hearts of my people are full of bitterness, resentment and questions towards me. Let them empty their hearts and I will come and fill them with my love."

Many tears flowed when Father's love began to touch the painful places in people's hearts. His love simply washed away unforgiveness and bitterness. We were amazed at the power of His love when we watched Him at work.

We took time, while we were in Gulu to visit different organisations to get a feel of what was being done to restore the region, now that peace had returned to this part of the country. When we were invited to an orphanage, all the children were dressed up for the visitors. The moment we entered the place God spoke to my heart, *"In my dictionary there is no such word as orphan, I only know children."*

Everyone was wearing orange T-shirts. All the children were dressed up for the visitors except for one little boy. The staff of the orphanage came to us and said, "Sorry, this boy is stubborn; he does not want to wear our uniform."

Winette and I looked at each other and we both knew God's heart for this child. He did not want to be one of the many orphans; he just wanted to be himself, Joshua. We applauded the little boy and tried to give him a big hug, but he hide from us.

I felt so hurt and sad for him; his young heart was already too wounded to receive a gentle touch.

One evening, when we were in Gulu, we went out for dinner with a friend. During the meal she got an emergency phone call; one of the ex-prostitutes she was working with had come home drunk and had started a fight. We asked her if we could support her and went with her to the home.

The picture I saw on arrival, I will not easily forget. In the cold, rainy night we found the young lady with her hands and feet tied to a tree. She had been so aggressive that no one knew how to handle her. The only solution was to tie her in the mud to a tree. We bent over, untied her and took her inside. The smell of alcohol was all over her. We wrapped her in a blanket and cleaned her up a bit. Than we surrounded her and asked Father God to come, with His love, and comfort her broken heart. Within a few minutes she started to cry and after twenty minutes she fell in a peaceful sleep. The following morning we visited her and shared with her that Jesus is the Way to the unconditional love, which she had experienced in her heart the night before. Immediately when we finished talking she walked up to us and confessed, "I need Jesus" in my life. Her encounter with the Father's love had led her to salvation.

People blessed us with donations so that we could organise youth weeks for orphans from Northern Uganda at Mto Moyoni.

George was one of the participants. He had fled the violence in Northern Uganda as a young boy. He told us his story:

His mother passed away when he was born and his father was desperate because he had no money to care for a new-born baby so he decided to bury the boy alive with the mother. An old lady in the village who watched the father put George in the coffin jumped forward and rescued the baby. She cared for him until he was four years old. His father was not willing to take care of him so he ended up in a house with relatives where he was severely mistreated. When he was 10 years old he left the village and moved to live on the streets of Kampala. An NGO cared for him and now, at 19 years of age, he was working as a night watchman at the NGO's offices. He was a deeply wounded young man.

During the seminar he received the revelation that he was born by the will of Father God and that God had an amazing plan for his life. With lots of tears he forgave his father for the rejection and the mistreatment he had received in his earlier years and asked God to become his perfect Father.

The following night, Father God gave him a dream. In the dream he received a phone-call from an unknown person who claimed to be his father and invited him to the village. When he came to the village, the father had made a feast with drinks and meat, celebrating the boy's homecoming. Two days after he left Mto Moyoni, the dream became a reality. He was invited to the village by his biological dad and restored back to his family. As he walked back home, a big four-wheel drive car stopped to give him a lift home. He asked the driver why he gave him a lift and the man replied, "Because I can see the love of God all over you."

A year later, we were back in Gulu. I stood on the top floor of our hotel, one morning. The pace at which Gulu town was developing surprised me; there was a lot of money coming into the town for development. There were traffic jams in the morning from all the relief cars and trucks from development agencies.

I heard Father God say, "*This is the time for Gulu's healing. In a few years time relief and development money will have filled the wounded and empty hearts of my children in Northern Uganda and they will continue to fight for survival.*" I had witnessed God's heart for this part of the country and made a decision not to refuse any invitation we would receive from the Northern part of the country to minister love and healing to the deeply wounded.

CHAPTER TWENTY-NINE

His Thoughts are Higher

I knew God was happy with the small beginnings but I was also curious what God's thoughts were about Mto Moyoni in the future. One morning, not long after we'd begun ministering, I asked Him, "Father what are your thoughts about Mto Moyoni's future?"

"Look straight ahead of you," came the reply.

I looked and saw the Four Star, 96-roomed hotel and began to laugh. Here we were, a small retreat centre with nine rooms! *"Is that what God has in mind?*

Perhaps we need more land," I thought to myself. We started to look for all the owners of the plots next to ours and asked if they would be willing to sell their land. No one was willing to sell and I did not pursue it any further. If Mto Moyoni had to grow it was for God to bring it to us.

"I hear you want to buy land." Six months after my little conversation with the Lord about Mto Moyoni's future, a young man came to the gate. "We have a plot in the next village, do you want to come and see it?"

We walked ten minutes to the land and when we saw it, we knew immediately that we should buy it; it was a beautiful piece of land. When we were signing the papers one of the village leaders said, "I have also a piece of land for sale; do you want to see it?"

"Sure, we would love to see it," we answered. He took us to his land and it was even more beautiful. We looked around and felt it was right to buy it too. At the same time, in The Netherlands, there was someone donating the exact amount for this plot of land. This was a real confirmation that it was Father God working on His greater plan.

There were three other plots in between these two and we decided to walk the land in faith. One day, eight months after signing the sales agreement of the other plots, my phone rang, "I have land for sale; do you want to buy it?"

I was excited and ran to Winette with the news. She said "If it is the middle plot then the other plots will also be ours too, in faith" When we walked over to see the land, it happened to be the middle plot!

Once more, God came through with His promise that He would bring everybody we needed. Winette and I were brainstorming about the development of our new land when the phone rang. "Do you have rooms for a tired mission team?" an American voice asked over the phone. We had just enough rooms to accommodate them and when they arrived, we found out that they were from Engineering Ministries International. We smiled at each other; this could be part of Father's bigger plan in helping us to develop our new land. We decided to wait with our request for technical advice on how to develop our new land, until they were rested enough.

Ten months later a thirteen-man international team of architects, engineers and surveyors were busy designing plans for our new land! Within four months we had a master plan ready for the land with an estimate budget of 1.2 million dollars. I lifted the plans to God and asked, "How will this be done?"

"Test Me in this and see if I will not throw open the floodgates of heaven and pour out so much blessing that you will not have room

enough for it."[39] I treasured these words in my heart in anticipation of their fulfilment.

Not only did God bring technical people, He blessed us with people that ministered to our hearts. God continued the inward journey as we gave Him our time. Lots of tears and pain still surfaced but it was no longer such a struggle because we knew that with every tear we cried more freedom was released.

Otto de Bruyne came from The Netherlands for a brief visit. He had worked in Africa for many years but was now back in The Netherlands, hosting a programme on a Christian TV channel. He had heard about Mto Moyoni through our friends in The Netherlands and decided to pay us a visit. We took him to see the new land and, while he was still enjoying the view, he suddenly knelt in the middle of the bush and told us, "God said to me one day, '*Otto, I am looking for a resting place in the hearts of my people.*'" He continued, "I said, 'No Lord, I need a resting place.'

"'*No,*' God said, '*I need a resting place.*'"

It was a Holy moment for us, as we dedicated our new land to become a resting place for God in the hearts of His children.

Over the years we developed an eagerness to receive an even deeper revelation of Father's love so we read every book on that subject that came into print. We had read Mark Stibbe's books on the Father-heart of God and were excited when we heard that he was doing a seminar for an organisation that we were also involved with. We asked if we could come and sit-in on his teaching. As soon as we met him, our hearts were bonded together as we saw in each other a similar passion of bringing the orphan-hearted people back to the heart of God, the Father, and to introduce them to their full inheritance as sons and daughters of God. After he returned to England, we remained in contact with each other and Mto Moyoni developed a relationship with his organisation,

---

39 *Malachi 3:10*

Fathershouse Trust, in the UK. Another of our prayers had been answered; we now had a man who was willing to be available to us for any questions we had with regards to the ministry.

Towards the end of 2009, a group of Japanese people entered the compound. We had not had many Japanese people visiting us yet, so I walked to the gate, welcomed them in and asked how I could help them.

"Sorry, sorry, sorry," they said. "We just want to see your compound. We are carrying out a survey for a new bridge over the Nile. We need to see your place."

"Please go ahead," I replied. I had an uneasy feeling in my heart when I saw the ten men walking down to the river. They returned the next day, and again the following day.

"What is so special about our compound?" I asked

The leader murmured, "A possible location of the bridge over river."

'Had I heard that right? What bridge?' The present bridge over the river Nile was in bad shape and needed replacing, but did they want to make a bridge through our compound? God forbid!

The next time they came, they entered with pickaxes, cement and paint on their way down to the river. I was just in time to stop them and ask, "Sorry Sir, where are you going? Can I help you?"

"We are the surveyors for the new bridge over the river Nile and we are setting out the possible location of the new bridge."

"Possible location? No, this is not a possible location because the land belongs to me and I don't want a bridge in my compound."

"We are government surveyors, madam, and we need to do our work."

"Please bring us an official letter requesting for permission, because we are still the owners," I insisted. My mind went into overdrive; I searched the internet and found out that our compound was one of three possible locations for a new bridge. I talked to the land officer to find out what the law of the country said.

"Madam, if the government wants your land," the man told me, "you have to give it. If you don't want to accept the compensation, then the money will be deposited with the court. They will bring bulldozers and go ahead with their development for the sake of national interest. You cannot stop them." As much as I had a land title, I had no rights!

There were times that we had joked about a pedestrian bridge to the other side, but this was out of all proportion; it meant we would lose our centre and our new land would be only 50 metres away from the Trans-African highway, in the middle of noise and pollution.

They came again, this time with a letter and the pickaxes, cement and paint. They marked out the bridge and the road right through our buildings. We had sent out prayer requests and were encouraged by so many responses from people affirming that they would pray for the situation. But my heart was still very disturbed.

I tried to find my solace in Father's presence and cried my heart out to Him, *'Don't you see what they are doing? This is your land; please act on our behalf.'*

"You are not a victim", I heard Him speak, *"You have my authority speak the word and believe."*

I jumped up from my bed, stood on my veranda, overlooking the marked road in the compound and declared aloud the promises of God over our land, *'His will be done in earth as it is in Heaven.'*

There was great relief and confessions when it was announced that another location for the bridge was more acceptable. "When they were doing their tests in the riverbed, we prayed that their equipment would fail," our staff confessed with smiles on their faces!

Mto Moyoni became better known in The Netherlands and

some teams that came to Uganda now spent some time at our centre. Many of them asked about the purpose of the centre and offered to pray over the new land. On one occasion, one of our friends saw a picture of huge Olympic Rings all over our land. He felt God saying, that it was going to be an international place, where people from all over the world would come and meet with God and find peace and rest. Winette and I looked at each other because not long before, just for fun and to encourage one another, we had counted the different nations that had been to our centre. Our vision was originally for African leaders to come, but when we counted the different nationalities that had been to Mto Moyoni we came to almost 50 different countries in the four years of our existence!

A few months later another Dutch mission group had come to encourage us and to seek God's face together. The worship was beautiful and the presence of God was so thick in the room. One of them had recently been released from prison; he had accepted Jesus while in custody and now joined this group to see God at work in the world. As he lay, soaking in God's presence, his friends had put an open Bible on his heart, and prayed that the word may become alive is his life. He took the Bible, read the opened scripture, stood up and stormed to the office. He looked for Winette and me and said, "God says I need to be baptized and I only have twenty minutes before we go. Will you please baptise me?"

Churches had used our compound for baptism services but we had never baptized people ourselves. There was no time for teaching any doctrine or theology about baptism. A quick thought crossed my mind, "Is that not a bit irresponsible?" But immediately I realised that Philip had done the same thing with the man from Ethiopia in the book of Acts.[40]

---

40 *Acts 8:26-39*

This man was so enthused that God had spoken to him, he grabbed our hands and the three of us ran to the river, jumped in with our clothes still on and baptized him, then and there, in the Name of the Father, the Son and the Holy Spirit!

After we had said goodbyes, I ran home to put some dry clothes on. As I went through my wardrobe to decide what to wear it suddenly dawned on me that there were no red clothes in my cupboard at all. From the moment I had been accused of being a witch, more than ten years ago, I had never bought anything red anymore. *'Had I unconsciously aligned my thinking with the lie of satan? Had I stopped wearing red clothes because of the accusations that red was for witches?'* I could not give satan that honour; I rushed to the market and bought myself a beautiful bright red second-hand blouse!

People came to visit us regularly and prophesied over Mto Moyoni. We wrote all the prophecies down and meditated on them, *"It will be a place where heaven touches earth; where God's will is done as it is in heaven. It will be a place of rest, restoration and healing."*

"Open heavens."

There were moments when I struggled with unbelief when I heard people prophesy over Mto Moyoni and I realised that the receiving capacity of my heart still needed to expand for me to move in faith and expect it all to happen. I had re-read the prophecy I had received in Toronto and slowly I saw it coming to pass. I realised once again that God was more than willing to share His heart with me but that I sometimes had difficulties with receiving it.

One way I liked to relax was to swim in the river. It was a good way of cooling down and getting some exercise. Usually the dogs would swim with us; they would chase the birds, while I would do my aqua-aerobics.

It was a beautiful wind-still afternoon, in the long dry season of 2009 and we were enjoying the cool of the river's flowing waters. It is always a joy to swim in the river. While we were swimming Winette told me about a dream she had the night before. She described what she'd seen, "In my dream there was a strong wind and it blew my bedroom door open. On my veranda I saw a lot of things connected with witchcraft, in Africa: stones, feathers, bones and leather pieces. Suddenly out of the river rose an Egyptian looking lady. She walked to my house and the expression on her face told me that she had the power over the river Nile. I stood up against her in my dream and told her that this land and the river belonged to Jesus and that she had to leave immediately in the name of Jesus. She left as suddenly as she had come."

It was a strange dream and while we were still wondering what its meaning could be, suddenly a strong whirlwind picked up around a specific tree at the riverside. The leaves of the tree were blown all over the place.

"That's strange," I said to Winette, "Did you see that? Now the wind is still again."

"Perhaps we need to pray there," she commented and then we forgot all about it.

Two weeks later, a Dutch lady with a special spiritual gift came to visit us. She was able to see in the spiritual world; she could see all the angels and demons. It was fascinating. I had never met anyone who had that gift and it opened up a whole new spiritual dimension for me. She was part of a group who had heard about us and were interested in what we are doing. It amazed us at how God brought likeminded people to our compound. She looked at us and said, "Your warring angels are very tired; you need more prayer support."

'Warring angels? Do I have warring angels?' this was new to me. I had gone through enough warfare in my life; I wanted rest, not

war. It confused me.

She looked at Snif, our German Shepherd and said, "This dog sees in the Spirit."

Winette and I had already suspected this, but whom could we have asked? I had never before heard anybody talk about dogs as spiritual beings. But we had noticed that Snif could see demons; at night she would go wild barking at a tree so we would go out and declare Jesus' Name over that area and she would calm down and sleep. Snif was also very aware of any demonic activities at the boundaries of our compound; we had also witnessed Droppie's deliverance, so it was not completely new to us but we hadn't shared these thoughts with anyone else because it was strange to us as well. But now this lady confirmed what we had already seen.

The group she was with consisted of young guys and ladies with a heart for Jesus. During their stay with us one prophetic guy had made a prayer walk through our compound.

"Did you see that dead man hanging on a tree near the river?" he asked us.

"No," I answered, "I am not a seer I don't know anything about a dead men."

He was followed by a lady; she walked up from the river and said, "Did you smell the sulphur down at the peninsula?"

"No," I answered, "I still don't smell in the Spirit." All I knew was that sulphur is often a representation of hell. I was about to learn new things and got excited in my spirit.

I laughed inside. A few years ago I would have thought these guys were not in their right mind and now I took them seriously. How much I'd changed!

"Friends, we need to pray down there at the peninsula," they shouted to the rest of the group. I went with them; this was all so new to me and it was very clear that there was a lot more between heaven and earth than I knew. I was very interested to learn more.

All ten of us went down to anoint the peninsula and to take authority over any spirits that were not supposed to be there. As soon as we began praying Snif started barking at a certain rock in the river. We anointed the place where she barked with oil and as soon as we had finished she ran to the next place barking like a wild beast. Wherever she barked, there was demonic activity and as we prayed over that place and anointed it with oil, peace returned. It was amazing to see.

Someone started singing, "There is power in the blood of Jesus." We all joined in. In the middle of the song someone shouted, "No, no, that is not possible, nobody touched that rock!" Our friend from Madagascar stopped singing looking in bewilderment at the river.

The sound of a big rock falling in the river made us all to stop singing. What had happened? A huge rock had broken off the peninsula. A demonic stronghold must have been removed, through the power of the Blood and, to our big surprise; it was right under the tree where we had seen the whirlwind!

I was aware that many people used the river for witchcraft purposes but today I was so excited; we were literally claiming back territory for Jesus. Every power on heaven and on earth has to submit to that mighty Name and surely the River Nile would become a river of healing instead of a river claiming people's lives.

Many people commented on the strategic location of the land, just one kilometre from the Source of the Nile, one of the biggest rivers in the world.

Early in 2010, Wytze, the leader of Daniel Prayer network in The Netherlands visited us. "I have been here before," he said, smiling as he entered our compound.

I had not met him before so I asked, "How and when?"

"Five months ago," he explained. "God asked us to pray for the rivers in the world and very soon we were focussing on the

River Nile. When we began interceding for the Nile, the Lord of Hosts came in our prayer room and the room was filled with the presence of God. Some people were unable to stay in the room, because God's presence was so overwhelming, while others were spontaneously healed in His presence. In the Spirit God took me to Uganda and placed me here at Mto Moyoni and I walked around this place."

We were astonished. We knew what walking in the Spirit was but travelling in the Spirit sounded otherworldly; we were entering a new spiritual territory that was unknown to all of us. At the beginning of the year God had given me a scripture, *"Do not lean on your own understanding"[41]* I thought I had let go of my understanding already but apparently there was a new spiritual dimension God wanted to lead us into.

We had kept a record of all the encouragements, scriptures and prophecies we had received over the years and decided to share them with our Advisory Board during one of our board meetings. The Archbishop asked an interesting question, "Have any of these words been given by Ugandans.

I suddenly realised that foreigners to this land had give all the prophetic words we had received. "Then it is high time that we listen for ourselves," he said and so he called a prayer meeting and also invited the other advisory and board members. It was an amazing day of prayer where God revealed His restoration plan not only for Uganda but also for the whole Nile region, leading up to Israel. He was in the business of claiming back the Source of the Nile for His own glory so that the river would become a river of life flowing through the Nations. Father God lifted the veil and gave us a glimpse of His amazing plan of redemption for Uganda and beyond; through the love He gave us in his Son Jesus.

God's presence was in our midst and He built faith in us

---

41 *Proverbs 3:5*

together to do the greater works than Jesus did.

I looked back at my life; how much had I lived a life of striving to achieve the greater works. What a relief it was to know that I no longer needed to be driven by the suffering around me, but that I simply needed to be led by the Spirit of God in order to walk in my Divine destiny and to do the works that the Father has already prepared for me to do.

After all the board members had left, I walked down to the River and contemplated the new things Father God was teaching me about who He is, about who I am as His child, about the authority and dominion that I have as His child. Thinking back I had so often felt defeated, but now I felt victorious because I knew that the same spirit of Him that raised Jesus from the dead was living in me. I began to see Romans 8 suddenly in a very different light. *'It is true, "the whole of creation is groaning for the Sons of God to be revealed".'* I saw it; it happened before my own eyes in our garden, almost every month we see new birds coming to our compound. The otters, that had disappeared long ago, were swimming again in the river near our peninsula; the fruit trees grew huge fruit. We were witnessing the restoring of God's creation in Mto Moyoni because we were beginning to live out of the revelation that we are children of God.

Now, looking back over the six years of Mto Moyoni's existence, I'm encouraged that 75% of the hundreds of people who have visited Mto Moyoni are Ugandans. We're also privileged to have people from other African nations and westerners visit us, each having had life changing encounters with Father God's unconditional love. Orphans are led home and God's servants become sons. Hope is being restored and marriages healed.

With deep assurance in my heart, I gaze at the Nile and know that the river of God's love will wash over the orphan spirit that has reigned over the African continent. I know for sure that we are playing a part in God's story a story of restoration, a story of the end times in which *'His will be done on earth as it is in Heaven.'*

There is no AIDS in heaven. In my heart I cry out to Father God, "Eradicate AIDS!" *There are no broken hearts in heaven.* "Father, heal Africa's broken hearts!"

There is no 'orphan' in Father's dictionary, so the orphans will be restored back to the heart of the Father that beats with unconditional love for His creation, yet I am so aware that none of this will happen in our own strength. It will be His presence; His love and His power manifested in us, the children of God, who live out of the revelation that we carry the same DNA Jesus has.

The Journey Continues...

Its 2016 now, and already five years ago that this book was first published. In those years Father continued to restore life back to my heart. As Father's love transforms my heart, I see more clearly that the world is the way it is because many people believe in two major lies: The lie of who God is and the lie in who we are as His children.

When we see that He is a loving Father and that He is not the creator of all the pain in this world, it becomes easier to open our heart to Him. Then we will see that He gave Jesus to be the way back to His heart. We than dare to live out of our identity as children of the King, and no longer as spiritual orphans. The whole of creation groans and waits for the time that God's children live in the deep assurance that they are in Him. That identity gives us the authority to do the things Jesus did and even more

His love is becoming more and more the foundation of my life. I know that I am invited to live in His presence and that His thoughts are becoming more of my thoughts. He desires to make me more like Jesus, because His plans are bigger than my own plans. Where He wants to lead me, I can not come in my own strength.

With my whole being I now know He is my Father. Now, I am in the process of learning what it is to be His daughter and that Jesus is my elder brother. I have the same DNA as Jesus!

I am receiving deeper revelation on John 14:20 where Jesus says that He is in the Father and that I am in Him,

All that the Father has for me, is already in me. I am invited to unpack it. The only thing He asks is that I keep my heart open to Him. His love connected my heart to His heart and filled that deep sense of loneliness. I am never alone anymore!

He is encouraging me to do things that I never thought possible. I am allowed to practice without fear of failure. On the contrary His heart rejoices when he sees me taking risks and stepping out in faith.

I am no longer driven by the needs around me, but hear that still small voice that says, this is the way walk in it. Even when I do not understand the way, He is encouraging me to influence the natural but also the spiritual world with His love.

He is a good Father and I am seeing that He is redeeming what the enemy stole. The rest and the peace in my heart are stronger than ever before because I know He cares.

I no longer need to perform to prove myself or impress others, because I know He has already approved of me. Not because of what I do but simply because I am His child.

There is no longer a force in me that tells me to become the Mother Theresa of Uganda or that I need to work harder in order to have the best and the biggest organisation, because I know what my Father thinks about me.

I am also getting more free from the Dutch culture where the word "have to" is so often used. Gods Kingdom is a Kingdom of freedom and choice. I don't have to obey Him, I want to obey Him. What an honour. I can love Him because He first loved me.

I no longer have to twist His arm with fasting and praying, because He knows what I need before I even ask.

My prayer life has changed into thanksgiving. I am still learning that the lowest path, in His Kingdom is the highest. That letting go means, giving the issues of life back to Father. He longs to carry me to His higher plan. I am learning that love is the strongest power in the world. I have a Father who fights for me and I can be still because it is His desire to protect me.

When life is hard, I can run back to His heart and His comforting love for me.

My eyes are opening more and more to the fact that the unseen world determines what is happening in the visible world.

As a Father He is joining his children's hearts world wide. We are working together with Fatherheart Ministries based in New Zealand. Our hearts are joined together. Their vision and values are very similar to Mto Moyoni.

Father takes me on exciting travels to give away His love, not only at Mto Moyoni and Africa but also in Europe, Israel, USA and Asia. This is my Father's world and He delights when He sees me enjoying my life.

More people are discovering Mto Moyoni as a place where they experience His loving presence. People receive deep encounters with love during the programmes or simply when they are enjoying nature or when they are asleep.

Our youth centre is well used and the Fatherheart Schools we do with orphans, ex-street children and ex- child soldiers have a life changing impact in these deeply wounded youth.

The people in the local village were very curious about what we are doing with the youth. This led to a small group of women coming together to receive love.

These women are testifying of peace and rest in their hearts. Their families are changing because they are receiving Father's love. His love opens their hearts and then, Father Himself will show His Son Jesus to them.

Father showed us a place for a bore hole to provide water to the community. The borehole gave very little water, but knowing that the invisible determines what happens in the visible we knew that this was going to change. Now that the village receives 'living water' we are very excited to see that the borehole also, gives enough water for the whole community.

Because that is what Father has given to us, A river of unending love.

Around the borehole we created a playground. The children, but also adults are learning to play. Life for many people has become too serious. Its when we become like children that we receive the Kingdom of God.

We are following the footsteps of Father with our eyes on His back. He goes so much slower than I would like to go, but His speed ensures that I am enjoying my life. I am still learning that I am more important to Him than what I do...

Mto Moyoni, placed so near the Source of the mighty River Nile, is a place from where Father's love will flow into Africa all the way to Israel.

We are only just beginning to see how strategic this location is and how huge God's plan of redemption is for each individual person, for this nation and for the whole world. He is bringing all of creation back to his original plan. What a tremendous honour to partner with Him!

Details of Ministries Mentioned in this Book

Looking back God has been so faithful. He has not let go of the work of His hands, as was His promise to me. In case you feel led to pray for these ministries, please visit their websites:

The vocational school is now a big school, having trained over 3000 students:
www.ccp-uganda.org

CRO has now four drop-in centres in Uganda and has worked with over 4500 street children in the nation.
www.croug.org

Mto Moyoni is now developing a youth centre to help young people receive the revelation of the Father's love and to help them see that they are not orphans but that they have a Father who has an amazing dream for their lives.
www.mto-moyoni.org

59909856R00171

Made in the USA
Charleston, SC
16 August 2016